flex & bison

John R. Levine

O'REILLY®

Beijing · Cambridge · Farnham · Köln · Sebastopol · Tokyo

flex & bison

by John R. Levine

Copyright © 2009 John Levine. All rights reserved.
Printed in the United States of America.

Published by O'Reilly Media, Inc., 1005 Gravenstein Highway North, Sebastopol, CA 95472.

O'Reilly books may be purchased for educational, business, or sales promotional use. Online editions are also available for most titles (*http://my.safaribooksonline.com*). For more information, contact our corporate/institutional sales department: (800) 998-9938 or *corporate@oreilly.com*.

Editor: Simon St.Laurent	**Indexer:** Fred Brown
Production Editor: Adam Witwer	**Cover Designer:** Karen Montgomery
Copyeditor: Kim Wimpsett	**Interior Designer:** David Futato
Proofreader: Teresa Berensfeld	**Illustrator:** Robert Romano
Production Services: Molly Sharp	

August 2009:   First Edition.

Revision History for the First Edition:
2009-08-04   First release
2013-07-19   Second release

See *http://oreilly.com/catalog/errata.csp?isbn=9780596155971* for release details.

ISBN: 978-0-596-15597-1

[LSI]

1374160575

Table of Contents

Preface

Flex and bison are tools designed for writers of compilers and interpreters, although they are also useful for many applications that will interest noncompiler writers. Any application that looks for patterns in its input or has an input or command language is a good candidate for flex and bison. Furthermore, they allow for rapid application prototyping, easy modification, and simple maintenance of programs. To stimulate your imagination, here are a few things people have used flex and bison, or their predecessors lex and yacc, to develop:

- The desktop calculator *bc*
- The tools *eqn* and *pic*, typesetting preprocessors for mathematical equations and complex pictures
- Many other "domain-specific languages" targeted for a particular application
- *PCC*, the Portable C Compiler used with many Unix systems
- Flex itself
- A SQL database language translator

Scope of This Book

Chapter 1, *Introducing Flex and Bison*, gives an overview of how and why flex and bison are used to create compilers and interpreters and demonstrates some simple applications including a calculator built in flex and bison. It also introduces basic terms we use throughout the book.

Chapter 2, *Using Flex*, describes how to use flex. It develops flex applications that count words in files, handle multiple and nested input files, and compute statistics on C programs.

Chapter 3, *Using Bison*, gives a full example using flex and bison to develop a fully functional desktop calculator with variables, procedures, loops, and conditional expressions. It shows the use of abstract syntax trees (ASTs), powerful and easy-to-use data structures for representing parsed input.

Chapter 4, *Parsing SQL*, develops a parser for the MySQL dialect of the SQL relational database language. The parser checks the syntax of SQL statements and translates them into an internal form suitable for an interpreter. It shows the use of Reverse Polish Notation (RPN), another powerful form used to represent and interpret parsed input.

Chapter 5, *A Reference for Flex Specifications*, and Chapter 6, *A Reference for Bison Specifications*, provide detailed descriptions of the features and options available to flex and bison programmers. These chapters and the two that follow provide technical information for the now-experienced flex and bison programmer to use while developing flex and bison applications.

Chapter 7, *Ambiguities and Conflicts*, explains bison ambiguities and conflicts, which are grammar problems that keep bison from creating a parser from a grammar. It then develops methods that can be used to locate and correct such problems.

Chapter 8, *Error Reporting and Recovery*, discusses techniques that compiler or interpreter designers can use to locate, recognize, and report errors in the compiler input.

Chapter 9, *Advanced Flex and Bison*, covers reentrant scanners and parsers, Generalized Left to Right (GLR) parsers that can handle grammars that regular bison parsers can't, and interfaces to C++.

The *appendix* provides the complete grammar and a cross-reference for the SQL parser discussed in Chapter 4.

The *glossary* lists technical terms from language and compiler theory.

We presume you are familiar with C, because most examples are in C, flex, or bison, with a few in C++ and the remainder in SQL or the special-purpose languages developed within the text.

Conventions Used in This Book

The following conventions are used in this book:

Italic
> Used for new terms and concepts when they are introduced.

`Constant Width`
> Used for program listings, as well as within paragraphs to refer to program elements such as statements, classes, macros, states, rules, all code terms, and files and directories.

`Constant Bold`
> Shows commands or other text that should be typed literally by the user.

`Constant width italic`
> Shows text that should be replaced with user-supplied values or by values determined by context.

$

is the shell prompt.

[]

surround optional elements in a description of program syntax. (Don't type the brackets themselves.)

 This icon signifies a tip, suggestion, or general note.

 This icon indicates a warning or caution.

Getting Flex and Bison

Flex and bison are modern replacements for the classic lex and yacc that were both developed at Bell Laboratories in the 1970s. Yacc was the first of the two, developed by Stephen C. Johnson. Lex was designed by Mike Lesk and Eric Schmidt (the same Eric Schmidt who now heads Google) to work with yacc. Both lex and yacc have been standard Unix utilities since Seventh Edition Unix in the 1970s.

The GNU Project of the Free Software Foundation distributes bison, a foreward-compatible replacement for yacc. It was originally written by Robert Corbett and Richard Stallman. The bison manual is excellent, especially for referencing specific features. Bison is included with all common distributions of BSD and Linux, but if you want the most up-to-date version, its home page is:

http://www.gnu.org/software/bison/

BSD and the GNU Project also distribute *flex* (Fast *Lex*ical Analyzer Generator), "a rewrite of lex intended to fix some of that tool's many bugs and deficiencies." Flex was originally written by Jef Poskanzer; Vern Paxson and Van Jacobson have considerably improved it. Common distributions of BSD and Linux include a copy of flex, but if you want the latest version, it's now hosted at SourceForge:

http://flex.sourceforge.net/

This Book's Example Files

The programs in this book are available online as:

ftp://ftp.iecc.com/pub/file/flexbison.zip

They can be downloaded by any web browser or FTP client. The zip format file can be decoded by the popular freeware *unzip* utility on Unix-ish and Linux systems or opened as a compressed folder on Windows XP or newer.

The examples in the book were all tested with flex version 2.5.35 and bison 2.4.1.

Using Code Examples

This book is here to help you get your job done. In general, you may use the code in this book in your programs and documentation. You do not need to contact us for permission unless you're reproducing a significant portion of the code. For example, writing a program that uses several chunks of code from this book does not require permission. Selling or distributing a CD-ROM of examples from O'Reilly books does require permission. Answering a question by citing this book and quoting example code does not require permission. Incorporating a significant amount of example code from this book into your product's documentation does require permission.

We appreciate, but do not require, attribution. An attribution usually includes the title, author, publisher, and ISBN. For example: "*Book Title* by Some Author. Copyright 2008 O'Reilly Media, Inc., 978-0-596-xxxx-x."

If you feel your use of code examples falls outside fair use or the permission given above, feel free to contact us at *permissions@oreilly.com*.

Safari® Books Online

 When you see a Safari® Books Online icon on the cover of your favorite technology book, that means the book is available online through the O'Reilly Network Safari Bookshelf.

Safari offers a solution that's better than e-books. It's a virtual library that lets you easily search thousands of top tech books, cut and paste code samples, download chapters, and find quick answers when you need the most accurate, current information. Try it for free at *http://my.safaribooksonline.com*.

How to Contact Us

Despite all the help, errors remain the author's responsibility. When you find some, or if you have other comments, email them to *fbook@iecc.com*, being sure to include the name of the book in the subject line to alert the spam filters that you are a real person rather than a deceased kleptocrat from a developing country. Or drop by the Usenet group `comp.compilers` where questions about compiler tools are always on topic.

You can also address comments and questions concerning this book to the publisher:

O'Reilly Media, Inc.

1005 Gravenstein Highway North
Sebastopol, CA 95472
800-998-9938 (in the United States or Canada)
707-829-0515 (international or local)
707 829-0104 (fax)

We have a web page for this book, where we list errata, examples, and any additional information. You can access this page at:

http://www.oreilly.com/catalog/9780596155971

To comment or ask technical questions about this book, send email to:

bookquestions@oreilly.com

For more information about our books, conferences, Resource Centers, and the O'Reilly Network, see our web site at:

http://www.oreilly.com

Acknowledgments

Every book is the work of many people, and this one is no exception. I thank Tony Mason and Doug Brown, my coauthors of *lex & yacc*, for permission to adapt parts of that book. Many people provided useful comments on the draft manuscript, including Lorenzo Bettini, Joel E. Denny, Danny Dubé, Ben Hanson, Jan Van Katwijk, Jeff Kenton, Timothy Knox, Chris Morley, Ken Rose, and Juha Vihavainen. I particularly thank Derek M. Jones, who provided a detailed page-by-page review in an unreasonably short time. Simon St. Laurent, my long-suffering editor, as always shepherded the book skillfully and without complaint through the editorial and production process.

# CHAPTER 1

Introducing Flex and Bison

Flex and Bison are tools for building programs that handle structured input. They were originally tools for building compilers, but they have proven to be useful in many other areas. In this first chapter, we'll start by looking at a little (but not too much) of the theory behind them, and then we'll dive into some examples of their use.

Lexical Analysis and Parsing

The earliest compilers back in the 1950s used utterly ad hoc techniques to analyze the syntax of the source code of programs they were compiling. During the 1960s, the field got a lot of academic attention, and by the early 1970s, syntax analysis was a well-understood field.

One of the key insights was to break the job into two parts: *lexical analysis* (also called *lexing* or *scanning*) and *syntax analysis* (or *parsing*).

Roughly speaking, scanning divides the input into meaningful chunks, called *tokens*, and parsing figures out how the tokens relate to each other. For example, consider this snippet of C code:

```
alpha = beta + gamma ;
```

A scanner divides this into the tokens `alpha`, `equal sign`, `beta`, `plus sign`, `gamma`, and `semicolon`. Then the parser determines that `beta + gamma` is an expression, and that the expression is assigned to `alpha`.

Getting Flex and Bison

Most Linux and BSD systems come with flex and bison as part of the base system. If your system doesn't have them, or has out-of-date versions, they're both easy to install.

Flex is a Sourceforge project, at *http://flex.sourceforge.net/*. The current version as of early 2009 was 2.5.35. Changes from version to version are usually minor, so it's not essential to update your version if it's close to .35, but some systems still ship with version 2.5.4 or 2.5.4a, which is more than a decade old.

Bison is available from *http://www.gnu.org/software/bison/*. The current version as of early 2009 was 2.4.1. Bison is under fairly active development, so it's worth getting an up-to-date version to see what's new. Version 2.4 added support for parsers in Java, for example. BSD users can generally install a current version of flex or bison using the ports collection. Linux users may be able to find current RPMs. If not, flex and bison both use the standard GNU build process, so to install them, download and unpack the current flex and bison tarballs from the web sites, run `./configure` and then `make` to build each, then become superuser and `make install` to install them.

Flex and bison both depend on the GNU m4 macroprocessor. Linux and BSD should all have m4, but in case they don't, or they have an ancient version, the current GNU m4 is at *http://www.gnu.org/software/m4/*.

For Windows users, both bison and flex are included in the Cygwin Linux emulation environment available at *http://www.cygwin.com/*. You can use the C or C++ code they generate either with the Cygwin development tools or with native Windows development tools.

Regular Expressions and Scanning

Scanners generally work by looking for patterns of characters in the input. For example, in a C program, an integer constant is a string of one or more digits, a variable name is a letter followed by zero or more letters or digits, and the various operators are single characters or pairs of characters. A straightforward way to describe these patterns is *regular expressions*, often shortened to *regex* or *regexp*. These are the same kind of patterns that the editors ed and vi and the search program egrep use to describe text to search for. A flex program basically consists of a list of regexps with instructions about what to do when the input matches any of them, known as *actions*. A flex-generated scanner reads through its input, matching the input against all of the regexps and doing the appropriate action on each match. Flex translates all of the regexps into an efficient internal form that lets it match the input against all the patterns simultaneously, so it's just as fast for 100 patterns as for one.[1]

Our First Flex Program

Unix systems (by which I also mean Unix-ish systems including Linux and the BSDs) come with a word count program, which reads through a file and reports the number of lines, words, and characters in the file. Flex lets us write wc in a few dozen lines, shown in Example 1-1.

---

1. The internal form is known as a deterministic finite automation (DFA). Fortunately, the only thing you really need to know about DFAs at this point is that they're fast, and the speed is independent of the number or complexity of the patterns.

Example 1-1. Word count fb1-1.l

```
/* just like Unix wc */
%{
int chars = 0;
int words = 0;
int lines = 0;
%}

%%

[a-zA-Z]+   { words++; chars += strlen(yytext); }
\n          { chars++; lines++; }
.           { chars++; }

%%

main(int argc, char **argv)
{
  yylex();
  printf("%8d%8d%8d\n", lines, words, chars);
}
```

Much of this program should look familiar to C programmers, since most of it is C. A flex program consists of three sections, separated by %% lines. The first section contains declarations and option settings. The second section is a list of patterns and actions, and the third section is C code that is copied to the generated scanner, usually small routines related to the code in the actions.

In the declaration section, code inside of %{ and %} is copied through verbatim near the beginning of the generated C source file. In this case it just sets up variables for lines, words, and characters.

In the second section, each pattern is at the beginning of a line, followed by the C code to execute when the pattern matches. The C code can be one statement or possibly a multiline block in braces, { }. (Each pattern *must* start at the beginning of the line, since flex considers any line that starts with whitespace to be code to be copied into the generated C program.)

In this program, there are only three patterns. The first one, [a-zA-Z]+, matches a word. The characters in brackets, known as a *character class*, match any single upper- or lowercase letter, and the + sign means to match one or more of the preceding thing, which here means a string of letters or a word. The action code updates the number of words and characters seen. In any flex action, the variable **yytext** is set to point to the input text that the pattern just matched. In this case, all we care about is how many characters it was so we can update the character count appropriately.

The second pattern, \n, just matches a new line. The action updates the number of lines and characters.

The final pattern is a dot, which is regex-ese for any character. (It's similar to a ? in shell scripts.) The action updates the number of characters. And that's all the patterns we need.[2]

The C code at the end is a main program that calls `yylex()`, the name that flex gives to the scanner routine, and then prints the results. In the absence of any other arrangements, the scanner reads from the standard input. So let's run it.

```
$ flex fb1-1.l
$ cc lex.yy.c -lfl
$ ./a.out
The boy stood on the burning deck
shelling peanuts by the peck
^D
2 12 63
$
```

First we tell flex to translate our program, and in classic Unix fashion since there are no errors, it does so and says nothing. Then we compile `lex.yy.c`, the C program it generated; link it with the flex library, `-lfl`; run it; and type a little input for it to count. Seems to work.

The actual `wc` program uses a slightly different definition of a word, a string of non-whitespace characters. Once we look up what all the whitespace characters are, we need only replace the line that matches words with one that matches a string of non-whitespace characters:

```
[^ \t\n\r\f\v]+ { words++; chars += strlen(yytext); }
```

The ^ at the beginning of the character class means to match any character other than the ones in the class, and the + once again means to match one or more of the preceding patterns. This demonstrates one of flex's strengths—it's easy to make small changes to patterns and let flex worry about how they might affect the generated code.

Programs in Plain Flex

Some applications are simple enough that you can write the whole thing in flex, or in flex with a little bit of C. For example, Example 1-2 shows the skeleton of a translator from English to American.

Example 1-2. English to American fb1-2.l

```
/* English -> American */
%%
"colour" { printf("color"); }
"flavour" { printf("flavor"); }
```

---

2. The observant reader may ask, if a dot matches anything, won't it also match the letters the first pattern is supposed to match? It does, but flex breaks a tie by preferring longer matches, and if two patterns match the same thing, it prefers the pattern that appears first in the flex program. This is an utter hack, but a very useful one we'll see frequently.

```
"clever" { printf("smart"); }
"smart" { printf("elegant"); }
"conservative" { printf("liberal"); }
 ... lots of other words ...
. { printf("%s", yytext); }
%%
```

It reads through its input, printing the American version when it matches an English word and passing everything else through. This example is somewhat unrealistic (*smart* can also mean hurt, after all), but flex is not a bad tool to use for doing modest text transformations and for programs that collect statistics on input. More often than not, though, you'll want to use flex to generate a scanner that divides the input into tokens that are then used by other parts of your program.

Putting Flex and Bison Together

The first program we'll write using both flex and bison is a desk calculator. First we'll write a scanner, and then we'll write a parser and splice the two of them together.

To keep things simple, we'll start by recognizing only integers, four basic arithmetic operators, and a unary absolute value operator (Example 1-3).

Example 1-3. A simple flex scanner fb1-3.l

```
/* recognize tokens for the calculator and print them out */
%%
"+"     { printf("PLUS\n"); }
"-"     { printf("MINUS\n"); }
"*"     { printf("TIMES\n"); }
"/"     { printf("DIVIDE\n"); }
"|"     { printf("ABS\n"); }
[0-9]+ { printf("NUMBER %s\n", yytext); }
\n      { printf("NEWLINE\n"); }
[ \t]  { }
.       { printf("Mystery character %s\n", yytext); }
%%
```

The first five patterns are literal operators, written as quoted strings, and the actions, for now, just print a message saying what matched. The quotes tell flex to use the strings as is, rather than interpreting them as regular expressions.

The sixth pattern matches an integer. The bracketed pattern [0-9]matches any single digit, and the following + sign means to match one or more of the preceding item, which here means a string of one or more digits. The action prints out the string that's matched, using the pointer yytext that the scanner sets after each match.

The seventh pattern matches a newline character, represented by the usual C \n sequence.

The eighth pattern ignores whitespace. It matches any single space or tab (\t), and the empty action code does nothing.

The final pattern is the catchall to match anything the other patterns didn't. Its action code prints a suitable complaint.

These nine patterns now provide rules to match anything that the user might enter. As we continue to develop the calculator, we'll add more rules to match more tokens, but these will do to get us started.

In this simple flex program, there's no C code in the third section. The flex library (-lfl) provides a tiny main program that just calls the scanner, which is adequate for this example.

So let's try out our scanner:

```
$ flex fb1-3.1
$ cc lex.yy.c -lfl
$ ./a.out
12+34
NUMBER 12
PLUS
NUMBER 34
NEWLINE
 5 6 / 7q
NUMBER 5
NUMBER 6
DIVIDE
NUMBER 7
Mystery character q
NEWLINE
^D
$
```

First we run flex, which translates the scanner into a C program called lex.yy.c, then we compile the C program, and finally we run it. The output shows that it recognizes numbers as numbers, it recognizes operators as operators, and the q in the last line of input is caught by the catchall pattern at the end. (That ^D is a Unix/Linux end-of-file character. On Windows you'd type ^Z.)

The Scanner as Coroutine

Most programs with flex scanners use the scanner to return a stream of tokens that are handled by a parser. Each time the program needs a token, it calls yylex(), which reads a little input and returns the token. When it needs another token, it calls yylex() again. The scanner acts as a coroutine; that is, each time it returns, it remembers where it was, and on the next call it picks up where it left off.

Within the scanner, when the action code has a token ready, it just returns it as the value from yylex(). The next time the program calls yylex(), it resumes scanning with the next input characters. Conversely, if a pattern doesn't produce a token for the calling program and doesn't return, the scanner will just keep going within the same call to yylex(), scanning the next input characters. This incomplete snippet shows two patterns that return tokens, one for the + operator and one for a number, and a white-space pattern that does nothing, thereby ignoring what it matched.

```
"+"    { return ADD; }
[0-9]+ { return NUMBER; }
[ \t] { /* ignore whitespace */ }
```

This apparent casualness about whether action code returns often confuses new flex users, but the rule is actually quite simple: If action code returns, scanning resumes on the next call to yylex(); if it doesn't return, scanning resumes immediately.

Now we'll modify our scanner so it returns tokens that a parser can use to implement a calculator.

Tokens and Values

When a flex scanner returns a stream of tokens, each token actually has two parts, the token and the token's *value*. The token is a small integer. The token numbers are arbitrary, except that token zero always means end-of-file. When bison creates a parser, bison assigns the token numbers automatically starting at 258 (this avoids collisions with literal character tokens, discussed later) and creates a .h with definitions of the tokens numbers. But for now, we'll just define a few tokens by hand:

```
NUMBER = 258,
ADD = 259,
SUB = 260,
MUL = 261,
DIV = 262,
ABS = 263,
EOL = 264  end of line
```

(Well, actually, it's the list of token numbers that bison will create, as we'll see a few pages ahead. But these token numbers are as good as any.)

A token's value identifies which of a group of similar tokens this one is. In our scanner, all numbers are NUMBER tokens, with the value saying what number it is. When parsing more complex input with names, floating-point numbers, string literals, and the like, the value says which name, number, literal, or whatever, this token is. Our first version of the calculator's scanner, with a small main program for debugging, is in Example 1-4.

Example 1-4. Calculator scanner fb1-4.l

```
/* recognize tokens for the calculator and print them out */
%{
   enum yytokentype {
     NUMBER = 258,
     ADD = 259,
     SUB = 260,
     MUL = 261,
     DIV = 262,
     ABS = 263,
     EOL = 264
```

```
    };

    int yylval;
%}

%%
"+"     { return ADD; }
"-"     { return SUB; }
"*"     { return MUL; }
"/"     { return DIV; }
"|"     { return ABS; }
[0-9]+ { yylval = atoi(yytext); return NUMBER; }
\n      { return EOL; }
[ \t]   { /* ignore whitespace */ }
.       { printf("Mystery character %c\n", *yytext); }
%%
main(int argc, char **argv)
{
  int tok;

  while(tok = yylex()) {
    printf("%d", tok);
    if(tok == NUMBER) printf(" = %d\n", yylval);
    else printf("\n");
  }
}
```

We define the token numbers in a C enum. Then we make yylval, the variable that stores the token value, an integer, which is adequate for the first version of our calculator. (Later we'll see that the value is usually defined as a union so that different kinds of tokens can have different kinds of values, e.g., a floating-point number or a pointer to a symbol's entry in a symbol table.)

The list of patterns is the same as in the previous example, but the action code is different. For each of the tokens, the scanner returns the appropriate code for the token; for numbers, it turns the string of digits into an integer and stores it in yylval before returning. The pattern that matches whitespace doesn't return, so the scanner just continues to look for what comes next.

For testing only, a small main program calls yylex(), prints out the token values, and, for NUMBER tokens, also prints yylval.

```
$ flex fb1-4.1
$ cc lex.yy.c -lfl
$ ./a.out
a / 34 + |45
Mystery character a
262
258 = 34
259
263
258 = 45
264
```

```
^D
$
```

Now that we have a working scanner, we turn our attention to parsing.

Where Did Flex and Bison Come From?

Bison is descended from yacc, a parser generator written between 1975 and 1978 by Stephen C. Johnson at Bell Labs. As its name, short for "yet another compiler compiler," suggests, many people were writing parser generators at the time. Johnson's tool combined a firm theoretical foundation from parsing work by D. E. Knuth, which made its parsers extremely reliable, and a convenient input syntax. These made it extremely popular among users of Unix systems, although the restrictive license under which Unix was distributed at the time limited its use outside of academia and the Bell System. In about 1985, Bob Corbett, a graduate student at the University of California, Berkeley, reimplemented yacc using somewhat improved internal algorithms, which evolved into Berkeley yacc. Since his version was faster than Bell's yacc and was distributed under the flexible Berkeley license, it quickly became the most popular version of yacc. Richard Stallman of the Free Software Foundation (FSF) adapted Corbett's work for use in the GNU project, where it has grown to include a vast number of new features as it has evolved into the current version of bison. Bison is now maintained as a project of the FSF and is distributed under the GNU Public License.

In 1975, Mike Lesk and summer intern Eric Schmidt wrote lex, a lexical analyzer generator, with most of the programming being done by Schmidt. They saw it both as a standalone tool and as a companion to Johnson's yacc. Lex also became quite popular, despite being relatively slow and buggy. (Schmidt nonetheless went on to have a fairly successful career in the computer industry where he is now the CEO of Google.)

In about 1987, Vern Paxson of the Lawrence Berkeley Lab took a version of lex written in ratfor (an extended Fortran popular at the time) and translated it into C, calling it flex, for "Fast *Lex*ical Analyzer Generator." Since it was faster and more reliable than AT&T lex and, like Berkeley yacc, available under the Berkeley license, it has completely supplanted the original lex. Flex is now a SourceForge project, still under the Berkeley license.

Grammars and Parsing

The parser's job is to figure out the relationship among the input tokens. A common way to display such relationships is a *parse tree*. For example, under the usual rules of arithmetic, the arithmetic expression 1 * 2 + 3 * 4 + 5 would have the parse tree in Figure 1-1.

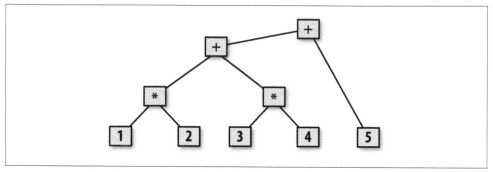

Figure 1-1. Expression parse tree

Multiplication has higher precedence than addition, so the first two expressions are
1 * 2 and 3 * 4. Then those two expressions are added together, and that sum is then
added to 5. Each branch of the tree shows the relationship between the tokens or subtrees below it. The structure of this particular tree is quite simple and regular with two
descendants under each node (that's why we use a calculator as the first example), but
any bison parser makes a parse tree as it parses its input. In some applications, it creates
the tree as a data structure in memory for later use. In others, the tree is just implicit in
the sequence of operations the parser does.

BNF Grammars

In order to write a parser, we need some way to describe the rules the parser uses to
turn a sequence of tokens into a parse tree. The most common kind of language that
computer parsers handle is a *context-free grammar* (CFG).[3] The standard form to write
down a CFG is *Backus-Naur Form* (BNF), created around 1960 to describe Algol 60
and named after two members of the Algol 60 committee.

Fortunately, BNF is quite simple. Here's BNF for simple arithmetic expressions enough
to handle 1 * 2 + 3 * 4 + 5:

```
<exp> ::= <factor>
        | <exp> + <factor>
<factor> ::= NUMBER
           | <factor> * NUMBER
```

Each line is a *rule* that says how to create a branch of the parse tree. In BNF, ::= can
be read "is a" or "becomes," and | is "or," another way to create a branch of the same
kind. The name on the left side of a rule is a *symbol* or *term*. By convention, all tokens
are considered to be symbols, but there are also symbols that are not tokens.

---

3. CFGs are also known as *phrase-structure grammars* or *type-2 languages*. Computer theorists and natural-
   language linguists independently developed them at about the same time in the late 1950s. If you're a
   computer scientist, you usually call them CFGs, and if you're a linguist, you usually call them PSGs or
   type-2, but they're the same thing.

Useful BNF is invariably quite recursive, with rules that refer to themselves directly or indirectly. These simple rules can match an arbitrarily complex sequence of additions and multiplications by applying them recursively.

Bison's Rule Input Language

Bison rules are basically BNF, with the punctuation simplified a little to make them easier to type. Example 1-5 shows the bison code, including the BNF, for the first version of our calculator.

Example 1-5. Simple calculator fb1-5.y

```
/* simplest version of calculator */
%{
#include <stdio.h>
%}

/* declare tokens */
%token NUMBER
%token ADD SUB MUL DIV ABS
%token EOL

%%

calclist: /* nothing */                       matches at beginning of input
  | calclist exp EOL { printf("= %d\n", $2); } EOL is end of an expression
  ;

exp: factor        default $$ = $1
  | exp ADD factor { $$ = $1 + $3; }
  | exp SUB factor { $$ = $1 - $3; }
  ;

factor: term       default $$ = $1
  | factor MUL term { $$ = $1 * $3; }
  | factor DIV term { $$ = $1 / $3; }
  ;

term: NUMBER   default $$ = $1
  | ABS term    { $$ = $2 >= 0? $2 : - $2; }
  ;
%%
main(int argc, char **argv)
{
  yyparse();
}

yyerror(char *s)
{
  fprintf(stderr, "error: %s\n", s);
}
```

Bison programs have (not by coincidence) the same three-part structure as flex programs, with declarations, rules, and C code. The declarations here include C code to be copied to the beginning of the generated C parser, again enclosed in %{ and %}. Following that are %token token declarations, telling bison the names of the symbols in the parser that are tokens. By convention, tokens have uppercase names, although bison doesn't require it. Any symbols not declared as tokens have to appear on the left side of at least one rule in the program. (If a symbol neither is a token nor appears on the left side of a rule, it's like an unreferenced variable in a C program. It doesn't hurt anything, but it probably means the programmer made a mistake.)

The second section contains the rules in simplified BNF. Bison uses a single colon rather than ::=, and since line boundaries are not significant, a semicolon marks the end of a rule. Again, like flex, the C action code goes in braces at the end of each rule.

Bison automatically does the parsing for you, remembering what rules have been matched, so the action code maintains the values associated with each symbol. Bison parsers also perform side effects such as creating data structures for later use or, as in this case, printing out results. The symbol on the left side of the first rule is the *start symbol*, the one that the entire input has to match. There can be, and usually are, other rules with the same start symbol on the left.

Each symbol in a bison rule has a value; the value of the target symbol (the one to the left of the colon) is called $$ in the action code, and the values on the right are numbered $1, $2, and so forth, up to the number of symbols in the rule. The values of tokens are whatever was in yylval when the scanner returned the token; the values of other symbols are set in rules in the parser. In this parser, the values of the factor, term, and exp symbols are the value of the expression they represent.

In this parser, the first two rules, which define the symbol calclist, implement a loop that reads an expression terminated by a newline and prints its value. The definition of calclist uses a common two-rule recursive idiom to implement a sequence or list: the first rule is empty and matches nothing; the second adds an item to the list. The action in the second rule prints the value of the exp in $2.

The rest of the rules implement the calculator. The rules with operators such as exp ADD factor and ABS term do the appropriate arithmetic on the symbol values. The rules with a single symbol on the right side are syntactic glue to put the grammar together; for example, an exp is a factor. In the absence of an explicit action on a rule, the parser assigns $1 to $$. This is a hack, albeit a very useful one, since most of the time it does the right thing.

How About Parsing English?

For a very long time, as far back as the 1950s, people have been trying to program computers to handle *natural languages*, languages spoken by people rather than by computers, a task that turns out to be extremely difficult. One approach is to parse them with the same techniques used for computer languages, as in this fragment:

```
simple_sentence: subject verb object
         |      subject verb object prep_phrase ;

subject:        NOUN
         |      PRONOUN
         |      ADJECTIVE subject ;

verb:           VERB
         |      ADVERB VERB
         |      verb VERB ;

object:         NOUN
         |      ADJECTIVE object ;

prep_phrase:    PREPOSITION NOUN ;
```

Unfortunately, it doesn't work beyond small and unrealistic subsets of natural languages. Although natural languages have grammars, the grammars are extremely complex and not easy to write down or to handle in software. It remains an interesting and open question why this should be. Why are languages we invent for our computers so much simpler than the ones we speak?

Compiling Flex and Bison Programs Together

Before we build the scanner and parser into a working program, we have to make some small changes to the scanner in Example 1-4 so we can call it from the parser. In particular, rather than defining explicit token values in the first part, we include a header file that bison will create for us, which includes both definitions of the token numbers and a definition of yylval. We also delete the testing main routine in the third section of the scanner, since the parser will now call the scanner. The first part of the scanner now looks like Example 1-6.

Example 1-6. Calculator scanner fb1-5.l

```
%{
# include "fb1-5.tab.h"
%}
%%  same rules as before, and no code in the third section
```

The build process is now complex enough to be worth putting into a Makefile:

```
# part of the makefile
fb1-5:  fb1-5.l fb1-5.y
        bison -d fb1-5.y
        flex fb1-5.l
        cc -o $@ fb1-5.tab.c lex.yy.c -lfl
```

First it runs bison with the -d (for "definitions" file) flag, which creates fb1-5.tab.c and fb1-5.tab.h, and it runs flex to create lex.yy.c. Then it compiles them together, along with the flex library. Try it out, and in particular verify that it handles operator precedence correctly, doing multiplication and division before addition and subtraction:

```
$ ./fb1-5
2 + 3 * 4
= 14
2 * 3 + 4
= 10
20 / 4 - 2
= 3
20 - 4 / 2
= 18
```

Ambiguous Grammars: Not Quite

The reader may be wondering at this point whether the grammar in Example 1-5 is needlessly complicated. Why not just write this?

```
exp: exp ADD exp
   | exp SUB exp
   | exp MUL exp
   | exp DIV exp
   | ABS exp
   | NUMBER
   ;
```

There are two answers: precedence and ambiguity. The separate symbols for term, factor, and exp tell bison to handle ABS, then MUL and DIV, and then ADD and SUB. In general, whenever a grammar has multiple levels of precedence where one kind of operator binds "tighter" than another, the parser will need a level of rule for each level.

Well, then, OK, how about this?

```
exp: exp ADD exp
   | exp SUB exp
   | factor
   ;
```
similarly for factor and term

One of bison's greatest strengths, and simultaneously one of its most annoying aspects, is that *it will not parse an ambiguous grammar*. That is, any parser that bison creates has exactly one way to parse any input that it parses, and the parser will accept exactly that grammar. The previous grammar is ambiguous, because input such as 1 - 2 + 3 could be parsed either as (1-2) + 3 or as 1 - (2+3), two different expressions with different values. Although there are some cases where ambiguity doesn't matter (e.g., 1+2+3), in most cases the ambiguity really is an error, and the grammar needs to be fixed. The way we wrote the grammar in Example 1-5 makes expressions unambiguously group to the left. If a grammar is ambiguous, bison reports *conflicts*, places where there are two different possible parses for a given bit of input. It creates a parser anyway, picking one option in each conflict, but that choice means the language it's parsing isn't necessarily the one you tried to specify. We discuss this at length in Chapter 7.

Bison's usual parsing algorithm can look ahead one token to decide what rules match the input. Some grammars aren't ambiguous but have places that require more than one token of lookahead to decide what rules will match. These also cause conflicts, although it is usually possible to rewrite the grammar so that one token lookahead is enough.

Actually, the previous discussion about ambiguity is not quite true. Since expression grammars are so common and useful, and since writing separate rules for each precedence level is tedious, bison has some special features that let you write an expression grammar in the natural way with one rule per operator in the form exp OP exp and just tell it what precedence and grouping rules to use to resolve the ambiguity. We'll learn about these in Chapter 3. Also, bison has an alternative parsing technique called GLR that can handle ambiguous grammars and arbitrary lookahead, tracking all the possible parses that match the input in parallel. We cover this in Chapter 9.

Adding a Few More Rules

One of the nicest things about using flex and bison to handle a program's input is that it's often quite easy to make small changes to the grammar. Our expression language would be a lot more useful if it could handle parenthesized expressions, and it would be nice if it could handle comments, using // syntax. To do this, we need only add one rule to the parser and three to the scanner.

In the parser we define two new tokens, OP and CP for open and close parentheses, and add a rule to make a parenthesized expression a term:

```
%token OP CP  in the declaration section
  ...
%%
term: NUMBER
 | ABS term { $$ = $2 >= 0? $2 : - $2; }
 | OP exp CP { $$ = $2; } New rule
 ;
```

Note the action code in the new rule assigns $2, the value of the expression in the parentheses, to $$.

The scanner has two new rules to recognize the two new tokens and one new rule to ignore two slashes followed by arbitrary text. Since a dot matches anything except a newline, .* will gobble up the rest of the line.

```
"("     { return OP; }
")"     { return CP; }
"//".*  /* ignore comments */
```

That's it—rebuild the calculator, and now it handles parenthesized expressions and comments.

Flex and Bison vs. Handwritten Scanners and Parsers

The two example programs in this chapter, word count and a calculator, are both simple enough that we could without too much trouble have written them directly in C. But there is little reason to do so when developing a program. The pattern-matching technique that flex uses is quite fast and is usually about the same speed as a handwritten scanner. For more complex scanners with many patterns, a flex scanner may even be faster, since handwritten code will usually do many comparisons per character, while flex always does one. The flex version of a scanner is invariably much shorter than the equivalent C, which makes it a lot easier to debug. In general, if the rules for breaking an input stream into tokens can be described by regular expressions, flex is the tool of choice.

A Handwritten Scanner

If the lexical syntax of a language isn't too complicated, a handwritten scanner can be a reasonable alternative to a flex scanner. Here's a handwritten C equivalent of the scanner in Example 1-6. This scanner will probably run a little faster than the flex version, but it's a lot harder to modify to add or change token types. If you do plan to use a handwritten scanner, prototype it in flex first.

```
/*
 * Handwritten version of scanner for calculator
 */

# include <stdio.h>
# include "fb1-5.tab.h"

FILE *yyin;
static int seeneof = 0;

int
yylex(void)
{
  if(!yyin) yyin = stdin;
  if(seeneof) return 0;        /* saw EOF last time */

  while(1) {
    int c = getc(yyin);

    if(isdigit(c)) {
      int i = c - '0';

      while(isdigit(c = getc(yyin)))
        i = (10*i) + c-'0';
      yylval = i;
      if(c == EOF) seeneof = 1;
      else ungetc(c, yyin);
      return NUMBER;
    }

    switch(c) {
    case '+': return ADD; case '-': return SUB;
```

```
        case '*': return MUL; case '|': return ABS;
        case '(': return OP;  case ')': return CP;
        case '\n': return EOL;
        case ' ': case '\t': break;    /* ignore these */
        case EOF: return 0;        /* standard end-of-file token */

        case '/': c = getc(yyin);
          if(c == '/') {        /* it's a comment */
        while((c = getc(yyin)) != '\n')
          if(c == EOF) return 0; /* EOF in comment line */
        break;
          }
          if(c == EOF) seeneof = 1; /* it's division */
          else ungetc(c, yyin);
          return DIV;

        default: yyerror("Mystery character %c\n", c); break;
        }
      }
    }
```

Similarly, a bison parser is much shorter and easier to debug than the equivalent hand-written parser, particularly because of bison's verification that the grammar is unambiguous.

Exercises

1. Will the calculator accept a line that contains only a comment? Why not? Would it be easier to fix this in the scanner or in the parser?

2. Make the calculator into a hex calculator that accepts both hex and decimal numbers. In the scanner add a pattern such as 0x[a-f0-9]+ to match a hex number, and in the action code use strtol to convert the string to a number that you store in yylval; then return a NUMBER token. Adjust the output printf to print the result in both decimal and hex.

3. (extra credit) Add bit operators such as AND and OR to the calculator. The obvious operator to use for OR is a vertical bar, but that's already the unary absolute value operator. What happens if you also use it as a binary OR operator, for example, exp ABS factor?

4. Does the handwritten version of the scanner from Example 1-4 recognize exactly the same tokens as the flex version?

5. Can you think of languages for which flex wouldn't be a good tool to write a scanner?

6. Rewrite the word count program in C. Run some large files through both versions. Is the C version noticeably faster? How much harder was it to debug?

# CHAPTER 2

Using Flex

In this chapter we'll take a closer look at flex as a standalone tool, with some examples that exercise most of its C language capabilities. All of flex's facilities are described in Chapter 5, and the usage of flex scanners in C++ programs is described in Chapter 9.

Regular Expressions

The patterns at the heart of every flex scanner use a rich regular expression language. A *regular expression* is a pattern description using a *metalanguage*, a language that you use to describe what you want the pattern to match. Flex's regular expression language is essentially POSIX-extended regular expressions (which is not surprising considering their shared Unix heritage). The metalanguage uses standard text characters, some of which represent themselves and others of which represent patterns. All characters other than the ones listed below, including all letters and digits, match themselves.

The characters with special meaning in regular expressions are:

.

Matches any single character except the newline character (\n).

[]

A *character class* that matches any character within the brackets. If the first character is a circumflex (^), it changes the meaning to match any character *except* the ones within the brackets. A dash inside the square brackets indicates a character range; for example, [0-9] means the same thing as [0123456789] and [a-z] means any lowercase letter. A - or] as the first character after the [is interpreted literally to let you include dashes and square brackets in character classes. POSIX introduced other special square bracket constructs that are useful when handling non-English alphabets, described later in this chapter. Other metacharacters do not have any special meaning within square brackets except that C escape sequences starting with \ are recognized. Character ranges are interpreted relative to the character coding in use, so the range [A-z] with ASCII character coding would match all uppercase and lowercase letters, as well as six punctuation characters whose codes fall between the code for Z and the code for a. In practice, useful ranges are ranges of digits, of uppercase letters, or of lowercase letters.

[a-z]{-}[jv]

A differenced character class, with the characters in the first class omitting the characters in the second class (only in recent versions of flex).

^

Matches the beginning of a line as the first character of a regular expression. Also used for negation within square brackets.

$

Matches the end of a line as the last character of a regular expression.

{}

If the braces contain one or two numbers, indicate the minimum and maximum number of times the previous pattern can match. For example, A{1,3} matches one to three occurrences of the letter *A*, and 0{5} matches 00000. If the braces contain a name, they refer to a named pattern by that name.

\

Used to escape metacharacters and as part of the usual C escape sequences; for example, \n is a newline character, while * is a literal asterisk.

*

Matches zero or more copies of the preceding expression. For example, [\t]* is a common pattern to match optional spaces and tabs, that is, whitespace, which matches " ", " <tab><tab>", or an empty string.

+

Matches one or more occurrences of the preceding regular expression. For example, [0-9]+ matches strings of digits such as 1, 111, or 123456 but not an empty string.

?

Matches zero or one occurrence of the preceding regular expression. For example, -?[0-9]+ matches a signed number including an optional leading minus sign.

|

The *alternation* operator; matches either the preceding regular expression or the following regular expression. For example, faith|hope|charity matches any of the three virtues.

"..."

Anything within the quotation marks is treated literally. Metacharacters other than C escape sequences lose their meaning. As a matter of style, it's good practice to quote any punctuation characters intended to be matched literally.

()

Groups a series of regular expressions together into a new regular expression. For example, (01) matches the character sequence 01, and a(bc|de) matches *abc* or *ade*. Parentheses are useful when building up complex patterns with *, +, ?, and |.

/
Trailing context, which means to match the regular expression preceding the slash but only if followed by the regular expression after the slash. For example, 0/1 matches 0 in the string 01 but would not match anything in the string 0 or 02. The material matched by the pattern following the slash is not "consumed" and remains to be turned into subsequent tokens. Only one slash is permitted per pattern.

The repetition operators affect the smallest preceding expression, so abc+ matches *ab* followed by one or more *c*'s. Use parentheses freely to be sure your expressions match what you want, such as (abc)+ to match one or more repetitions of *abc*.

Regular Expression Examples

We can combine these characters to make quite complex and useful regular expression patterns. For example, consider the surprisingly difficult job of writing a pattern to match Fortran-style numbers, which consist of an optional sign, a string of digits that may contain a decimal point, optionally an exponent that is the letter E, an optional sign, and a string of digits. A pattern for an optional sign and a string of digits is simple enough:

    [-+]?[0-9]+

Note that we put the hyphen as the first thing in [-+] so it wouldn't be taken to mean a character range.

Writing the pattern to match a string of digits with an optional decimal point is harder, because the decimal point can come at the beginning or end of the number. Here's a few near misses:

    [-+]?[0-9.]+   matches too much, like 1.2.3.4
    [-+]?[0-9]+\.?[0-9]+ matches too little, misses .12 or 12.
    [-+]?[0-9]*\.?[0-9]+ doesn't match 12.
    [-+]?[0-9]+\.?[0-9]* doesn't match .12
    [-+]?[0-9]*\.?[0-9]* matches nothing, or a dot with no digits at all

It turns out that no combination of character classes, ?, *, and + will match a number with an optional decimal point. Fortunately, the alternation operator | does the trick by allowing the pattern to combine two versions, each of which individually isn't quite sufficient:

    [-+]?([0-9]*\.?[0-9]+|[0-9]+\.)
    [-+]?([0-9]*\.?[0-9]+|[0-9]+\.[0-9]*) *This is overkill but also works*

The second example is internally ambiguous, because there are many strings that match either of the alternates, but that is no problem for flex's matching algorithm. (Flex also allows two *different* patterns to match the same input, which is also useful but requires more care by the programmer.)

Now we need to add on the optional exponent, for which the pattern is quite simple:

    E(+|-)?[0-9]+

(We did the two sign characters as an alternation here rather than a character class; it's purely a matter of taste.) Now we glue the two together to get a Fortran number pattern:

```
[-+]?([0-9]*\.?[0-9]+|[0-9]+\.)(E(+|-)?[0-9]+)?
```

Since the exponent part is optional, we used parens and a question mark to make it an optional part of the pattern. Note that our pattern now includes nested optional parts, which work fine and as shown here are often very useful.

This is about as complex a pattern as you'll find in most flex scanners. It's worth reiterating that complex patterns do *not* make the scanner any slower.[1] Write your patterns to match what you need to match, and trust flex to handle them.

How Flex Handles Ambiguous Patterns

Most flex programs are quite ambiguous, with multiple patterns that can match the same input. Flex resolves the ambiguity with two simple rules:

- Match the longest possible string every time the scanner matches input.
- In the case of a tie, use the pattern that appears first in the program.

These turn out to do the right thing in the vast majority of cases. Consider this snippet from a scanner for C source code:

```
"+"                       { return ADD; }
"="                       { return ASSIGN; }
"+="                      { return ASSIGNADD; }

"if"                      { return KEYWORDIF; }
"else"                    { return KEYWORDELSE; }
[a-zA-Z_][a-zA-Z0-9_]*    { return IDENTIFIER; }
```

For the first three patterns, the string += is matched as one token, since += is longer than +. For the last three patterns, so long as the patterns for keywords precede the pattern that matches an identifier, the scanner will match keywords correctly.

Context-Dependent Tokens

In some languages, scanning is context dependent. For example, in Pascal, 1. is usually a floating-point number, but in a declaration, 1..2 is two integers separated by a .. token. Flex provides *start states*, which can turn patterns on and off dynamically and are generally sufficient to handle such context dependencies. We discuss start states later in this chapter.

---

1. There's one exception: If there are any / operators at all in a flex program, the whole scanner is slightly slower because of the added logic to handle backing up over the input that is matched but not consumed by trailing context. But in practice such scanners are usually still plenty fast.

File I/O in Flex Scanners

Flex scanners will read from the standard input unless you tell them otherwise. In practice, most scanners read from files. We'll modify the word count program from Example 1-1 to read from files, like the real wc program does.

The I/O options available in scanners generated by flex and its predecessor lex have undergone extensive evolution over the past 30 years, so there are several different ways to manage a scanner's input and output. Unless you make other arrangements, a scanner reads from the stdio FILE called yyin, so to read a single file, you need only set it before the first call to yylex. In Example 2-1, we add the ability to specify an input file to the word count program from Example 1-1.

Example 2-1. Word count, reading one file

```
/* even more like Unix wc */
%option noyywrap
%{
int chars = 0;
int words = 0;
int lines = 0;
%}

%%

[a-zA-Z]+   { words++; chars += strlen(yytext); }
\n          { chars++; lines++; }
.           { chars++; }

%%

main(argc, argv)
int argc;
char **argv;
{
  if(argc > 1) {
    if(!(yyin = fopen(argv[1], "r"))) {
      perror(argv[1]);
      return (1);
    }
  }

  yylex();
  printf("%8d%8d%8d\n", lines, words, chars);
}
```

The only differences from Example 1-1 are in the code in the third section. The main routine opens a filename passed on the command line, if the user specified one, and assigns the FILE to yyin. Otherwise, yyin is left unset, in which case yylex automatically sets it to stdin.

The Flex Library

Lex and flex have always come with a small library now known as -lfl that defines a default main routine, as well as a default version of yywrap, a wart left over from the earliest days of lex.

When a lex scanner reached the end of yyin, it called yywrap(). The idea was that if there was another input file, yywrap could adjust yyin and return 0 to resume scanning. If that was really the end of the input, it returned 1 to the scanner to say that it was done. Although subsequent versions of lex and flex have faithfully preserved yywrap, in 30 years I have never seen a use of yywrap that wouldn't be better handled by flex's other I/O management features. In practice, everyone used the default yywrap from the flex library, which always returns 1, or put a one-line equivalent in their programs. Modern versions of flex let you say %option noyywrap at the top of your scanner to tell it not to call yywrap, and from here on, we'll always do that.

The default main program is slightly useful for testing and for quick flex hacks, although, again, in any nontrivial flex program, you always have your own main program that at least sets up the scanner's input. Here's what the library version does:

```
int main()
{
    while (yylex() != 0) ;
    return 0;
}
```

Most flex programs now use %option noyywrap and provide their own main routine, so they don't need the flex library.

Reading Several Files

The real version of wc handles multiple files, so Example 2-2 is an improved version of our program that does so as well. For programs with simple I/O needs that read each input file from beginning to end, flex provides the routine yyrestart(f), which tells the scanner to read from stdio file f.

Example 2-2. Word count, reading many files

```
/* fb2-2 read several files */
%option noyywrap

%{
int chars = 0;
int words = 0;
int lines = 0;

int totchars = 0;
int totwords = 0;
int totlines = 0;
%}
```

```
%%

[a-zA-Z]+  { words++; chars += strlen(yytext); }
\n         { chars++; lines++; }
.            { chars++; }

%%

main(argc, argv)
int argc;
char **argv;
{
  int i;

  if(argc < 2) { /* just read stdin */
    yylex();
    printf("%8d%8d%8d\n", lines, words, chars);
    return 0;
  }

  for(i = 1; i < argc; i++) {
    FILE *f = fopen(argv[i], "r");

    if(!f) {
      perror(argv[i]);
      return (1);
    }
    yyrestart(f);
    yylex();
    fclose(f);
    printf("%8d%8d%8d %s\n", lines, words, chars, argv[i]);
    totchars += chars; chars = 0;
    totwords += words; words = 0;
    totlines += lines; lines = 0;
  }
  if(argc > 2) /* print total if more than one file */
    printf("%8d%8d%8d total\n", totlines, totwords, totchars);
  return 0;
}
```

For each file, it opens the file, uses yyrestart() to make it the input to the scanner, and calls yylex() to scan it. Like the real wc, it also tracks the overall total items read and reports the overall totals if there was more than one input file.

The I/O Structure of a Flex Scanner

Basically, a flex scanner reads from an input source and optionally writes to an output sink. By default, the input and output are stdin and stdout, but as we've seen, they're often changed to something else.

Input to a Flex Scanner

In programs that include scanners, the performance of the scanner frequently determines the performance of the entire program. Early versions of lex read from yyin one character at a time. Since then, flex has developed a flexible (perhaps overly so) three-level input system that allows programmers to customize it at each level to handle any imaginable input structure.

In most cases, a flex scanner reads its input using stdio from a file or the standard input, which can be the user console. There's a subtle but important difference between reading from a file and reading from the console—readahead. If the scanner is reading from a file, it should read big chunks to be as fast as possible. But if it's reading from the console, the user is probably typing one line at a time and will expect the scanner to process each line as soon as it's typed. In this case, speed doesn't matter, since a very slow scanner is still a lot faster than a fast typist, so it reads one character at a time. Fortunately, a flex scanner checks to see whether its input is from the terminal and generally does the right thing automatically.[2]

To handle its input, a flex scanner uses a structure known as a YY_BUFFER_STATE, which describes a single input source. It contains a string buffer and a bunch of variables and flags. Usually it contains a FILE* for the file it's reading from, but it's also possible to create a YY_BUFFER_STATE not connected a file to scan a string already in memory.

The default input behavior of a flex scanner is approximately this:

```
YY_BUFFER_STATE bp;
extern FILE* yyin;
```

... whatever the program does before the first call to the scanner

```
if(!yyin) yyin = stdin; default input is stdin
bp = yy_create_buffer(yyin,YY_BUF_SIZE );
    YY_BUF_SIZE defined by flex, typically 16K
yy_switch_to_buffer(bp); tell it to use the buffer we just made
```

```
yylex(); or yyparse() or whatever calls the scanner
```

If yyin isn't already set, set it to stdin. Then use yy_create_buffer to create a new buffer reading from yyin, use yy_switch_to_buffer to tell the scanner to read from it, then scan.

When reading from several files in sequence, after opening each file, call yyrestart(fp) to switch the scanner input to the stdio file fp. For the common case where a new file is assigned to yyin, YY_NEW_FILE is equivalent to yyrestart(yyin).[3]

---

2. There's a separate issue for interactive scanners related to whether the scanning process itself needs to peek ahead at the character after the one being processed, but we'll save that for later in this chapter. Fortunately, flex generally does the right thing in that case, too.

3. If the previous yyin was read all the way to EOF, YY_NEW_FILE isn't strictly necessary, but it's good to use anyway for defensive programming. This is particularly the case if a scanner or parse error might return from the scanner or parser without reading the whole file.

There are several other functions to create scanner buffers, including yy_scan_string("string") to scan a null-terminated string and yy_scan_buffer(char *base, size) to scan a buffer of known size. Later in this chapter we'll also see functions to maintain a stack of buffers, which is handy when handling nested include files. They're all listed in Chapter 5, under "Input Management."

Finally, for maximum flexibility, you can redefine the macro that flex uses to read input into the current buffer:

```
#define YY_INPUT(buf,result,max_size) ...
```

Whenever the scanner's input buffer is empty, it invokes YY_INPUT, where buf and maxsize are the buffer and its size, respectively, and result is where to put the actual amount read or zero at EOF. (Since this is a macro, it's result, not *result.) The ability to redefine YY_INPUT predates the addition of YY_BUFFER_STATE, so most of what people used to do with the former is now better done with the latter. At this point, the main use for a custom YY_INPUT is in event-driven systems where the input arrives from something that can't be preloaded into a string buffer and that stdio can't handle.

Whenever the scanner reaches the end of an input file, it matches the pseudopattern <<EOF>>, which is often used to clean up, switch to other files, and so forth.

Flex offers two macros that can be useful in action code, input() and unput(). Each call to input() returns the next character from the input stream. It's sometimes a convenient way to read through a little input without having to write patterns to match it. Each call to unput(c) pushes character c back into the input stream. It's an alternative to the / operator to peek ahead into the input but not to process it.

To summarize, the three levels of input management are:

- Setting yyin to read the desired file(s)
- Creating and using YY_BUFFER_STATE input buffers
- Redefining YY_INPUT

Flex Scanner Output

Scanner output management is much simpler than input management and is completely optional. Again, harking back to the earliest versions of lex, unless you tell it otherwise, flex acts as though there is a default rule at the end of the scanner that copies otherwise unmatched input to yyout.

```
.    ECHO;
```

```
#define ECHO fwrite( yytext, yyleng, 1, yyout )
```

This is of some use in flex programs that do something with part of the input and leave the rest untouched, as in the English to American translator in Example 1-2, but in general it is more likely to be a source of bugs than to be useful. Flex lets you say %option nodefault at the top of the scanner to tell it not to add a default rule and rather to report an error if the input rules don't cover all possible input. I recommend that scanners always use `nodefault` and include their own default rule if one is needed.

Start States and Nested Input Files

We'll try out our knowledge of flex I/O with a simple program that handles nested include files and prints them out. To make it a little more interesting, it prints the input files with the line number of each line in its file. To do that, the program keeps a stack of nested input files and line numbers, pushing an entry each time it encounters a `#include` and popping an entry off the stack when it gets to the end of a file.

We also use a very powerful flex feature called *start states* that let us control which patterns can be matched when. The `%x` line near the top of the file defines `IFILE` as a start state that we'll use when we're looking for the filename in a `#include` statement. At any point, the scanner is in one start state and can match patterns active in that start state only. In effect, the state defines a different scanner, with its own rules.

You can define as many start states as needed, but in this program we need only one in addition to the `INITIAL` state that flex always defines. Patterns are tagged with start state names in angle brackets to indicate in which state(s) the pattern is active. The `%x` marks `IFILE` as an **exclusive** start state, which means that when that state is active, only patterns specifically marked with the state can match. (There are also *inclusive* start states declared with `%s`, in which patterns not marked with any state can also match. Exclusive states are usually more useful.) In action code, the macro `BEGIN` switches to a different start state. Example 2-3 shows a code skeleton for a scanner that handles included files.

Example 2-3. Skeleton for include files

```
/* fb2-3 skeleton for include files */
%option noyywrap yylineno
%x IFILE

%{
  struct bufstack {
    struct bufstack *prev;      /* previous entry */
    YY_BUFFER_STATE bs;         /* saved buffer */
    int lineno;                 /* saved line number */
    char *filename;             /* name of this file */
    FILE *f;                    /* current file */
  } *curbs = 0;

  char *curfilename;            /* name of current input file */

  int newfile(char *fn);
  int popfile(void);
%}
%%
    match #include statement up through the quote or <
^"#"[ \t]*include[ \t]*[\"<]  { BEGIN IFILE; }
```

handle filename up to the closing quote, >, or end of line
```
<IFILE>[^ \t\n\">]+      {
                         { int c;
                           while((c = input()) && c != '\n') ;
                         }
                         yylineno++;
                         if(!newfile(yytext))
                           yyterminate(); /* no such file */
                         BEGIN INITIAL;
                         }
```

handle bad input in IFILE state
```
<IFILE>.|\n              { fprintf(stderr, "%4d bad include line\n", yylineno);
                                 yyterminate();
                         }
```

pop the file stack at end of file, terminate if it's the outermost file
```
<<EOF>>                  { if(!popfile()) yyterminate(); }
```

print the line number at the beginning of each line
and bump the line number each time a \n is read
```
^.                       { fprintf(yyout, "%4d %s", yylineno, yytext); }
^\n                      { fprintf(yyout, "%4d %s", yylineno++, yytext); }
\n                       { ECHO; yylineno++; }
.                        { ECHO; }

%%

main(int argc, char **argv)
{
  if(argc < 2) {
    fprintf(stderr, "need filename\n");
    return 1;
  }
  if(newfile(argv[1]))
    yylex();
}

int
  newfile(char *fn)
{
  FILE *f = fopen(fn, "r");
  struct bufstack *bs = malloc(sizeof(struct bufstack));

  /* die if no file or no room */
  if(!f) { perror(fn); return 0; }
  if(!bs) { perror("malloc"); exit(1); }

  /* remember state */
  if(curbs)curbs->lineno = yylineno;
  bs->prev = curbs;

  /* set up current entry */
  bs->bs = yy_create_buffer(f, YY_BUF_SIZE);
```

```
    bs->f = f;
    bs->filename = strdup(fn);
    yy_switch_to_buffer(bs->bs);
    curbs = bs;
    yylineno = 1;
    curfilename = bs->filename;
    return 1;
}

int
    popfile(void)
{
    struct bufstack *bs = curbs;
    struct bufstack *prevbs;

    if(!bs) return 0;

    /* get rid of current entry */
    fclose(bs->f);
    free(bs->fn);
    yy_delete_buffer(bs->bs);

    /* switch back to previous */
    prevbs = bs->prev;
    free(bs);

    if(!prevbs) return 0;

    yy_switch_to_buffer(prevbs->bs);
    curbs = prevbs;
    yylineno = curbs->lineno;
    curfilename = curbs->filename;
    return 1;
}
```

The first part of the program defines the start state and also has the C code to declare the bufstack structure that will hold an entry in the list of saved input files.

In the patterns, the first pattern matches a #include statement up through the double quote that precedes the filename. The pattern permits optional whitespace in the usual places. It switches to IFILE state to read the next input filename. In IFILE state, the second pattern matches a filename, characters up to a closing quote, whitespace, or end-of-line. The filename is passed to newfile to stack the current input file and set up the next level of input, but first there's the matter of dealing with whatever remains of the #include line. One possibility would be to use another start state and patterns that absorb the rest of the line, but that would be tricky, since the action switches to the included file, so the start state and pattern would have to be used *after* the end of the included file. Instead, this is one of the few places where input() makes a scanner simpler. A short loop reads until it finds the \n at the end of the line or EOF. Then, when scanning returns to this file after the end of the included one, it resumes at the beginning of the next line.

Since an exclusive start state in effect defines its own mini-scanner, that scanner has to be prepared for any possible input. The next pattern deals with the case of an ill-formed #include line that doesn't have a filename after the double quote. It simply prints an error message and uses the macro yyterminate(), which immediately returns from the scanner.[4] This definition of #include is fairly casual and makes no effort to verify that the punctuation around the filename matches or that there isn't extra junk after the filename. It's not hard to write code to check those issues and diagnose errors, and a more polished version of this program should do so.[5]

Next is the special pattern <<EOF>>, which matches at the end of each input file. We call popfile(), defined later, to return to the previous input file. If it returns 0, meaning that was the last file, we terminate. Otherwise, the scanner will resume reading the previous file when it resumes scanning.

The last four patterns do the actual work of printing out each line with a preceding line number. Flex provides a variable called yylineno that is intended to track line numbers, so we might as well use it. The pattern ^. matches any character at the beginning of a line, so the action prints the current line number and the character. Since a dot doesn't match a newline, ^\n matches a newline at the beginning of a line, that is, an empty line, so the code prints out the line number and the new line and increments the line number. A newline or other character not at the beginning of the line is just printed out with ECHO, incrementing the line number for a new line.

The routine newfile(fn) prepares to read from the file named fn, saving any previous input file. It does so by keeping a linked list of bufstack structures, each of which has a link to the previous bufstack along with the saved yylineno and filename. It opens the file; creates and switches to a flex buffer; and saves the previous open file, filename, and buffer. (In this program nothing uses the filename after the file is open, but we'll reuse this code later in this chapter in a program that does.)

The routine popfile undoes what newfile did. It closes the open file, deletes the current flex buffer, and then restores the buffer, filename, and line number from the prior stack entry. Note that it doesn't call yyrestart() when it restores the prior buffer; if it did, it would lose any input that had already been read into the buffer.

This is a fairly typical albeit somewhat simplistic example of code for handling include files. Although flex can handle a stack of input buffers using the routines yypush_buffer_state and yypop_buffer_state, I rarely find them to be useful since they don't handle the other information invariably associated with the stacked files.

---

4. It returns the value YY_NULL, defined as 0, which a bison parser interprets as the end of input.

5. Or to put it another way, the error diagnostics are left as an exercise for the reader.

Symbol Tables and a Concordance Generator

Nearly every flex or bison program uses a *symbol table* to keep track of the names used in the input. We'll start with a very simple program that makes a *concordance*, which is a list of the line numbers where each word in the input appears, and then we'll modify it to read C source to make a C cross-referencer.

Managing Symbol Tables

Many long and dense chapters have been written in compiler texts on the topic of symbol tables, but this (I hope) is not one of them. The symbol table for the concordance simply tracks each word and the files and line numbers of each. Example 2-4 shows the declarations part of the concordance generator.

Example 2-4. Concordance generator

```
/* fb2-4 text concordance */
%option noyywrap nodefault yylineno case-insensitive

/* the symbol table */
%{
  struct symbol {              /* a word */
    char *name;
    struct ref *reflist;
  };

  struct ref {
    struct ref *next;
    char *filename;
    int flags;
    int lineno;
  };

  /* simple symtab of fixed size */
  #define NHASH 9997
  struct symbol symtab[NHASH];

  struct symbol *lookup(char*);
  void addref(int, char*, char*,int);

  char *curfilename;           /* name of current input file */

%}
%%
```

The %option line has two options we haven't seen before, both of which are quite useful. The %yylineno option tells flex to define an integer variable called yylineno and to maintain the current line number in it. What that means is that every time the scanner reads a newline character, it increments yylineno, and if the scanner backs up over a newline (using some features we'll get to later), it decrements it. It's still up to you to initialize yylineno to 1 at the beginning of each file and to save and restore it if you're handling include files. Even with those limitations, it's still easier than doing line numbers by hand. (In this example, there's only a single pattern that matches \n, which wouldn't be hard to get right, but it's quite common to have several patterns that match, causing hard-to-track bugs when some but not all of them update the line number.)

The other new option is `case-insensitive`, which tells flex to build a scanner that treats upper- and lowercase the same. What this means is that a pattern like abc will match *abc*, *Abc*, *ABc*, *AbC*, and so forth. It does *not* have any effect on your input; in particular, the matched string in yytext is not case folded or otherwise modified.

The symbol table is just an array of `symbol` structures, each of which contains a pointer to the name (i.e., the word in the concordance) and a list of references. The references are a linked list of line numbers and pointers to the filename. We also define `curfilename`, a static pointer to the name of the current file, for use when adding references.

```
%%
 /* rules for concordance generator */
 /* skip common words */
a |
an |
and |
are |
as |
at |
be |
but |
for |
in |
is |
it |
of |
on |
or |
that |
the |
this |
to                      /* ignore */

[a-z]+(\'(s|t))?   { addref(yylineno, curfilename, yytext, 0); }
.|\n                      /* ignore everything else */
%%
```

Concordances usually don't index common short words, so the first set of patterns matches and ignores them. An action consisting solely of a vertical bar tells flex that the action for this rule is the same as the action for the next rule. The action on the last ignored word to does nothing, which is all we need to do to ignore a word.

The next rule is the meat of the scanner and matches a reasonable approximation of an English word. It matches a string of letters, [a-z]+, optionally followed by an apostrophe and either s or t, to match words such as *owner's* and *can't*. Each matched word is passed to addref(), described in a moment, along with the current filename and line number.

The final pattern is a catchall to match whatever the previous patterns didn't.

Note that this scanner is extremely ambiguous, but flex's rules for resolving ambiguity make it do what we want. It prefers longer matches to shorter ones, so the word *toad* will be matched by the main word pattern, not *to*. If two patterns make an exact match, it prefers the earlier one in the program, which is why we put the ignore rules first and the catchall last.

```
/* concordance main routine */
main(argc, argv)
int argc;
char **argv;
{
  int i;

  if(argc < 2) { /* just read stdin */
    curfilename = "(stdin)";
    yylineno = 1;
    yylex();
  } else
  for(i = 1; i < argc; i++) {
    FILE *f = fopen(argv[i], "r");

    if(!f) {
      perror(argv[i]);
      return (1);
    }
    curfilename = argv[i];      /* for addref */

    yyrestart(f);
    yylineno = 1;
    yylex();
    fclose(f);
  }

  printrefs();
}
```

The main routine looks a lot like the one in the word count program that reads multiple files. It opens each file in turn, uses yyrestart to arrange to read the file, and calls yylex. The additions are setting curfilename to the name of the file, for use when building the list of references, and setting yylineno to 1 for each file. (Otherwise, the line numbers would continue from one file to another, which might be desirable in some situations, but not here.) Finally, printrefs alphabetizes the symbol table and prints the references.

Using a Symbol Table

The code section of the scanner includes a simple symbol table routine, a routine to add a word to the symbol table, and a routine to print out the concordance after all the input is run.

This symbol table is minimal but quite functional. It contains one routine, `lookup`, which takes a string and returns the address of the table entry for that name, creating a new entry if there isn't one already. The lookup technique is known as *hashing with linear probing*. It uses a hash function to turn the string into an entry number in the table, then checks the entry, and, if it's already taken by a different symbol, scans linearly until it finds a free entry.

The hash function is also quite simple: For each character, multiply the previous hash by 9 and then `xor` the character, doing all the arithmetic as unsigned, which ignores overflows. The lookup routine computes the symbol table entry index as the hash value modulo the size of the symbol table, which was chosen as a number with no even factors, again to mix the hash bits up.

```
/* hash a symbol */
static unsigned
symhash(char *sym)
{
  unsigned int hash = 0;
  unsigned c;

  while(c = *sym++) hash = hash*9 ^ c;

  return hash;
}

struct symbol *
lookup(char* sym)
{
  struct symbol *sp = &symtab[symhash(sym)%NHASH];
  int scount = NHASH;           /* how many have we looked at */

  while(--scount >= 0) {
    if(sp->name && !strcasecmp(sp->name, sym)) return sp;

    if(!sp->name) {             /* new entry */
      sp->name = strdup(sym);
      sp->reflist = 0;
      return sp;
    }

    if(++sp >= symtab+NHASH) sp = symtab; /* try the next entry */
  }
  fputs("symbol table overflow\n", stderr);
  abort(); /* tried them all, table is full */

}
```

Note that whenever `lookup` makes a new entry, it calls `strdup` to make a copy of the string to put into the symbol table entry. Flex and bison programs often have hard-to-track string storage management bugs, because it is easy to forget that the string in `yytext` will be there only until the next token is scanned.

This simple hash function and lookup routine works pretty well. I ran a group of text files through an instrumented version of the concordance program, with 4,429 different words and a total of 70,775 lookups. The average lookup took 1.32 probes, not far from the ideal minimum of 1.0.

```
void
addref(int lineno, char *filename, char *word, int flags)
{
  struct ref *r;
  struct symbol *sp = lookup(word);

  /* don't do dups of same line and file */
  if(sp->reflist &&
     sp->reflist->lineno == lineno &&
     sp->reflist->filename == filename) return;

  r = malloc(sizeof(struct ref));
  if(!r) {fputs("out of space\n", stderr); abort(); }
  r->next = sp->reflist;
  r->filename = filename;
  r->lineno = lineno;
  r->flags = flags;
  sp->reflist = r;
}
```

Next is `addref`, the routine called from inside the scanner to add a reference to a particular word; it's implemented as a linked list of reference structures chained from the symbol. In order to make the report a little shorter, it doesn't add a reference if the symbol already has a reference to the same line number and filename. Note that in this routine, we don't make a copy of the filename, because we know that the caller handed us a string that won't change. We don't copy the word either, since `lookup` will handle that if needed. Each reference has a `flags` value that isn't used here but will be when we reuse this code in the next example.

```
/* print the references
 * sort the table alphabetically
 * then flip each entry's reflist to get it into forward order
 * and print it out
 */

/* aux function for sorting */
static int
symcompare(const void *xa, const void *xb)
{
  const struct symbol *a = xa;
  const struct symbol *b = xb;

  if(!a->name) {
```

```
    if(!b->name) return 0;        /* both empty */
    return 1;                     /* put empties at the end */
  }
  if(!b->name) return -1;
  return strcmp(a->name, b->name);
}

void
printrefs()
{
  struct symbol *sp;

  qsort(symtab, NHASH, sizeof(struct symbol), symcompare); /* sort the symbol table */

  for(sp = symtab; sp->name && sp < symtab+NHASH; sp++) {
    char *prevfn = NULL;          /* last printed filename, to skip dups */

    /* reverse the list of references */
    struct ref *rp = sp->reflist;
    struct ref *rpp = 0;          /* previous ref */
    struct ref *rpn;      /* next ref */

    do {
      rpn = rp->next;
      rp->next = rpp;
      rpp = rp;
      rp = rpn;
    } while(rp);

    /* now print the word and its references */
    printf("%10s", sp->name);
    for(rp = rpp; rp; rp = rp->next) {
      if(rp->filename == prevfn) {
        printf(" %d", rp->lineno);
      } else {
        printf(" %s:%d", rp->filename, rp->lineno);
        prevfn = rp->filename;
      }
    }
    printf("\n");
  }
}
```

The final routines sort and print the symbol table. The symbol table is created in an order that depends on the hash function, which is not one that is useful to human readers, so we sort the symbol table alphabetically using the standard qsort function. Since the symbol table probably won't be full, the sort function puts unused symbol entries after used ones, so the sorted entries will end up at the front of the table.

Then printrefs runs down the table and prints out the references to each word. The references are in a linked list, but since each reference was pushed onto the front of the list, it is in reverse order. So, we make a pass over the list to flip the links and put it in forward order, and we then print it out.[6] To make the concordance somewhat more readable, we print the filename only if it's different from the one in the previous entry. We just compare the pointer to the filename, on the reasonable assumption that all entries for the same file will point to the same copy of the filename.

C Language Cross-Reference

The final example in this chapter takes all the techniques we've learned so far and uses them in one program, a fairly realistic C language cross-referencer (Example 2-5). It uses nested input files to handle #include statements, start states to handle includes and comments, a lexical hack to track when a mention of a symbol is a definition rather than a reference, and a symbol table to keep track of it all.

Example 2-5. C cross-referencer

```
/* fb2-5 C cross-ref */
%option noyywrap nodefault yylineno

%x COMMENT
%x IFILE

/* some complex named patterns */
/* Universal Character Name */
UCN     (\\u[0-9a-fA-F]{4}|\\U[0-9a-fA-F]{8})
/* float exponent */
EXP     ([Ee][-+]?[0-9]+)
/* integer length */
ILEN    ([Uu](L|l|LL|ll)?|(L|l|LL|ll)[Uu]?)
```

The options here are the same as for the concordance, except that there's no case folding, since C treats upper- and lowercase text differently. The two exclusive start states are COMMENT, used to skip text inside C comments, and IFILE, used in #include.

Next come three named patterns, for use later in the rule section. There's a style of flex programming that names every tiny subpattern, for example, DIGIT for [0-9]. I don't find that useful, but I do find it useful to name patterns that are both fairly complex and used inside other larger patterns. The first pattern matches a universal character name, which is a cumbersome way of putting non-ASCII characters into strings and identifiers. A UCN is \u followed by four hex digits or else \U followed by eight hex digits. The second pattern is for the exponent of a floating-point number, the letter E in upper- or lowercase, an optional sign, and a string of digits. The third pattern matches the length and type suffix on an integer constant, which is an optional U for unsigned or an optional L or LL for length, in either order, each in either upper- or lowercase. Each pattern is enclosed in parentheses to avoid an old lex/flex incompatibility: When

---

6. This trick of building the list in the wrong order and then reversing it is a handy one that we'll see again when building parse trees. It turns out to be quite efficient, since the reversal step takes just one pass over the list and requires no extra space in each individual entry.

flex interpolates a named pattern, it acts as though the pattern was enclosed in parens, but lex didn't, leading to some very obscure bugs.

```
/* the symbol table */
%{
  struct symbol {                /* a variable name */
    struct ref *reflist;
    char *name;
  };

  struct ref {
    struct ref *next;
    char *filename;
    int flags;                   /* 01 - definition */
    int lineno;
  };

  /* simple symtab of fixed size */
  #define NHASH 9997
  struct symbol symtab[NHASH];

  struct symbol *lookup(char*);
  void addref(int, char*, char*, int);

  char *curfilename;             /* name of current input file */
/* include file stack */
  struct bufstack {
    struct bufstack *prev;       /* previous entry */
    YY_BUFFER_STATE bs;          /* saved buffer */
    int lineno;                  /* saved line number in this file */
    char *filename;              /* name of this file */
    FILE *f;                     /* current file */
  } *curbs;

  int newfile(char *fn);
  int popfile(void);

  int defining;                  /* names are probably definitions */

%}
```

The rest of the front section should look familiar. The symbol table is the same as the one in the previous example. The file stack is the same as in Example 2-3.

Last is a new variable, `defining`, which is set when a mention of a name is likely to be a definition rather than a reference.

Next comes the rules section, which is much longer than any rules section we've seen before; this one is more typical of practical flex programs. Many of the token-matching rules are long and complicated but were actually quite easy to write by transliterating the BNF descriptions in the C standard. Although flex can't handle general BNF (you need bison for that), the tokens were deliberately designed to be matched by regular expressions, so the transliterations all work.

```
%%
 /* comments */
"/*"                    { BEGIN(COMMENT); }
<COMMENT>"*/"           { BEGIN(INITIAL); }
<COMMENT>([^*]|\n)+|.
<COMMENT><<EOF>>        { printf("%s:%d: Unterminated comment\n",
              curfilename, yylineno); return 0; }

 /* C++ comment, a common extension */
"//".*\n
```

An exclusive start state makes it easy to match C comments. The first rule starts the COMMENT state when it sees /*, and the second rule switches back to the normal INITIAL state on */. The third rule matches everything in between. Although the complexity of patterns doesn't affect the speed of a flex scanner, it is definitely faster to match one big pattern than several little ones. So, this rule could have just been .|\n, but the ([^*]|\n)+ can match a long string of text at once. Note that it has to exclude * so that the second rule can match */. The <COMMENT><<EOF>> rule catches and reports unterminated comments. Next is a bonus rule that matches C++-style comments, a common extension to C compilers.

Patterns for C Comments

Although it's possible to match C comments with a single flex pattern, it's generally not a great idea to do so. For reference, here's the pattern:

```
/\*([^*]|\*+[^/*])*\*+/
```

It matches the two characters that begin a comment, /*; then a sequence of nonstars or strings of stars followed by something other than a star or slash, ([^*]|*+[^/*])*; followed by at least one star and a closing slash, *+/.

There are two reasons to prefer the approach with multiple patterns and a start state. One is that comments can potentially be very long, if one comments out a couple of pages of code, but a flex token is limited to the size of the input buffer, typically 16K. (This is the kind of bug that is likely to be missed in testing.) The other is that it's much easier to catch and diagnose unclosed comments. It'd be possible to use a modified version of the previous pattern to match unclosed comments, but they'd be even more likely to run afoul of the 16K limit.

```
 /* declaration keywords */
_Bool |
_Complex |
_Imaginary |
auto |
char |
const |
double |
enum |
extern |
float |
```

```
inline |
int |
long |
register |
restrict |
short |
signed |
static |
struct |
typedef |
union |
unsigned |
void |
volatile { defining = 1; }

 /* keywords */
break
case
continue
default
do
else
for
goto
if
return
sizeof
switch
while
```

Next are patterns to match all of the C keywords. The keywords that introduce a definition or declaration set the `defining` flag; the other keywords are just ignored.

Another way to handle keywords is to put them into the symbol table with a flag saying they're keywords, treat them as ordinary symbols in the scanner, and recognize them via the symbol table lookup. This is basically a space versus time trade-off. Putting them into the scanner makes the scanner bigger but recognizes the keywords without an extra lookup. On modern computers the size of the scanner tables is rarely an issue, so it is easier to put them in the scanner; even with all the keywords, the tables in this program are less than 18K bytes.

```
 /* constants */

 /* integers */
0[0-7]*{ILEN}?
[1-9][0-9]*{ILEN}?
0[Xx][0-9a-fA-F]+{ILEN}?

 /* decimal float */
([0-9]*\.[0-9]+|[0-9]+\.){EXP}?[flFL]?
[0-9]+{EXP}[flFL]?

 /* hex float */
0[Xx]([0-9a-fA-F]*\.[0-9a-fA-F]+|[0-9a-fA-F]+\.?)[Pp][-+]?[0-9]+[flFL]?
```

Next come the patterns for numbers. The syntax for C numbers is surprisingly complicated, but the named ILEN and EXP subpatterns make the rules manageable. There's one pattern for each form of integer, octal, decimal, and hex, each with an optional unsigned and/or integer prefix. (This could have been done as one larger pattern, but it seems easier to read this way, and of course it's the same speed.)

Decimal floating-point numbers are very similar to the Fortran example earlier in the chapter. The first pattern matches a number that includes a decimal point and has an optional exponent. The second matches a number that doesn't have a decimal point, in which case the exponent is mandatory to make it floating point. (Without the exponent, it'd just be an integer.)

Finally comes the hex form of a floating-point number, with a binary exponent separated by P rather than E, so it can't use the EXP pattern.

```
/* char const */
\'([^'\\]|\\['"?\\abfnrtv]|\\[0-7]{1,3}|\\[Xx][0-9a-fA-F]+|{UCN})+\'

/* string literal */
L?\"([^"\\]|\\['"?\\abfnrtv]|\\[0-7]{1,3}|\\[Xx][0-9a-fA-F]+|{UCN})*\"
```

Next come very messy patterns for character and string literals. A character literal is a single quote followed by one or more of an ordinary character other than a quote or a backslash, a single character backslash escape such as \n, an octal escape with up to three octal digits, a hex escape with an arbitrary number of hex digits, or a UCN, all followed by a close quote. A string literal is the same syntax, except that it's enclosed in double quotes, has an optional prefix L to indicate a wide string, and doesn't have to contain any characters. (Note the + at the end of the character constant and the * at the end of the string.)

```
/* punctuators */
"{"|"<%"|";"              { defining = 0; }

"["|"]"|"("|")"|"{"|"}"|"."|"->"
"++"|"--"|"&"|"*"|"+"|"-"|"~"|"!"
"/"|"%"|"<<"|">>"|"<"|">"|"<="|">="|"=="|"!="|"^"|"|"|"&&"|"||"
"?"|":"|";"|"..."
"="|"*="|"/="|"%="|"+="|"-="|"<<="|">>="|"&="|"^="|"|="
","|"#"|"##"
"<:"|":>"|"%>"|"%:"|"%:%:"
```

C calls all of the operators and punctuation *punctuators*. For our purposes, we separately treat three that usually indicate the end of the names in a variable or function definition, and we ignore the rest.

```
/* identifier */
([_a-zA-Z]|{UCN})([_a-zA-Z0-9]|{UCN})* {
                        addref(yylineno, curfilename, yytext, defining); }

/* whitespace */
[ \t\n]+
```

```
    /* continued line */
    \\$
```

The C syntax of an identifier is a letter, underscore, or UCN, optionally followed by more letters, underscores, UCNs, and digits. When we see an identifier, we add a reference to it to the symbol table.

Two more patterns match and ignore whitespace and a backslash at the end of the line.

```
    /* some preprocessor stuff */
    "#"" "*if.*\n
    "#"" "*else.*\n
    "#"" "*endif.*\n
    "#"" "*define.*\n
    "#"" "*line.*\n

    /* recognize an include */
    ^"#"[ \t]*include[ \t]*[\"<] { BEGIN IFILE; }
    <IFILE>[^>\"]+  {
                        { int c;
                while((c = input()) && c != '\n') ;
                    }
                    newfile(strdup(yytext));
                    BEGIN INITIAL;
                    }

    <IFILE>.|\n     { fprintf(stderr, "%s:%d bad include line\n",
                    curfilename, yylineno);
                        BEGIN INITIAL;
                    }

    <<EOF>>         { if(!popfile()) yyterminate(); }
```

There's no totally satisfactory solution to handling preprocessor commands in a cross-referencer. One possibility would be to run the source program through the preprocessor first, but that would mean the cross-reference wouldn't see any of the symbols handled by the preprocessor, just the code it expanded to. We take a very simple approach here and just ignore all preprocessor commands other than #include. (A reasonable alternative would be to read whatever follows #define and #if and add that to the cross-reference.) The code to handle include files is nearly the same as the example earlier in this chapter, slightly modified to handle C's include syntax. One pattern matches #include up to the quote or < that precedes the filename, and then it switches to IFILE state. The next pattern collects the file name, skips the rest of the line, and switches to the new file. It's a little sloppy and doesn't try to ensure that the punctuation before and after the filename matches. The next two patterns complain if there's no filename and return to the previous file at the end of each included one.

```
    /* invalid character */
    .               { printf("%s:%d: Mystery character '%s'\n",
                    curfilename, yylineno, yytext);
                    }
    %%
```

The final pattern is a simple . to catch anything that none of the previous patterns did. Since the patterns cover every token that can appear in a valid C program, this pattern shouldn't ever match.

The contents of the code section are very similar to code we've already seen. The first two routines, symhash and lookup, are identical to the versions in the previous example and aren't shown again here. The version of addref is the same as in the earlier include example. This version of printrefs is slightly different. It has a line to print a * for each reference that's flagged as being a definition.

```
void
printrefs()
{
  struct symbol *sp;

  qsort(symtab, NHASH, sizeof(struct symbol), symcompare); /* sort the symbol table */

  for(sp = symtab; sp->name && sp < symtab+NHASH; sp++) {
    char *prevfn = NULL;    /* last printed filename, to skip dups */

    /* reverse the list of references */
    struct ref *rp = sp->reflist;
    struct ref *rpp = 0;     /* previous ref */
    struct ref *rpn;     /* next ref */

    do {
      rpn = rp->next;
      rp->next = rpp;
      rpp = rp;
      rp = rpn;
    } while(rp);

    /* now print the word and its references */
    printf("%10s", sp->name);
    for(rp = rpp; rp; rp = rp->next) {
      if(rp->filename == prevfn) {
    printf(" %d", rp->lineno);
      } else {
    printf(" %s:%d", rp->filename, rp->lineno);
    prevfn = rp->filename;
      }
      if(rp->flags & 01) printf("*");
    }
    printf("\n");
  }
}
```

The versions of newfile and popfile are the same as the ones earlier in this chapter, so they aren't repeated here. In this program, if newfile can't open a file, it just prints an error message, returning 1 if it opened the file and 0 if it didn't, and the include code in the rules section just goes on to the next line. This wouldn't be a good idea in a regular compiler. For a cross-referencer, it has the reasonable effect of processing include files in the same directory that are specific to the current program, while skipping library files in other directories.

Finally, the main program just calls newfile and, if it succeeds, yylex for each file.

```
int
main(argc, argv)
int argc;
char **argv;
{
    int i;

    if(argc < 2) {
        fprintf(stderr, "need filename\n");
        return 1;
    }
    for(i = 1; i < argc; i++) {
        if(newfile(argv[i]))
            yylex();
    }

    printrefs();
    return 0;
}
```

This concludes our first realistically large flex program. It has a fairly complex set of patterns, has somewhat complex file I/O, and does something with the text it reads.

Exercises

1. Example 2-3 matches characters one at a time. Why doesn't it match them a line at a time with a pattern like ^.*\n? Suggest a pattern or combination of patterns that would match larger chunks of text, keeping in mind the reason ^.* won't work.

2. The concordance program treats upper- and lowercase text separately. Modify it to handle them together. You can do this without making extra copies of the words. In symhash(), use tolower to hash lowercase versions of the characters, and use strcasecmp() to compare words.

3. The symbol table routine in the concordance and cross-referencer programs uses a fixed-size symbol table and dies if it fills up. Modify the routine so it doesn't do that. The two standard techniques to allow variable-sized hash tables are *chaining* and *rehashing*. Chaining turns the hash table into a table of pointers to a list of symbol entries. Lookups run down the chain to find the symbol, and if it's not found, allocate a new entry with malloc() and add it to the chain. Rehashing creates an initial fixed-size symbol table, again using malloc(). When the symbol table fills up, create a new larger symbol table and copy all the entries into it, using the hash function to decide where each entry goes in the new table. Both techniques work, but one would make it a lot messier to produce the cross-reference. Which one? Why?

# CHAPTER 3

Using Bison

The previous chapter concentrated on flex alone. In this chapter we turn our attention to bison, although we use flex to generate our lexical analyzers. Where flex recognizes regular expressions, bison recognizes entire grammars. Flex divides the input stream into pieces (*tokens*), and then bison takes these pieces and groups them together logically. In this chapter we'll finish the desk calculator we started in Chapter 1, starting with simple arithmetic and then adding built-in functions, user variables, and finally user-defined functions.

How a Bison Parser Matches Its Input

Bison takes a grammar that you specify and writes a parser that recognizes valid "sentences" in that grammar. We use the term *sentence* here in a fairly general way—for a C language grammar, the sentences are syntactically valid C programs. Programs can be syntactically valid but semantically invalid, for example, a C program that assigns a string to an int variable. Bison handles only the syntax; other validation is up to you. As we saw in Chapter 1, a grammar is a series of rules that the parser uses to recognize syntactically valid input. For example, here is a version of the grammar we'll use later in this chapter in a calculator:

```
statement:   NAME '=' expression

expression:  NUMBER '+' NUMBER
          |  NUMBER '-' NUMBER
```

The vertical bar, |, means there are two possibilities for the same symbol; that is, an expression can be either an addition or a subtraction. The symbol to the left of the : is known as the *left-hand side* of the rule, often abbreviated LHS, and the symbols to the right are the *right-hand side*, usually abbreviated RHS. Several rules may have the same left-hand side; the vertical bar is just shorthand for this. Symbols that actually appear in the input and are returned by the lexer are terminal symbols or tokens, while those that appear on the left-hand side of each rule are nonterminal symbols or nonterminals.

Terminal and nonterminal symbols must be different; it is an error to write a rule with a token on the left side.

The usual way to represent a parsed sentence is as a tree. For example, if we parsed the input `fred = 12 + 13` with this grammar, the tree would look like Figure 3-1.

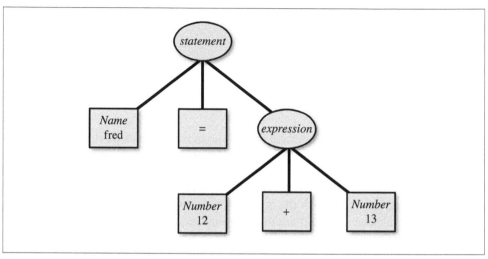

Figure 3-1. Expression parse tree

In this example, `12 + 13` is an expression, and `fred = expression` is a statement. A bison parser doesn't automatically create this tree as a data structure, although as we will see, it is not hard to do so yourself. Every grammar includes a start symbol, the one that has to be at the root of the parse tree. In this grammar, `statement` is the start symbol. Rules can refer directly or indirectly to themselves; this important ability makes it possible to parse arbitrarily long input sequences. Let's extend our grammar to handle longer arithmetic expressions:

```
expression: NUMBER
          | expression '+' NUMBER
          | expression '-' NUMBER
```

Now we can parse a sequence like `fred = 14 + 23 - 11 + 7` by applying the expression rules repeatedly, as in Figure 3-2. Bison can parse recursive rules very efficiently, so we will see recursive rules in nearly every grammar we use.

Shift/Reduce Parsing

A bison parser works by looking for rules that might match the tokens seen so far. When bison processes a parser, it creates a set of states, each of which reflects a possible position in one or more partially parsed rules. As the parser reads tokens, each time it reads a token that doesn't complete a rule, it pushes the token on an internal stack and

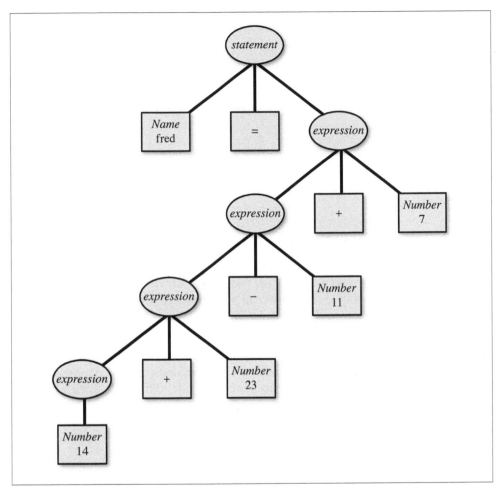

Figure 3-2. Parse tree with recursive rules

switches to a new state reflecting the token it just read. This action is called a *shift*. When it has found all the symbols that constitute the right-hand side of a rule, it pops the right-hand side symbols off the stack, pushes the left-hand side symbol onto the stack, and switches to a new state reflecting the new symbol on the stack. This action is called a *reduction*, since it usually reduces the number of items on the stack.[1] Whenever bison reduces a rule, it executes user code associated with the rule. This is how you actually do something with the material that the parser parses. Let's look how it parses the input `fred = 12 + 13` using the simple rules in Figure 3-1. The parser starts by shifting tokens on to the internal stack one at a time:

---

1. It is possible to have rules with empty right-hand sides, in which case a reduction ends up with one more item than it started with, but we call them reductions anyway.

```
fred
fred =
fred = 12
fred = 12 +
fred = 12 + 13
```

At this point it can reduce the rule expression: NUMBER + NUMBER, so it pops the 12, the plus, and the 13 from the stack and replaces them with *expression*:

```
fred = expression
```

Now it reduces the rule statement: NAME = expression, so it pops fred, =, and *expression* and replaces them with *statement*. We've reached the end of the input and the stack has been reduced to the start symbol, so the input was valid according to the grammar.

What Bison's LALR(1) Parser Cannot Parse

Bison parsers can use either of two parsing methods, known as LALR(1) (Look Ahead Left to Right with a one-token lookahead) and GLR (Generalized Left to Right). Most parsers use LALR(1), which is less powerful but considerably faster and easier to use than GLR. In this chapter we'll describe LALR parsing and save GLR for Chapter 9.

Although LALR parsing is quite powerful, you can write grammars that it cannot handle. It cannot deal with ambiguous grammars, ones in which the same input can match more than one parse tree. It also cannot deal with grammars that need more than one token of lookahead to tell whether it has matched a rule. (But bison has a wonderful hack to deal with the most common kind of ambiguous grammars, which we'll come to in a few pages.) Consider this extremely contrived example:

```
phrase:  cart_animal AND CART
       | work_animal AND PLOW

cart_animal: HORSE | GOAT

work_animal: HORSE | OX
```

This grammar isn't ambiguous, since there is only one possible parse tree for any valid input, but bison can't handle it because it requires two symbols of lookahead. In particular, in the input HORSE AND CART it cannot tell whether HORSE is a cart_animal, or a work_animal until it sees CART, and bison cannot look that far ahead. If we changed the first rule to this:

```
phrase: cart_animal CART
      | work_animal PLOW
```

bison would have no trouble, since it can look one token ahead to see whether an input of HORSE is followed by CART, in which case the horse is a cart_animal, or by PLOW, in which case it is a work_animal. In practice, the rules about what bison can handle are not as complex and confusing as they may seem here. One reason is that bison knows exactly what grammars it can parse and what it cannot. If you give it one that it cannot handle, it will tell you, so there is no problem of overcomplex parsers silently failing. Another reason is that the grammars that bison can handle correspond pretty well to ones that people really write. As often as not, a grammatical construct that confuses bison will confuse people as well, so if you have some latitude in your language design, you should consider changing the language to make it more understandable both to bison and to its users. For more information on shift/reduce parsing, see Chapter 7. For a discussion of what bison has to do to turn your specification into a working C program, a good reference is Dick Grune's *Parsing Techniques: A Practical Guide*. He offers a download of an old but quite adequate edition at *http://www.cs.vu.nl/~dick/ PTAPG.html*.

A Bison Parser

A bison specification has the same three-part structure as a flex specification. (Flex copied its structure from the earlier lex, which copied its structure from yacc, the predecessor of bison.) The first section, the definition section, handles control information for the parser and generally sets up the execution environment in which the parser will operate. The second section contains the rules for the parser, and the third section is C code copied verbatim into the generated C program.

Bison creates the C program by plugging pieces into a standard skeleton file. The rules are compiled into arrays that represent the state machine that matches the input tokens. The actions have the $N and @N values translated into C and then are put into a switch statement within yyparse() that runs the appropriate action each time there's a reduction. Some bits of the skeleton have multiple versions from which bison chooses depending on what options are in use; for example, if the parser uses the locations feature, it includes code to handle location data.

In this chapter we take the simple calculator example from Chapter 1 and extend it significantly. First, we rewrite it to take advantage of some handy bison shortcuts and change it to produce a reusable data structure rather than computing the values on the fly. Later, we'll add more complex syntax for loops and functions and show how to implement them in a simple interpreter.[2]

Abstract Syntax Trees

One of the most powerful data structures used in compilers is an *abstract syntax tree* (AST). In Chapter 1 we saw a parse tree, a tree that has a node for every rule used to parse the input string. In most real grammars, there are rules that exist to manage grouping but that add no meaning to the program. In the calculator example, the rules

---

2. Then we'll stop; the world has plenty of script interpreter programs already. For practical purposes, you'll be much better off adding a few extensions to an existing well-debugged scripting language such as Python, Perl, or Lua rather than writing yet another one.

exp: term and term: factor exist only to tell the parser the relative precedence of the operators. An AST is basically a parse tree that omits the nodes for the uninteresting rules.

Once a parser creates an AST, it's straightforward to write recursive routines that "walk" the tree. We'll see several tree walkers in this example.

An Improved Calculator That Creates ASTs

This example is big enough to be worth dividing into several source files, so we'll put most of the C code into a separate file, which means we also need a C header file to declare the routines and data structures used in the various files (Example 3-1).

Example 3-1. Calculator that builds an AST: header fb3-1.h

```
/*
 * Declarations for a calculator fb3-1
 */

/* interface to the lexer */
extern int yylineno; /* from lexer */
void yyerror(char *s, ...);

/* nodes in the abstract syntax tree */
struct ast {
  int nodetype;
  struct ast *l;
  struct ast *r;
};

struct numval {
  int nodetype;    /* type K for constant */
  double number;
};

/* build an AST */
struct ast *newast(int nodetype, struct ast *l, struct ast *r);
struct ast *newnum(double d);

/* evaluate an AST */
double eval(struct ast *);

/* delete and free an AST */
void treefree(struct ast *);
```

The variable yylineno and routine yyerror are familiar from the flex example. Our yyerror is slightly enhanced to take multiple arguments in the style of printf.

The AST consists of nodes, each of which has a node type. Different nodes have different fields, but for now we have just two kinds, one that has pointers to up to two subnodes and one that contains a number. Two routines, newast and newnum, create AST nodes;

`eval` walks an AST and returns the value of the expression it represents; and `treefree` walks an AST and deletes all of its nodes.

Example 3-2. Bison parser for AST calculator

```
/* calculator with AST */

%{
#  include <stdio.h>
#  include <stdlib.h>
#  include "fb3-1.h"
%}

%union {
  struct ast *a;
  double d;
}

/* declare tokens */
%token <d> NUMBER
%token EOL

%type <a> exp factor term
```

Example 3-2 shows the bison parser for the AST calculator. The first section of the parser uses the `%union` construct to declare types to be used in the values of symbols in the parser. In a bison parser, every symbol, both tokens and nonterminals, can have a value associated with it. By default, the values are all integers, but useful programs generally need more sophisticated values. The `%union` construct, as its name suggests, is used to create a C language `union` declaration for symbol values. In this case, the union has two members; `a`, which is a pointer to an AST, and `d`, which is a double precision number.

Once the union is defined, we need to tell bison what symbols have what types of values by putting the appropriate name from the union in angle brackets (`< >`). The token `NUMBER`, which represents numbers in the input, has the value `<d>` to hold the value of the number. The new declaration `%type` assigns the value `<a>` to exp, `factor`, and `term`, which we'll use as we build up our AST.

You don't have to declare a type for a token or declare a nonterminal at all if you don't use the symbol's value. If there is a `%union` in the declarations, bison will give you an error if you attempt to use the value of a symbol that doesn't have an assigned type. Keep in mind that any rule without explicit action code gets the default action `$$ = $1;`, and bison will complain if the LHS symbol has a type and the RHS symbol doesn't have the same type.

```
%%
calclist: /* nothing */
 | calclist exp EOL {
     printf("= %4.4g\n", eval($2));      evaluate and print the AST
     treefree($2);                       free up the AST
```

```
        printf("> ");
    }

    | calclist EOL { printf("> "); } /* blank line or a comment */
    ;

exp: factor
    | exp '+' factor { $$ = newast('+', $1,$3); }
    | exp '-' factor { $$ = newast('-', $1,$3);}
    ;

factor: term
    | factor '*' term { $$ = newast('*', $1,$3); }
    | factor '/' term { $$ = newast('/', $1,$3); }
    ;

term: NUMBER { $$ = newnum($1); }
    | '|' term { $$ = newast('|', $2, NULL); }
    | '(' exp ')' { $$ = $2; }
    | '-' term { $$ = newast('M', $2, NULL); }
    ;
%%
```

Literal Character Tokens

The rules section has two significant changes from the version in Chapter 1. One is that the rules now use literal tokens for the operators. Rather than giving every token a name, it's also possible to use a single quoted character as a token, with the ASCII value of the token being the token number. (Bison starts the numbers for named tokens at 258, so there's no problem of collisions.) By convention, literal character tokens are used to represent input tokens consisting of the same character; for example, the token '+' represents the input token +, so in practice they are used only for punctuation and operators. There's no need to declare literal character tokens unless you need to declare the type of their values.

The other change to the parser is that it creates an AST for each expression rather than evaluating it on the fly. In this version of the calculator, we create an AST for each expression and then evaluate the AST, print the result, and free the AST. We call newast() to create each node in the AST. Each node has an operator type, which is generally the same as the token name. Notice that unary minus creates a node of type M to distinguish it from binary subtraction.

Example 3-3. Lexer for AST calculator

```
/* recognize tokens for the calculator */
%option noyywrap nodefault yylineno
%{
# include "fb3-1.h"
# include "fb3-1.tab.h"
%}
```

```
/* float exponent */
EXP     ([Ee][-+]?[0-9]+)

%%
"+" |
"-" |
"*" |
"/" |
"|" |
"(" |
")"     { return yytext[0]; }
[0-9]+"."[0-9]*{EXP}? |
"."?[0-9]+{EXP}? { yylval.d = atof(yytext); return NUMBER; }

\n      { return EOL; }
"//".*
[ \t]   { /* ignore whitespace */ }
.       { yyerror("Mystery character %c\n", *yytext); }
%%
```

The lexer, shown in Example 3-3, is a little simpler than the version in Chapter 1. We use a common idiom for the single-character operators, handling them all with the same rule that returns yytext[0], the character itself, as the token. We do still have names for NUMBER and EOL. We also handle floating-point numbers, using a version of the pattern from Chapter 2, and change the internal representation of numbers to double. Since yylval is now a union, the double value has to be assigned to yylval.d. (Flex does not automate the management of token values as bison does.)

Example 3-4. C routines for AST calculator

```
#   include <stdio.h>
#   include <stdlib.h>
#   include <stdarg.h>
#   include "fb3-1.h"

struct ast *
newast(int nodetype, struct ast *l, struct ast *r)
{
  struct ast *a = malloc(sizeof(struct ast));

  if(!a) {
    yyerror("out of space");
    exit(0);
  }
  a->nodetype = nodetype;
  a->l = l;
  a->r = r;
  return a;
}

struct ast *
newnum(double d)
{
  struct numval *a = malloc(sizeof(struct numval));
```

```
  if(!a) {
    yyerror("out of space");
    exit(0);
  }
  a->nodetype = 'K';
  a->number = d;
  return (struct ast *)a;
}
```

Finally, there is a file of routines called from the parser, shown in Example 3-4.[3] First come the two routines to create AST nodes, by malloc-ing a node and filling it in. All AST nodes have a nodetype as the first field, so a tree walk can tell what kind of nodes it's walking through.

```
double
eval(struct ast *a)
{
  double v;   calculated value of this subtree

  switch(a->nodetype) {
  case 'K': v = ((struct numval *)a)->number; break;

  case '+': v = eval(a->l) + eval(a->r); break;
  case '-': v = eval(a->l) - eval(a->r); break;
  case '*': v = eval(a->l) * eval(a->r); break;
  case '/': v = eval(a->l) / eval(a->r); break;
  case '|': v = eval(a->l); if(v < 0) v = -v; break;
  case 'M': v = -eval(a->l); break;
  default: printf("internal error: bad node %c\n", a->nodetype);
  }
  return v;
}

void
treefree(struct ast *a)
{
  switch(a->nodetype) {

    /* two subtrees */
  case '+':
  case '-':
  case '*':
  case '/':
    treefree(a->r);

    /* one subtree */
  case '|':
  case 'M':
    treefree(a->l);
```

---

3. These could have gone in the third section of the parser, but it's easier to debug your program if you don't put a lot of extra code in the parser file.

```
    /* no subtree */
  case 'K':
    free(a);
    break;

  default: printf("internal error: free bad node %c\n", a->nodetype);
  }
}
```

Next we have the two tree-walking routines. They each make what's known as a *depth-first* traversal of the tree, recursively visiting the subtrees of each node and then the node itself. The **eval** routine returns the value of the tree or subtree from each call, and the **treefree** doesn't have to return anything.

```
void
yyerror(char *s, ...)
{
  va_list ap;
  va_start(ap, s);

  fprintf(stderr, "%d: error: ", yylineno);
  vfprintf(stderr, s, ap);
  fprintf(stderr, "\n");
}

int
main()
{
  printf("> ");
  return yyparse();
}
```

Finally, we have **yyerror** and **main**. This version of **yyerror** uses varargs to accept a printf-style argument list, which turns out to be convenient when generating error messages.

Building the AST Calculator

This program now has three source files and a header file, so of course we use make to build it.

```
fb3-1:  fb3-1.l fb3-1.y fb3-1.h
        bison -d fb3-1.y
        flex -ofb3-1.lex.c fb3-1.l
        cc -o $@ fb3-1.tab.c fb3-1.lex.c fb3-1funcs.c
```

Notice the -o flag to flex. Bison automatically names its generated C file to match the .y file, but flex always calls its C file lex.yy.c unless you tell it otherwise.

Shift/Reduce Conflicts and Operator Precedence

The expression parser uses three different symbols, exp, factor, and term, to set the precedence and associativity of operators. Although this parser is still reasonably legible, as grammars add more operators with more levels of precedence, they become increasingly hard to read and maintain. Bison provides a clever way to describe the precedence separately from the rules in the grammar, which makes the grammar and parser smaller and easier to maintain. First, we'll just make all expressions use exp symbols:

```
%type <a> exp

%%
...
exp: exp '+' exp { $$ = newast('+', $1,$3); }
   | exp '-' exp { $$ = newast('-', $1,$3);}
   | exp '*' exp { $$ = newast('*', $1,$3); }
   | exp '/' exp { $$ = newast('/', $1,$3); }
   | '|' exp     { $$ = newast('|', $2, NULL); }
   | '(' exp ')' { $$ = $2; }
   | '-' exp     { $$ = newast('M', $2, NULL); }
   | NUMBER      { $$ = newnum($1); }
   ;
%%
```

But this grammar has a problem: It is extremely ambiguous. For example, the input 2+3*4 might mean (2+3)*4 or 2+(3*4), and the input 3-4-5-6 might mean 3-(4-(5-6)) or (3-4)-(5-6) or any of a lot of other possibilities. Figure 3-3 shows the two possible parses for 2+3*4.

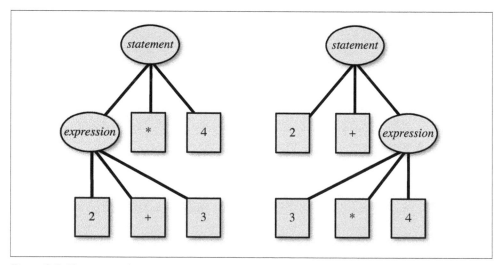

Figure 3-3. Two expression parse trees

If you compile this grammar as it stands, bison will tell you that there are 24 *shift/reduce conflicts*, which are states where it cannot tell whether it should shift the token on the stack or reduce a rule first. For example, when parsing 2+3*4, the parser goes through these steps (we abbreviate exp as E here):

```
2           shift NUMBER
E           reduce E → NUMBER
E +         shift +
E + 3       shift NUMBER
E + E       reduce E → NUMBER
```

At this point, the parser looks at the * and could either reduce 2+3 using:

```
exp:        exp '+' exp
```

to an expression or shift the *, expecting to be able to reduce:

```
exp:        exp '*' exp
```

later on.

The problem is that we haven't told bison about the precedence and associativity of the operators. *Precedence* controls which operators execute first in an expression. Mathematical and programming tradition (dating back past the first Fortran compiler in 1956) says that multiplication and division take precedence over addition and subtraction, so a+b*c means a+(b*c), and d/e-f means (d/e)-f. In any expression grammar, operators are grouped into levels of precedence from lowest to highest. The total number of levels depends on the language. The C language is notorious for having too many precedence levels, a total of 15 levels.

Associativity controls the grouping of operators at the same precedence level. Operators may group to the left, for example, a-b-c in C means (a-b)-c, or to the right, for example, a=b=c in C means a=(b=c). In some cases, operators do not group at all; for example, in Fortran A.LE.B.LE.C is invalid.

There are two ways to specify precedence and associativity in a grammar, implicitly and explicitly. So far, we've specified them implicitly, by using separate nonterminal symbols for each precedence level. This is a perfectly reasonable way to write a grammar, and if bison didn't have explicit precedence rules, it would be the only way.

But bison also lets you specify precedence explicitly. We can add these lines to the declaration section to tell it how to resolve the conflicts:

```
%left '+' '-'
%left '*' '/'
%nonassoc '|' UMINUS

%type <a> exp

%%
 ...
exp: exp '+' exp { $$ = newast('+', $1,$3); }
   | exp '-' exp { $$ = newast('-', $1,$3);}
```

```
        | exp '*' exp { $$ = newast('*', $1,$3); }
        | exp '/' exp { $$ = newast('/', $1,$3); }
        | '|' exp     { $$ = newast('|', $2, NULL); }
        | '(' exp ')' { $$ = $2; }
        | '-' exp %prec UMINUS{ $$ = newast('M', NULL, $2); }
        | NUMBER      { $$ = newnum($1); }
    ;
```

Each of these declarations defines a level of precedence, with the order of the `%left`, `%right`, and `%nonassoc` declarations defining the order of precedence from lowest to highest. They tell bison that + and - are left associative and at the lowest precedence level; * and / are left associative and at a higher precedence level; and | and `UMINUS`, a pseudotoken standing for unary minus, have no associativity and are at the highest precedence. (We don't have any right-associative operators here, but if we did, they'd use `%right`.) Bison assigns each rule the precedence of the rightmost token on the right-hand side; if that token has no precedence assigned, the rule has no precedence of its own. When bison encounters a shift/reduce conflict, it consults the table of precedence, and if all the rules involved in the conflict have a precedence assigned, it uses precedence to resolve the conflict.

In our grammar, all of the conflicts occur in the rules of the form `exp OP exp`, so setting precedence for the four operators allows it to resolve all of the conflicts. This parser using precedence is slightly smaller and faster than the one with the extra rules for implicit precedence, since it has fewer rules to reduce.

The rule for negation includes `%prec UMINUS`. The only operator in this rule is -, which has low precedence, but we want unary minus to have higher precedence than multiplication rather than lower. The `%prec` tells bison to use the precedence of `UMINUS` for this rule.

When Not to Use Precedence Rules

You can use precedence rules to fix any shift/reduce conflict that occurs in the grammar. This is usually a terrible idea. In expression grammars, the cause of the conflicts is easy to understand, and the effect of the precedence rules is clear. In other situations, precedence rules fix shift/reduce problems, but it can be extremely difficult to understand just what effect they have on the grammar.

Use precedence in only two situations: in expression grammars and to resolve the "dangling else" conflict in grammars for if/then/else language constructs. (See the section "IF/THEN/ELSE" on page 185 for examples of the latter.) Otherwise, if you can, you should fix the grammar to remove the conflict. Remember that conflicts mean that bison can't create a parser for a grammar, probably because it's ambiguous. This means there are multiple possible parses for the same input and the parser that bison created chose one of them. Except in the two previous cases, this usually points to a problem in your language definition. In some cases, if a grammar is ambiguous to bison, it's almost certainly ambiguous to humans, too. See Chapter 8 for more information on finding and repairing conflicts, as well as the advanced bison features that let you use ambiguous grammars if you really want to do so.

An Advanced Calculator

The final example in this chapter extends the calculator to make it a small but somewhat realistic compiler. We'll add named variables and assignments; comparison expressions (greater, less, equal, etc.); flow control with if/then/else and while/do; built-in and user-defined functions; and a little error recovery. The previous version of the calculator didn't take much advantage of the AST representation of expressions, but in this one, the AST is the key to the implementation of flow control and user functions. Here's an example of defining a user function, and then calling it, using a built-in function as one of the arguments:

```
> let avg(a,b) = (a+b)/2;
Defined avg
> avg(3, sqrt(25))
=    4
```

As before, we start with the declarations, shown in Example 3-5.

Example 3-5. Advanced calculator header fb3-2.h

```
/*
 * Declarations for a calculator fb3-1
 */

/* interface to the lexer */
extern int yylineno; /* from lexer */
void yyerror(char *s, ...);

/* symbol table */
struct symbol {          /* a variable name */
  char *name;
  double value;
  struct ast *func;      /* stmt for the function */
  struct symlist *syms; /* list of dummy args */
};

/* simple symtab of fixed size */
#define NHASH 9997
struct symbol symtab[NHASH];

struct symbol *lookup(char*);

/* list of symbols, for an argument list */
struct symlist {
  struct symbol *sym;
  struct symlist *next;
};
```

```
struct symlist *newsymlist(struct symbol *sym, struct symlist *next);
void symlistfree(struct symlist *sl);
```

The symbol table is adapted from the one used in the previous chapter. In the calculator, each symbol can potentially be both a variable and a user-defined function. The value field holds the symbol's value as a variable, the func field points to the AST for the user code for the function, and syms points to a linked list of the dummy arguments, which are themselves symbols. (In the previous example, avg is the function, and a and b are the dummy arguments.) The C functions newsymlist and symlistfree create and free them.

```
/* node types
 *  + - * / |
 *  0-7 comparison ops, bit coded 04 equal, 02 less, 01 greater
 *  M unary minus
 *  L expression or statement list
 *  I IF statement
 *  W WHILE statement
 *  N symbol ref
 *  = assignment
 *  S list of symbols
 *  F built in function call
 *  C user function call
 */

enum bifs {                      /* built-in functions */
  B_sqrt = 1,
  B_exp,
  B_log,
  B_print
};

/* nodes in the abstract syntax tree */
/* all have common initial nodetype */

struct ast {
  int nodetype;
  struct ast *l;
  struct ast *r;
};

struct fncall {                  /* built-in function */
  int nodetype;                  /* type F */
  struct ast *l;
  enum bifs functype;
};

struct ufncall {                 /* user function */
  int nodetype;                  /* type C */
  struct ast *l;                 /* list of arguments */
  struct symbol *s;
};

struct flow {
```

```
  int nodetype;              /* type I or W */
  struct ast *cond;          /* condition */
  struct ast *tl;            /* then branch or do list */
  struct ast *el;            /* optional else branch */
};

struct numval {
  int nodetype;              /* type K */
  double number;
};

struct symref {
  int nodetype;              /* type N */
  struct symbol *s;
};

struct symasgn {
  int nodetype;              /* type = */
  struct symbol *s;
  struct ast *v;             /* value */
};

/* build an AST */
struct ast *newast(int nodetype, struct ast *l, struct ast *r);
struct ast *newcmp(int cmptype, struct ast *l, struct ast *r);
struct ast *newfunc(int functype, struct ast *l);
struct ast *newcall(struct symbol *s, struct ast *l);
struct ast *newref(struct symbol *s);
struct ast *newasgn(struct symbol *s, struct ast *v);
struct ast *newnum(double d);
struct ast *newflow(int nodetype, struct ast *cond, struct ast *tl, struct ast *tr);

/* define a function */
void dodef(struct symbol *name, struct symlist *syms, struct ast *stmts);

/* evaluate an AST */
double eval(struct ast *);

/* delete and free an AST */
void treefree(struct ast *);
```

This version has considerably more kinds of nodes in the AST. As before, each kind of node starts with a nodetype that the tree-walking code can use to tell what kind of node it is.[4] The basic ast node is also used for comparisons, with each kind of comparison (less, less-equal, equal, etc.) being a different type, and for lists of expressions.

Built-in functions have a fncall node with the AST of the argument (the built-ins each take one argument) and an enum that says which built-in function it is. There are three standard functions, sqrt, exp, and log, as well as print, a function that prints its argument and returns the argument as its value. Calls to user functions have a ufncall node

---

4. This is a classic C trick that doesn't work in C++. If you write your parser in C++, as we describe in Chapter 9, you'll have to use an explicit union of structures within the AST structure to get a similar result.

with a pointer to the function, which is an entry in the symbol table, and an AST, which is a list of the arguments.

Flow control expressions if/then/else and while/do use a flow node with the control expression, the then branch or do list, and the optional else branch.

Constants are numval as before; references to symbols are symref with a pointer to the symbol in the symbol table; and assignments are symasgn with a pointer to the symbol to be assigned and the AST of the value to assign to it.

Every AST has a value. The value of an if/then/else is the value of the branch taken; the value of while/do is the last value of the do list; and the value of a list of expressions is the last expression.[5] Finally, we have C procedures to create each kind of AST node and a procedure to create a user-defined function.

Advanced Calculator Parser

Example 3-6 shows the parser for the advanced AST calculator.

Example 3-6. Advanced calculator parser fb3-2.y

```
/* calculator with AST */

%{
#   include <stdio.h>
#   include <stdlib.h>
#   include "fb3-2.h"
%}

%union {
  struct ast *a;
  double d;
  struct symbol *s;          /* which symbol */
  struct symlist *sl;
  int fn;                    /* which function */
}

/* declare tokens */
%token <d> NUMBER
%token <s> NAME
%token <fn> FUNC
%token EOL

%token IF THEN ELSE WHILE DO LET

%nonassoc <fn> CMP
%right '='
%left '+' '-'
```

---

5. This design is vaguely based on the ancient BLISS system programming language. It would be perfectly possible to design an AST that treated expressions and statements separately, but the implementation is a little simpler this way.

```
%left '*' '/'
%nonassoc '|' UMINUS

%type <a> exp stmt list explist
%type <sl> symlist

%start calclist
%%
```

The **%union** here defines many kinds of symbol values, which is typical in realistic bison parsers. As well as a pointer to an AST and a numeric value, a value can be a pointer to the symbol table for a user symbol, a list of symbols, or a subtype of a comparison or function token. (We use the word *symbol* somewhat confusingly here, both for names used in the bison grammar and for names that the user types into the compiled program. We'll say *user symbol* for the latter when the context isn't otherwise clear.)

There's a new token FUNC for the built-in functions, with the value indicating which function, and six reserved words, IF through LET. The token CMP is any of the six comparison operators, with the value indicating which operator. (This trick of using one token for several syntactically similar operators helps keep down the size of the grammar.)

The list of precedence declarations starts with the new CMP and = operators.

A **%start** declaration identifies the top-level rule, so we don't have to put it at the beginning of the parser.

Calculator Statement Syntax

```
stmt: IF exp THEN list            { $$ = newflow('I', $2, $4, NULL); }
    | IF exp THEN list ELSE list  { $$ = newflow('I', $2, $4, $6); }
    | WHILE exp DO list           { $$ = newflow('W', $2, $4, NULL); }
    | exp
;

list: /* nothing */ { $$ = NULL; }
    | stmt ';' list { if ($3 == NULL)
                          $$ = $1;
                      else
                          $$ = newast('L', $1, $3);
                    }
    ;
```

Our grammar distinguishes between statements (stmt) and expressions (exp). A statement is either a flow of control (if/then/else or while/do) or an expression. The if and while statements take lists of statements, with each statement in the list being followed by a semicolon. Each rule that matches a statement calls a routine to build an appropriate AST node.

The design of the syntax here is largely arbitrary, and one of the nice things about using bison to build a parser is that it's easy to experiment with variations. The interplay among bits of the syntax can be quite subtle; if, for example, the definition of list had put semicolons between rather than after each statement, the grammar would be ambiguous unless the grammar also added closing FI and ENDDO tokens to indicate the end of if/then and while/do statements.

The definition of list is right recursive, that is, stmt ; list rather than list stmt ;. It doesn't make any difference to the language recognized, but it makes it easier to build the list of statements linked from head to tail rather than from tail to head. Each time the stmt ; list rule is reduced, it creates a link that adds the statement to the head of the list so far. If the rule were list stmt ;, the statement would need to go at the tail of the list, which would require either a more complex circularly linked list or else reversing the list at the end (as we did with the list of references in Chapter 1).

One disadvantage of right recursion rather than left is that right recursion puts up all of the yet-to-be-reduced statements on the parser stack and then reduces them all at the end of the list, while left recursion builds the list a statement at a time as the input is parsed. In a situation like this, where the list is unlikely to be more than a few items long, it doesn't matter, but in a language where the list might be a list of thousands of items, it's worth making the list with a left recursive rule and then reversing it to prevent parser stack overflow. Some programmers also find left recursion to be easier to debug, since it tends to produce output after each statement rather than all at once at the end.

Calculator Expression Syntax

```
exp: exp CMP exp          { $$ = newcmp($2, $1, $3); }
   | exp '+' exp          { $$ = newast('+', $1,$3); }
   | exp '-' exp          { $$ = newast('-', $1,$3);}
   | exp '*' exp          { $$ = newast('*', $1,$3); }
   | exp '/' exp          { $$ = newast('/', $1,$3); }
   | '|' exp              { $$ = newast('|', $2, NULL); }
   | '(' exp ')'          { $$ = $2; }
   | '-' exp %prec UMINUS { $$ = newast('M', $2, NULL); }
   | NUMBER               { $$ = newnum($1); }
   | NAME                 { $$ = newref($1); }
   | NAME '=' exp         { $$ = newasgn($1, $3); }
   | FUNC '(' explist ')' { $$ = newfunc($1, $3); }
   | NAME '(' explist ')' { $$ = newcall($1, $3); }
;

explist: exp
   | exp ',' explist  { $$ = newast('L', $1, $3); }
;
symlist: NAME          { $$ = newsymlist($1, NULL); }
   | NAME ',' symlist  { $$ = newsymlist($1, $3); }
;
```

The expression syntax is a modestly expanded version of the expression syntax in the previous example. A new rule for CMP handles the six comparison operators, using the value of the CMP to tell which operator it was, and a rule for assignments creates an assignment node.

There are separate rules for built-in functions identified by a reserved name (FUNC) and user functions identified by a user symbol (NAME).

A rule for **explist**, a list of expressions, builds an AST of the expressions used for the actual arguments to a function call. A separate rule for **symlist**, a list of symbols, builds a linked list of symbols for the dummy arguments in a function definition. Both are right recursive to make it easier to build the list in the desired order.

Top-Level Calculator Grammar

```
calclist: /* nothing */
  | calclist stmt EOL {
      printf("= %4.4g\n> ", eval($2));
      treefree($2);
    }
  | calclist LET NAME '(' symlist ')' '=' list EOL {
                      dodef($3, $5, $8);
                      printf("Defined %s\n> ", $3->name); }

  | calclist error EOL { yyerrok; printf("> "); }
  ;
```

The last bit of grammar is the top level, which recognizes a list of statements and function declarations. As before, the top level evaluates the AST for a statement, prints the result, and then frees the AST. A function definition is just saved for future use.

Basic Parser Error Recovery

The last rule in the parser provides a small amount of error recovery. Because of the way that bison parsers work, it's rarely worth the effort to try to correct errors, but it's at least possible to recover to a state where the parser can continue. The special pseudo-token **error** indicates an error recovery point. When a bison parser encounters an error, it starts discarding symbols from the parser stack until it reaches a point where an **error** token would be valid; then it discards input tokens until it finds one it can shift in its current state, and then continues parsing from there. If the parse fails again, it discards more stack symbols and input tokens until either it can resume parsing or the stack is empty and the parse fails. To avoid a cascade of misleading error messages, the parser normally suppresses any parse error messages after the first one until it has successfully shifted three tokens in a row. The macro **yyerrok** in an action tells the parser that recovery is done, so subsequent error messages will be produced.

Although it's possible in principle to add lots of error rules to try to do lots of error recovery, in practice it's rare to have more than one or two error rules. The error token is almost always used to resynchronize at a punctuation character in a top-level recursive rule as we do here.

If the symbols discarded in error recovery from the stack have values that point to allocated storage, the error recovery process will leak storage, since the discarded values are never freed. In this example, we don't worry about it, but bison does provide a feature to tell the parser to call your code to free discarded values, described in Chapter 6.

The Advanced Calculator Lexer

Example 3-7. Advanced calculator lexer fb3-2.l

```
/* recognize tokens for the calculator */
%option noyywrap nodefault yylineno
%{
# include "fb3-2.h"
# include "fb3-2.tab.h"
%}

/* float exponent */
EXP     ([Ee][-+]?[0-9]+)

%%
 /* single character ops */
"+" |
"-" |
"*" |
"/" |
"=" |
"|" |
"," |
";" |
"(" |
")"     { return yytext[0]; }

 /* comparison ops, all are a CMP token */
">"     { yylval.fn = 1; return CMP; }
"<"     { yylval.fn = 2; return CMP; }
"<>"    { yylval.fn = 3; return CMP; }
"=="    { yylval.fn = 4; return CMP; }
">="    { yylval.fn = 5; return CMP; }
"<="    { yylval.fn = 6; return CMP; }

 /* keywords */

"if"    { return IF; }
"then"  { return THEN; }
"else"  { return ELSE; }
"while" { return WHILE; }
"do"    { return DO; }
"let"   { return LET;}

 /* built-in functions */
"sqrt"  { yylval.fn = B_sqrt; return FUNC; }
"exp"   { yylval.fn = B_exp; return FUNC; }
"log"   { yylval.fn = B_log; return FUNC; }
"print" { yylval.fn = B_print; return FUNC; }
```

```
 /* names */
[a-zA-Z][a-zA-Z0-9]*  { yylval.s = lookup(yytext); return NAME; }

[0-9]+"."[0-9]*{EXP}? |
"."?[0-9]+{EXP}? { yylval.d = atof(yytext); return NUMBER; }

"//".*
[ \t]  /* ignore whitespace */

\\\n { printf("c> "); } /* ignore line continuation */

\n   { return EOL; }

.        { yyerror("Mystery character %c\n", *yytext); }
%%
```

The lexer, shown in Example 3-7, adds a few new rules to the previous example. There are a few new single-character operators. The six comparison operators all return a CMP token with a lexical value to distinguish them.

The six keywords and four built-in functions are recognized by literal patterns. Note that they have to precede the general pattern to match a name so that they're matched in preference to the general pattern. The name pattern looks up the name in the symbol table and returns a pointer to the symbol.

As before, a newline (EOL) marks the end of an input string. Since a function or expression might be too long to type on a single line, we allow continuation lines. A new lexer rule matches a backslash and newline and doesn't return anything to the parser, making the continuation invisible to the parser. But it does print a prompt for the user.

Reserved Words

In this grammar, the words if, then, else, while, do, let, sqrt, exp, log, and print are *reserved* and can't be used as user symbols. Whether you want to allow users to use the same name for two things in the same program is debatable. On the one hand, it can make programs harder to understand, but on the other hand, users are otherwise forced to invent names that do not conflict with the reserved names.

Either can be taken to extremes. COBOL has more than 300 reserved words, so nobody can remember them all, and programmers resort to strange conventions like starting every variable name with a digit to be sure it doesn't conflict with a reserved word. On the other hand, PL/I has no reserved words at all, so you can write the following:

```
IF IF = THEN THEN ELSE = THEN; ELSE ELSE = IF;
```

Bison parsers are a lot easier to write if you reserve the keywords; otherwise, you need to carefully design your language so at each point where the lexer is reading a token, either a name or a keyword is valid, but not both, and you have to provide extensive feedback to the lexer so it knows which to do. Having written lexers for Fortran, which has no reserved words and (in its classic versions) ignores all whitespace, I strongly encourage you to reserve your keywords.

Building and Interpreting ASTs

Finally, we have the file of helper code, shown in Example 3-8. Some of this file is the same as the previous example; the main and yyerror are unchanged and aren't repeated here.

The key code builds and evaluates the ASTs. First, we have the symbol table management, which should be familiar from the examples in Chapter 2.

Example 3-8. Advanced calculator helper functions fb3-2func.c

```
/*
 * helper functions for fb3-2
 */
# include <stdio.h>
# include <stdlib.h>
# include <stdarg.h>
# include <string.h>
# include <math.h>
# include "fb3-2.h"

/* symbol table */
/* hash a symbol */
static unsigned
symhash(char *sym)
{
  unsigned int hash = 0;
  unsigned c;

  while(c = *sym++) hash = hash*9 ^ c;

  return hash;
}

struct symbol *
lookup(char* sym)
{
  struct symbol *sp = &symtab[symhash(sym)%NHASH];
  int scount = NHASH;            /* how many have we looked at */

  while(--scount >= 0) {
    if(sp->name && !strcmp(sp->name, sym)) { return sp; }

    if(!sp->name) {              /* new entry */
      sp->name = strdup(sym);
      sp->value = 0;
      sp->func = NULL;
      sp->syms = NULL;
      return sp;
    }
```

```
    if(++sp >= symtab+NHASH) sp = symtab; /* try the next entry */
  }
  yyerror("symbol table overflow\n");
  abort(); /* tried them all, table is full */

}
```

Next come the procedures to build the AST nodes and symlists. They all allocate a node and then fill in the fields appropriately for the node type. An extended version of treefree recursively walks an AST and frees all of the nodes in the tree.

```
struct ast *
newast(int nodetype, struct ast *l, struct ast *r)
{
  struct ast *a = malloc(sizeof(struct ast));

  if(!a) {
    yyerror("out of space");
    exit(0);
  }
  a->nodetype = nodetype;
  a->l = l;
  a->r = r;
  return a;
}

struct ast *
newnum(double d)
{
  struct numval *a = malloc(sizeof(struct numval));

  if(!a) {
    yyerror("out of space");
    exit(0);
  }
  a->nodetype = 'K';
  a->number = d;
  return (struct ast *)a;
}

struct ast *
newcmp(int cmptype, struct ast *l, struct ast *r)
{
  struct ast *a = malloc(sizeof(struct ast));

  if(!a) {
    yyerror("out of space");
    exit(0);
  }
  a->nodetype = '0' + cmptype;
  a->l = l;
  a->r = r;
  return a;
}
```

```
struct ast *
newfunc(int functype, struct ast *l)
{
  struct fncall *a = malloc(sizeof(struct fncall));

  if(!a) {
    yyerror("out of space");
    exit(0);
  }
  a->nodetype = 'F';
  a->l = l;
  a->functype = functype;
  return (struct ast *)a;
}

struct ast *
newcall(struct symbol *s, struct ast *l)
{
  struct ufncall *a = malloc(sizeof(struct ufncall));

  if(!a) {
    yyerror("out of space");
    exit(0);
  }
  a->nodetype = 'C';
  a->l = l;
  a->s = s;
  return (struct ast *)a;
}

struct ast *
newref(struct symbol *s)
{
  struct symref *a = malloc(sizeof(struct symref));

  if(!a) {
    yyerror("out of space");
    exit(0);
  }
  a->nodetype = 'N';
  a->s = s;
  return (struct ast *)a;
}

struct ast *
newasgn(struct symbol *s, struct ast *v)
{
  struct symasgn *a = malloc(sizeof(struct symasgn));

  if(!a) {
    yyerror("out of space");
    exit(0);
  }
  a->nodetype = '=';
```

```
  a->s = s;
  a->v = v;
  return (struct ast *)a;
}

struct ast *
newflow(int nodetype, struct ast *cond, struct ast *tl, struct ast *el)
{
  struct flow *a = malloc(sizeof(struct flow));

  if(!a) {
    yyerror("out of space");
    exit(0);
  }
  a->nodetype = nodetype;
  a->cond = cond;
  a->tl = tl;
  a->el = el;
  return (struct ast *)a;
}

/* free a tree of ASTs */
void
treefree(struct ast *a)
{
  switch(a->nodetype) {

    /* two subtrees */
  case '+':
  case '-':
  case '*':
  case '/':
  case '1':  case '2':  case '3':  case '4':  case '5':  case '6':
  case 'L':
    treefree(a->r);

    /* one subtree */
  case '|':
  case 'M': case 'C': case 'F':
    treefree(a->l);

    /* no subtree */
  case 'K': case 'N':
    break;

  case '=':
    free( ((struct symasgn *)a)->v);
    break;

    /* up to three subtrees */
  case 'I': case 'W':
    free( ((struct flow *)a)->cond);
    if( ((struct flow *)a)->tl) treefree( ((struct flow *)a)->tl);
    if( ((struct flow *)a)->el) treefree( ((struct flow *)a)->el);
    break;
```

```
    default: printf("internal error: free bad node %c\n", a->nodetype);
    }

    free(a); /* always free the node itself */
}

struct symlist *
newsymlist(struct symbol *sym, struct symlist *next)
{
  struct symlist *sl = malloc(sizeof(struct symlist));

  if(!sl) {
    yyerror("out of space");
    exit(0);
  }
  sl->sym = sym;
  sl->next = next;
  return sl;
}

/* free a list of symbols */
void
symlistfree(struct symlist *sl)
{
  struct symlist *nsl;

  while(sl) {
    nsl = sl->next;
    free(sl);
    sl = nsl;
  }
}
```

The heart of the calculator is eval, which evaluates an AST built up in the parser. Following the practice in C, comparisons return 1 or 0 depending on whether the comparison succeeds, and tests in if/then/else and while/do treat any nonzero as true.

For expressions, we do the familiar depth-first tree walk to compute the value. An AST makes it straightforward to implement if/then/else: Evaluate the condition AST to decide which branch to take, and then evaluate the AST for the path to be taken. To evaluate while/do loops, a loop in eval evaluates the condition AST, then the body AST, repeating as long as the condition AST remains true. Any AST that references variables that are changed by an assignment will have a new value each time it's evaluated.

```
static double callbuiltin(struct fncall *);
static double calluser(struct ufncall *);

double
eval(struct ast *a)
{
  double v;

  if(!a) {
```

```
    yyerror("internal error, null eval");
    return 0.0;
  }

  switch(a->nodetype) {
    /* constant */
  case 'K': v = ((struct numval *)a)->number; break;

    /* name reference */
  case 'N': v = ((struct symref *)a)->s->value; break;

    /* assignment */
  case '=': v = ((struct symasgn *)a)->s->value =
      eval(((struct symasgn *)a)->v); break;

    /* expressions */
  case '+': v = eval(a->l) + eval(a->r); break;
  case '-': v = eval(a->l) - eval(a->r); break;
  case '*': v = eval(a->l) * eval(a->r); break;
  case '/': v = eval(a->l) / eval(a->r); break;
  case '|': v = fabs(eval(a->l)); break;
  case 'M': v = -eval(a->l); break;

    /* comparisons */
  case '1': v = (eval(a->l) > eval(a->r))? 1 : 0; break;
  case '2': v = (eval(a->l) < eval(a->r))? 1 : 0; break;
  case '3': v = (eval(a->l) != eval(a->r))? 1 : 0; break;
  case '4': v = (eval(a->l) == eval(a->r))? 1 : 0; break;
  case '5': v = (eval(a->l) >= eval(a->r))? 1 : 0; break;
  case '6': v = (eval(a->l) <= eval(a->r))? 1 : 0; break;

  /* control flow */
  /* null expressions allowed in the grammar, so check for them */

  /* if/then/else */
  case 'I':
    if( eval( ((struct flow *)a)->cond) != 0) { check the condition
      if( ((struct flow *)a)->tl) {            the true branch
        v = eval( ((struct flow *)a)->tl);
      } else
        v = 0.0;               /* a default value */
    } else {
      if( ((struct flow *)a)->el) {            the false branch
        v = eval(((struct flow *)a)->el);
      } else
        v = 0.0;               /* a default value */
    }
    break;

  /* while/do */
  case 'W':
    v = 0.0;               /* a default value */

    if( ((struct flow *)a)->tl) {
      while( eval(((struct flow *)a)->cond) != 0) evaluate the condition
```

```
      v = eval(((struct flow *)a)->tl);        evaluate the target statements
    }
    break;                          /* value of last statement is value of while/do */

  /* list of statements */
  case 'L': eval(a->l); v = eval(a->r); break;

  case 'F': v = callbuiltin((struct fncall *)a); break;

  case 'C': v = calluser((struct ufncall *)a); break;

  default: printf("internal error: bad node %c\n", a->nodetype);
  }
  return v;
}
```

Evaluating Functions in the Calculator

The trickiest bits of code in the evaluator handle functions. Built-in functions are relatively straightforward: They determine which function it is and call specific code to do the function.

```
static double
callbuiltin(struct fncall *f)
{
  enum bifs functype = f->functype;
  double v = eval(f->l);

  switch(functype) {
  case B_sqrt:
    return sqrt(v);
  case B_exp:
    return exp(v);
  case B_log:
    return log(v);
  case B_print:
    printf("= %4.4g\n", v);
    return v;
  default:
    yyerror("Unknown built-in function %d", functype);
    return 0.0;
  }
}
```

User-Defined Functions

A function definition consists of the name of the function, a list of dummy arguments, and an AST that represents the body of the function. Defining the function simply saves the argument list and AST in the function's symbol table entry, replacing any previous version.

```
/* define a function */
void
```

```
dodef(struct symbol *name, struct symlist *syms, struct ast *func)
{
  if(name->syms) symlistfree(name->syms);
  if(name->func) treefree(name->func);
  name->syms = syms;
  name->func = func;
}
```

Say you define a function to calculate the maximum of its two arguments:

```
> let max(x,y) = if x >= y then x; else y;;
> max(4+5,6+7)
```

The function has two dummy arguments, x and y. When the function is called, the evaluator does this:

1. Evaluate the actual arguments, 4+5 and 6+7 in this case.
2. Save the current values of the dummy arguments and assign the values of the actual arguments to them.
3. Evaluate the body of the function, which will now use the actual argument values when it refers to the dummy arguments.
4. Put back the old values of the dummies.
5. Return the value of the body expression.

The code to do this counts the arguments, allocates two temporary arrays for the old and new values of the dummy arguments, and then does the steps described earlier.

```
static double
calluser(struct ufncall *f)
{
  struct symbol *fn = f->s;       /* function name */
  struct symlist *sl;             /* dummy arguments */
  struct ast *args = f->l;        /* actual arguments */
  double *oldval, *newval;        /* saved arg values */
  double v;
  int nargs;
  int i;

  if(!fn->func) {
    yyerror("call to undefined function %s", fn->name);
    return 0;
  }

  /* count the arguments */
  sl = fn->syms;
  for(nargs = 0; sl; sl = sl->next)
    nargs++;

  /* prepare to save them */
  oldval = (double *)malloc(nargs * sizeof(double));
  newval = (double *)malloc(nargs * sizeof(double));
  if(!oldval || !newval) {
    yyerror("Out of space in %s", fn->name); return 0.0;
```

```
    }

    /* evaluate the arguments */
    for(i = 0; i < nargs; i++) {
      if(!args) {
        yyerror("too few args in call to %s", fn->name);
        free(oldval); free(newval);
        return 0.0;
      }

      if(args->nodetype == 'L') { /* if this is a list node */
        newval[i] = eval(args->l);
        args = args->r;
      } else {                    /* if it's the end of the list */
        newval[i] = eval(args);
        args = NULL;
      }
    }

    /* save old values of dummies, assign new ones */
    sl = fn->syms;
    for(i = 0; i < nargs; i++) {
      struct symbol *s = sl->sym;

      oldval[i] = s->value;
      s->value = newval[i];
      sl = sl->next;
    }

    free(newval);

    /* evaluate the function */
    v = eval(fn->func);

    /* put the real values of the dummies back */
    sl = fn->syms;
    for(i = 0; i < nargs; i++) {
      struct symbol *s = sl->sym;

      s->value = oldval[i];
      sl = sl->next;
    }

    free(oldval);
    return v;
}
```

Using the Advanced Calculator

This calculator is flexible enough to do some useful calculations. Example 3-9 shows the function **sq** to compute square roots iteratively using Newton's method, as well as an auxiliary function **avg** to compute the average of two numbers.

Example 3-9. Computing square roots with the calculator

```
> let sq(n)=e=1; while |((t=n/e)-e)>.001 do e=avg(e,t);;
Defined sq
> let avg(a,b)=(a+b)/2;
Defined avg
> sq(10)
= 3.162
> sqrt(10)
= 3.162
> sq(10)-sqrt(10)
= 0.000178      accurate to better than the .001 cutoff
```

Exercises

1. Try some variants of the syntax in the enhanced calculator. In the previous example, the sq function has to end with two semicolons to close off both the while loop and the let statement, which is pretty clunky. Can you change the syntax to make it more intuitive? If you add closing symbols to conditional statements if/then/else/fi and loops while/do/done, can you make the syntax of statement lists more flexible?

2. In the last example, user functions evaluate all of the actual arguments, put them in a temporary array, and then assign them to the dummy arguments. Why not just do them one at a time and set the dummies as the actuals are evaluated?

# CHAPTER 4

Parsing SQL

SQL (which stands for Structured Query Language and is usually pronounced *sequel*) is the most common language used to handle relational databases.[1] We'll develop a SQL parser that produces a compact tokenized version of SQL statements.

This parser is based on the version of SQL used in the popular MySQL open source database. MySQL actually uses a bison parser to parse its SQL input, although for a variety of reasons this parser isn't based on mySQL's parser but rather is based on the description of the language in the manual.

MySQL's parser is much longer and more complex, since this pedagogical example leaves out many of the less heavily used parts. MySQL's parser is written in an odd way that uses bison to generate a C parser that's compiled by the C++ compiler, with a handwritten C++ lexer. There's also the detail that its license doesn't allow excerpting in a book like this one. But if you're interested, it's the file `sql/sql_yacc.yy`, which is part of the source code at *http://dev.mysql.com/downloads/mysql/5.1.html*.

The ultimate definitions for SQL are the standards documents published by ANSI and ISO including ISO/IEC 9075-2:2003, which defines SQL, and a variety of related documents that define the way to embed SQL in other programming languages and in XML.

A Quick Overview of SQL

SQL is a special-purpose language for relational databases. Rather than manipulating data in memory, it manipulates data in database tables, referring to memory only incidentally.

---

1. SQL is the Fortran of databases—nobody likes it much, the language is ugly and ad hoc, every database supports it, and we all use it.

Relational Databases

A *database* is a collection of *tables*, which are analogous to files. Each table contains *rows* and *columns*, which are analogous to records and fields. The rows in a table are not kept in any particular order. You create a set of tables by giving the name and type of each column:

```
CREATE TABLE Foods (
       name CHAR(8) NOT NULL,
       type CHAR(5),
       flavor    CHAR(6),
       PRIMARY KEY ( name )
)

CREATE TABLE Courses (
       course     CHAR(8) NOT NULL PRIMARY KEY,
       flavor     CHAR(6),
       sequence INTEGER
)
```

The syntax is completely free-format, and there are often several different syntactic ways to write the same thing—notice the two different ways we gave the PRIMARY KEY specifier. (The *primary key* in a table is a column, or set of columns, that uniquely specifies a row.) Table 4-1 shows the two tables we just created after loading in data.

Table 4-1. Two relational tables

Foods				Courses		
name	*type*	*flavor*		*course*	*flavor*	*sequence*
peach	fruit	sweet		salad	savory	1
tomato	fruit	savory		main	savory	2
lemon	fruit	sour		dessert	sweet	3
lard	fat	bland				
cheddar	fat	savory				

SQL implements what's known as a *tuple calculus*, where *tuple* is relational-ese for a record, which is an ordered list of fields or expressions. To use a database, you tell the database what tuples you want it to extract from your data. It's up to the database to figure out how to get it from the tables it has. (That's the calculus part.) The specification of a set of desired data is a *query*. For example, using the two tables in Table 4-1, to get a list of fruits, you would say the following:

```
SELECT name, flavor
FROM   Foods
WHERE Foods.type = "fruit"
```

The response is shown in Table 4-2.

Table 4-2. SQL response table

name	flavor
peach	sweet
tomato	savory
lemon	sour

You can also ask questions spanning more than one table. To get a list of foods suitable to each course of the meal, you say the following:

```
SELECT course, name, Foods.flavor, type
FROM   Courses, Foods
WHERE  Courses.flavor = Foods.flavor
```

The response is shown in Table 4-3.

Table 4-3. Second SQL response table

course	name	flavor	type
salad	tomato	savory	fruit
salad	cheddar	savory	fat
main	tomato	savory	fruit
main	cheddar	savory	fat
dessert	peach	sweet	fruit

When listing the column names, we can leave out the table name if the column name is unambiguous.

Manipulating Relations

SQL has a rich set of table manipulation commands. You can read and write individual rows with SELECT, INSERT, UPDATE, and DELETE commands. The SELECT statement has a very complex syntax that lets you look for values in columns; compare columns to each other; do arithmetic; and compute minimum, maximum, average, and group totals.

Three Ways to Use SQL

In the original version of SQL, users typed commands into a file or directly at the terminal and received responses immediately. People still sometimes use it this way for creating tables and for debugging, but for the vast majority of applications, SQL commands come from inside programs, and the results are returned to those programs. The SQL standard defines a "module language" to embed SQL in a variety of programming languages, but MySQL avoids the issue by using subroutine calls for communication between a user program and the database, and it doesn't use the module language at all.

Since the syntax of SQL is so large, we have reproduced the entire grammar in one place in the Appendix, with a cross-reference for all of the symbols in the grammar.

SQL to RPN

Our tokenized version of SQL will use a version of Reverse Polish Notation (RPN), familiar to users of HP calculators. In 1920, Polish logician Jan Łukasiewicz[2] realized that if you put the operators before the operands in logical expressions, you don't need any parentheses or other punctuation to describe the order of evaluation:

```
(a+b)*c          * + a b c
a+(b*c)          + a * b c
```

It works equally well in reverse, if you put the operators after the operands:

```
(a+b)*c          a b + c *
a+(b*c)          a b c * +
```

On a computer, RPN has the practical advantage that it is very easy to interpret using a stack. The computer processes each token in order. If it's an operand, it pushes the token on the stack. If it's an operator, it pops the right number of operands off the stack, does the operation, and pushes the result. This trick is very well known and has been used since 1954 to build software and hardware that interprets RPN code using a stack.

RPN has two other advantages for compiler developers. One is that if you're using a bottom-up parser like the ones that bison generates, it is amazingly easy to generate RPN. If you emit the action code for each operator or operand in the rule that recognizes it, your code will come out in RPN order. Here's a sneak preview of part of the SQL parser:

```
expr: NAME          { emit("NAME %s", $1); }
    | INTNUM        { emit("NUMBER %d", $1); }
    | expr '+' expr { emit("ADD"); }
    | expr '-' expr { emit("SUB"); }
    | expr '*' expr { emit("MUL"); }
    | expr '/' expr { emit("DIV"); }
```

When it parses a+2*3, it emits NAME a, NUMBER 2, NUMBER 3, MUL, ADD. This lovely property comes directly from the way a LALR parser works, pushing the symbols for partially parsed rules on its internal stack and then at the end of each rule popping the symbols and pushing the new LHS symbol, which is a sequence of operations just the same as what an RPN interpreter does.

The other advantage is that it is very easy to turn a string of RPN tokens into an AST, and vice versa. To turn RPN into an AST, you run through the RPN pushing each operand and, for each operator, pop the operands, build an AST tree node with the

---

2. It's called Polish notation because people don't know how to pronounce Łukasiewicz. It's roughly WOO-ka-shay-vits.

operands and operator, and then push the address of the new tree node. When you're done, the stack will contain the root of the AST. To go the other way, you do a depth-first walk of the AST. Starting from the root of the AST, at each node you visit the subnodes (by recursively calling the tree-walking subroutine) and then emit the operator for the node. At leaf nodes, you just emit the operand for that node.

Classic RPN has a fixed number of operands for each operator, but we're going to relax the rules a little and have some operators that take a variable number of operands, with the number as part of the operator. For example:

```
select a,b,c from d;

rpn: NAME a
rpn: NAME b
rpn: NAME c
rpn: TABLE d
rpn: SELECT 3
```

The 3 in the SELECT tells the RPN interpreter that the statement is selecting three things, so after it pops the table name, it should take the three field names off the stack. I've written interpreters for RPN code, and this trick makes the code a lot simpler than the alternative of using extra tree-building operators to combine the variable number of operands into one before handing the combined operand to the main operator.

The Lexer

First we need a lexer for the tokens that SQL uses. The syntax is free-format, with whitespace ignored except to separate words. There is a fairly long but fixed set of reserved words. The other tokens are conventional: names, strings, numbers, and punctuation. Comments are Ada-style, from a pair of dashes to the end of the line, with a MySQL extension also allowing C comments.

Example 4-1. MySQL lexer

```
/*
 * Scanner for mysql subset
 * $Header: /usr/home/johnl/flnb/RCS/ch04.tr,v 1.7 2009/05/19 18:28:27 johnl Exp $
 */

%option noyywrap nodefault yylineno case-insensitive
%{
#include "pmysql.tab.h"
#include <stdarg.h>
#include <string.h>

void yyerror(char *s, ...);

int oldstate;

%}
```

```
%x COMMENT
%s BTWMODE

%%
```

The lexer, shown in Example 4-1, starts with a few include files, notably
pmysql.tab.h, the token name definition file generated by bison. It also defines two
start states, an exclusive COMMENT state used in C-style comments and an inclusive
BTWMODE state used in a kludge to deal with a SQL expression that has its own idea of
the keyword AND.

Scanning SQL Keywords

SQL has a lot of keywords:

```
/* keywords */

ADD     { return ADD; }
ALL     { return ALL; }
ALTER   { return ALTER; }
ANALYZE { return ANALYZE; }

  /* Hack for BETWEEN ... AND ...
   * return special AND token if BETWEEN seen
   */
<BTWMODE>AND    { BEGIN INITIAL; return AND; }
AND     { return ANDOP; }
ANY     { return ANY; }
AS      { return AS; }
ASC     { return ASC; }
AUTO_INCREMENT  { return AUTO_INCREMENT; }
BEFORE  { return BEFORE; }
BETWEEN { BEGIN BTWMODE; return BETWEEN; }
INT8|BIGINT     { return BIGINT; }
BINARY  { return BINARY; }
BIT     { return BIT; }
BLOB    { return BLOB; }
BOTH    { return BOTH; }
BY      { return BY; }
CALL    { return CALL; }
CASCADE { return CASCADE; }
CASE    { return CASE; }
CHANGE  { return CHANGE; }
CHAR(ACTER)?    { return CHAR; }
CHECK   { return CHECK; }
COLLATE { return COLLATE; }
COLUMN  { return COLUMN; }
COMMENT { return COMMENT; }
CONDITION       { return CONDITION; }
CONSTRAINT      { return CONSTRAINT; }
CONTINUE        { return CONTINUE; }
CONVERT { return CONVERT; }
CREATE  { return CREATE; }
```

```
CROSS    { return CROSS; }
CURRENT_DATE    { return CURRENT_DATE; }
CURRENT_TIME    { return CURRENT_TIME; }
CURRENT_TIMESTAMP        { return CURRENT_TIMESTAMP; }
CURRENT_USER    { return CURRENT_USER; }
CURSOR   { return CURSOR; }
DATABASE         { return DATABASE; }
DATABASES        { return DATABASES; }
DATE     { return DATE; }
DATETIME         { return DATETIME; }
DAY_HOUR         { return DAY_HOUR; }
DAY_MICROSECOND { return DAY_MICROSECOND; }
DAY_MINUTE      { return DAY_MINUTE; }
DAY_SECOND       { return DAY_SECOND; }
NUMERIC|DEC|DECIMAL      { return DECIMAL; }
DECLARE { return DECLARE; }
DEFAULT { return DEFAULT; }
DELAYED { return DELAYED; }
DELETE  { return DELETE; }
DESC    { return DESC; }
DESCRIBE         { return DESCRIBE; }
DETERMINISTIC   { return DETERMINISTIC; }
DISTINCT         { return DISTINCT; }
DISTINCTROW      { return DISTINCTROW; }
DIV      { return DIV; }
FLOAT8|DOUBLE   { return DOUBLE; }
DROP     { return DROP; }
DUAL     { return DUAL; }
EACH     { return EACH; }
ELSE     { return ELSE; }
ELSEIF  { return ELSEIF; }
END      { return END; }
ENUM { return ENUM; }
ESCAPED { return ESCAPED; }
EXISTS  { yylval.subtok = 0; return EXISTS; }
NOT[ \t\n]+EXISTS        { yylval.subtok = 1; return EXISTS; }
EXIT     { return EXIT; }
EXPLAIN { return EXPLAIN; }
FETCH    { return FETCH; }
FLOAT4? { return FLOAT; }
FOR      { return FOR; }
FORCE    { return FORCE; }
FOREIGN { return FOREIGN; }
FROM     { return FROM; }
FULLTEXT         { return FULLTEXT; }
GRANT    { return GRANT; }
GROUP    { return GROUP; }
HAVING  { return HAVING; }
HIGH_PRIORITY   { return HIGH_PRIORITY; }
HOUR_MICROSECOND         { return HOUR_MICROSECOND; }
HOUR_MINUTE     { return HOUR_MINUTE; }
HOUR_SECOND      { return HOUR_SECOND; }
IF       { return IF; }
IGNORE  { return IGNORE; }
IN       { return IN; }
```

```
INFILE  { return INFILE; }
INNER   { return INNER; }
INOUT   { return INOUT; }
INSENSITIVE     { return INSENSITIVE; }
INSERT  { return INSERT; }
INT4?|INTEGER   { return INTEGER; }
INTERVAL        { return INTERVAL; }
INTO    { return INTO; }
IS      { return IS; }
ITERATE { return ITERATE; }
JOIN    { return JOIN; }
INDEX|KEY       { return KEY; }
KEYS    { return KEYS; }
KILL    { return KILL; }
LEADING { return LEADING; }
LEAVE   { return LEAVE; }
LEFT    { return LEFT; }
LIKE    { return LIKE; }
LIMIT   { return LIMIT; }
LINES   { return LINES; }
LOAD    { return LOAD; }
LOCALTIME       { return LOCALTIME; }
LOCALTIMESTAMP  { return LOCALTIMESTAMP; }
LOCK    { return LOCK; }
LONG    { return LONG; }
LONGBLOB        { return LONGBLOB; }
LONGTEXT        { return LONGTEXT; }
LOOP    { return LOOP; }
LOW_PRIORITY    { return LOW_PRIORITY; }
MATCH   { return MATCH; }
MEDIUMBLOB      { return MEDIUMBLOB; }
MIDDLEINT|MEDIUMINT     { return MEDIUMINT; }
MEDIUMTEXT      { return MEDIUMTEXT; }
MINUTE_MICROSECOND      { return MINUTE_MICROSECOND; }
MINUTE_SECOND   { return MINUTE_SECOND; }
MOD     { return MOD; }
MODIFIES        { return MODIFIES; }
NATURAL { return NATURAL; }
NOT     { return NOT; }
NO_WRITE_TO_BINLOG      { return NO_WRITE_TO_BINLOG; }
NULL    { return NULLX; }
NUMBER  { return NUMBER; }
ON      { return ON; }
ON[ \t\n]+DUPLICATE { return ONDUPLICATE; } /* hack due to limited lookahead */
OPTIMIZE        { return OPTIMIZE; }
OPTION  { return OPTION; }
OPTIONALLY      { return OPTIONALLY; }
OR      { return OR; }
ORDER   { return ORDER; }
OUT     { return OUT; }
OUTER   { return OUTER; }
OUTFILE { return OUTFILE; }
PRECISION       { return PRECISION; }
PRIMARY { return PRIMARY; }
PROCEDURE       { return PROCEDURE; }
```

```
PURGE    { return PURGE; }
QUICK    { return QUICK; }
READ     { return READ; }
READS    { return READS; }
REAL     { return REAL; }
REFERENCES      { return REFERENCES; }
REGEXP|RLIKE    { return REGEXP; }
RELEASE { return RELEASE; }
RENAME { return RENAME; }
REPEAT { return REPEAT; }
REPLACE { return REPLACE; }
REQUIRE { return REQUIRE; }
RESTRICT        { return RESTRICT; }
RETURN { return RETURN; }
REVOKE { return REVOKE; }
RIGHT  { return RIGHT; }
ROLLUP { return ROLLUP; }
SCHEMA { return SCHEMA; }
SCHEMAS { return SCHEMAS; }
SECOND_MICROSECOND      { return SECOND_MICROSECOND; }
SELECT  { return SELECT; }
SENSITIVE       { return SENSITIVE; }
SEPARATOR       { return SEPARATOR; }
SET     { return SET; }
SHOW    { return SHOW; }
INT2|SMALLINT   { return SMALLINT; }
SOME    { return SOME; }
SONAME  { return SONAME; }
SPATIAL { return SPATIAL; }
SPECIFIC        { return SPECIFIC; }
SQL     { return SQL; }
SQLEXCEPTION    { return SQLEXCEPTION; }
SQLSTATE        { return SQLSTATE; }
SQLWARNING      { return SQLWARNING; }
SQL_BIG_RESULT  { return SQL_BIG_RESULT; }
SQL_CALC_FOUND_ROWS     { return SQL_CALC_FOUND_ROWS; }
SQL_SMALL_RESULT        { return SQL_SMALL_RESULT; }
SSL     { return SSL; }
STARTING        { return STARTING; }
STRAIGHT_JOIN   { return STRAIGHT_JOIN; }
TABLE   { return TABLE; }
TEMPORARY       { return TEMPORARY; }
TERMINATED      { return TERMINATED; }
TEXT    { return TEXT; }
THEN    { return THEN; }
TIME    { return TIME; }
TIMESTAMP       { return TIMESTAMP; }
INT1|TINYINT    { return TINYINT; }
TINYTEXT        { return TINYTEXT; }
TO      { return TO; }
TRAILING        { return TRAILING; }
TRIGGER { return TRIGGER; }
UNDO    { return UNDO; }
UNION   { return UNION; }
UNIQUE  { return UNIQUE; }
```

```
UNLOCK   { return UNLOCK; }
UNSIGNED         { return UNSIGNED; }
UPDATE   { return UPDATE; }
USAGE    { return USAGE; }
USE      { return USE; }
USING    { return USING; }
UTC_DATE         { return UTC_DATE; }
UTC_TIME         { return UTC_TIME; }
UTC_TIMESTAMP    { return UTC_TIMESTAMP; }
VALUES? { return VALUES; }
VARBINARY        { return VARBINARY; }
VARCHAR(ACTER)? { return VARCHAR; }
VARYING { return VARYING; }
WHEN     { return WHEN; }
WHERE    { return WHERE; }
WHILE    { return WHILE; }
WITH     { return WITH; }
WRITE    { return WRITE; }
XOR      { return XOR; }
YEAR     { return YEAR; }
YEAR_MONTH       { return YEAR_MONTH; }
ZEROFILL         { return ZEROFILL; }
```

All of the reserved words are separate tokens in the parser, because it is the easiest thing to do. Notice that CHARACTER and VARCHARACTER can be abbreviated to CHAR and VAR CHAR, and INDEX and KEY are the same as each other.

The keyword BETWEEN switches into start state BTWMODE, in which the word AND returns the token AND rather than ANDOP. The reason is that normally AND is treated the same as the && logical-and operator, except in the SQL operator BETWEEN ... AND:

```
IF(a && b, ...)    normally these mean the same thing
IF(a AND b, ...)

... WHERE a BETWEEN c AND d, ... except here
```

There's a variety of ways to deal with problems like this, but lexical special cases are often the easiest.

Also note that the phrases NOT EXISTS and ON DUPLICATE are recognized as single tokens; this is to avoid shift/reduce conflicts in the parser because of other contexts where NOT and ON can appear. To remember the difference between EXISTS and NOT EXISTS, the lexer returns a value along with the token that the parser uses when generating the token code. These two don't actually turn out to be ambiguous, but parsing them needs more than the single-token lookahead that bison usually uses. We revisit these in Chapter 9 where the alternate GLR parser can handle them directly.

Scanning Numbers

Numbers come in a variety of forms:

```
/* numbers */
```

```
-?[0-9]+                    { yylval.intval = atoi(yytext); return INTNUM; }

-?[0-9]+"."[0-9]* |
-?"."[0-9]+      |
-?[0-9]+E[-+]?[0-9]+    |
-?[0-9]+"."[0-9]*E[-+]?[0-9]+ |
-?"."[0-9]+E[-+]?[0-9]+ { yylval.floatval = atof(yytext) ;
                                      return APPROXNUM; }
    /* booleans */
TRUE    { yylval.intval = 1; return BOOL; }
UNKNOWN { yylval.intval = -1; return BOOL; }
FALSE   { yylval.intval = 0; return BOOL; }

    /* strings */

'(\\.|''|[^'\n])*'    |
\"(\\.|\"\"|[^"\n])*\"  { yylval.strval = strdup(yytext); return STRING; }

'(\\.|[^'\n])*$      { yyerror("Unterminated string %s", yytext); }
\"(\\.|[^"\n])*$     { yyerror("Unterminated string %s", yytext); }

    /* hex strings */
X'[0-9A-F]+' |
0X[0-9A-F]+ { yylval.strval = strdup(yytext); return STRING; }

    /* bit strings */

0B[01]+    |
B'[01]+'   { yylval.strval = strdup(yytext); return STRING; }
```

SQL numbers are similar to the numbers we've seen in previous chapters. The rules to scan them turn them into C integers or doubles and store them in the token values. Boolean values are true, false, and unknown, so they're recognized as reserved words and returned as variations on a BOOL token.

SQL strings are enclosed in single quotes, using a pair of quotes to represent a single quote in the string. MySQL extends this to add double-quoted strings, and \x escapes within strings. The first two string patterns match valid, quoted strings that don't extend past a newline and return the string as the token value, remembering to make a copy since the value in **yytext** doesn't stay around.[3] The next two patterns catch unterminated strings and print a suitable diagnostic.

The next four patterns match hex and binary strings, each of which can be written in two ways. A more realistic example would convert them to binary, but for our purposes we just return them as strings.

Scanning Operators and Punctuation

Operators and punctuation can be captured with a few patterns:

---

3. MySQL actually accepts multiline strings, but we're keeping this example simple.

```
        /* operators */
[-+&~|^/%*(),.;!]    { return yytext[0]; }

"&&"               { return ANDOP; }
"||"               { return OR; }

"="      { yylval.subtok = 4; return COMPARISON; }
"<=>"    { yylval.subtok = 12; return COMPARISON; }
">="     { yylval.subtok = 6; return COMPARISON; }
">"      { yylval.subtok = 2; return COMPARISON; }
"<="     { yylval.subtok = 5; return COMPARISON; }
"<"      { yylval.subtok = 1; return COMPARISON; }
"!="     |
"<>"     { yylval.subtok = 3; return COMPARISON; }

"<<"     { yylval.subtok = 1; return SHIFT; }
">>"     { yylval.subtok = 2; return SHIFT; }

":="     { return ASSIGN; }
```

Next come the punctuation tokens, using the standard trick to match all of the single-character operators with the same pattern. MySQL has the usual range of comparison operators, which are all treated as one COMPARISON operator with the token value telling which one. We'll see later that this doesn't work perfectly, since the = token is used in a few places where it's not a comparison, but we can work around it.

Scanning Functions and Names

The last pieces to capture are functions and names:

```
        /* functions */

SUBSTR(ING)?/"(" { return FSUBSTRING; }
TRIM/"("          { return FTRIM; }
DATE_ADD/"("      { return FDATE_ADD; }
DATE_SUB/"("      { return FDATE_SUB; }

        /* check trailing context manually */
COUNT    { int c = input(); unput(c);
           if(c == '(') return FCOUNT;
           yylval.strval = strdup(yytext);
           return NAME; }

        /* names */

[A-Za-z][A-Za-z0-9_]*    { yylval.strval = strdup(yytext);
                           return NAME; }

`[^`/\\.\n]+`              { yylval.strval = strdup(yytext+1);
                           yylval.strval[yyleng-2] = 0;
                           return NAME; }

`[^`\n]*$                 { yyerror("unterminated quoted name %s", yytext); }
```

```
        /* user variables */
@[0-9a-z_.$]+ |
@\"[^"\n]+\" |
@`[^`\n]+` |
@'[^'\n]+' { yylval.strval = strdup(yytext+1); return USERVAR; }

@\"[^"\n]*$ |
@`[^`\n]*$ |
@'[^'\n]*$ { yyerror("unterminated quoted user variable %s", yytext); }
```

Standard SQL has a small fixed list of functions whose names are effectively key-words, but MySQL adds its long list of functions and lets you define your own, so they have to be recognized by context in the parser. MySQL usually considers them to be function names only when they are immediately followed by an open parenthesis, so the patterns use trailing context to check. However, MySQL provides an option to turn off the open parenthesis test. The pattern for COUNT shows an alternative way to do trailing context, by peeking at the next character with input() and unput(). This is less elegant than a trailing context pattern but has the advantage that your code can decide at runtime whether to do the test and what token to report back.

Names start with a letter and are composed of letters, digits, and underscores. The pattern to match them has to follow all of the reserved words, so the reserved word patterns take precedence. When a name is recognized, the scanner returns a copy of it. Names can also be quoted in backticks, which allow arbitrary characters in names. The scanner returns a quoted name the same way as an unquoted one, stripping off the backticks. The next pattern catches a missing close backtick, by matching a string that starts with a backtick, and runs to the end of the line.

User variables are a MySQL extension to standard SQL and are variables that are part of a user's session rather than part of a database. Their names start with an @ sign and can use any of three quoting techniques to include arbitrary characters.

We also have some patterns to catch unclosed quoted user variable names. They end with \n rather than $ to avoid a "dangerous trailing context" warning from flex; a $ at the end of a pattern is equivalent to /\n, and multiple patterns with trailing context that share an action turn out to be inefficient to handle. In this case, since we didn't have any other plans for the \n, we just make the pattern match the newline, but if that were a problem, the alternative would just be to copy the action code separately for each of the three patterns.

Comments and Miscellany

```
        /* comments */
#.*              ;
"--"[ \t].*      ;

"/*"             { oldstate = YY_START; BEGIN COMMENT; }
<COMMENT>"*/"    { BEGIN oldstate; }
<COMMENT>.|\n    ;
```

```
<COMMENT><<EOF>> { yyerror("unclosed comment"); }

        /* everything else */
[ \t\n]         /* whitespace */
.               { yyerror("mystery character '%c'", *yytext); }

%%
```

The last few patterns skip whitespace, counting lines when the whitespace is a newline; skip comments; and complain if any invalid character appears in the input. The C comment patterns use the exclusive start state COMMENT to absorb the contents of the comment. The <<EOF>> pattern catches an unclosed C-style comment that runs to the end of the input file.

The Parser

The SQL parser, shown in Example 4-2, is larger than any of the parsers we've seen up to this point, but we can understand it in pieces.

Example 4-2. MySQL subset parser

```
/*
 * Parser for mysql subset
 * $Header: /usr/home/johnl/flnb/RCS/ch04.tr,v 1.7 2009/05/19 18:28:27 johnl Exp $
 */
%{
#include <stdlib.h>
#include <stdarg.h>
#include <string.h>

void yyerror(char *s, ...);
void emit(char *s, ...);
%}

%union {
        int intval;
        double floatval;
        char *strval;
        int subtok;
}
```

The parser starts out with the usual include statements and two function prototypes, one for **yyerror()**, which is the same as in Chapter 3, and one for emit(), the routine used to emit the RPN code, which takes a printf-style format string and arguments.

The **%union** has four members, all of which we met in the lexer: integer and float numeric values, a pointer to copies of strings, and subtok for tokens that have subtypes. Since intval and subtok are both integers, the parser would work just as well if we'd used a single field for both, but separating them helps document the two different purposes, numeric value and subtype, that the token value is used for.

```
            /* names and literal values */

%token <strval> NAME
%token <strval> STRING
%token <intval> INTNUM
%token <intval> BOOL
%token <floatval> APPROXNUM

        /* user @abc names */

%token <strval> USERVAR

        /* operators and precedence levels */

%right ASSIGN
%left OR
%left XOR
%left ANDOP
%nonassoc IN IS LIKE REGEXP
%left NOT '!'
%left BETWEEN
%left <subtok> COMPARISON /* = <> < > <= >= <=> */
%left '|'
%left '&'
%left <subtok> SHIFT /* << >> */
%left '+' '-'
%left '*' '/' '%' MOD
%left '^'
%nonassoc UMINUS
```

Next come token declarations, matching the tokens used in the lexer. Like C, MySQL has a dauntingly large number of precedence levels, but bison has no trouble handling them if you can define them. The COMPARISON and SHIFT tokens are both declared here to have subtok values where the lexer returns the particular operator or shift direction.

Next comes a long list of reserved words. Some of these are duplicates of tokens already defined. Bison doesn't object to duplicate token declarations, and it's convenient to have one master alphabetical list of all the reserved word tokens. The full list of tokens is in the cross-reference in the Appendix, so here we just show a representative part of the list. Note the special definition of EXISTS, which can correspond to EXISTS or NOT EXISTS when the lexer reads the input.

```
%token ADD
%token ALL
  ...
%token ESCAPED
%token <subtok> EXISTS /* NOT EXISTS or EXISTS */
  ...
 /* functions with special syntax */
%token FSUBSTRING
%token FTRIM
%token FDATE_ADD FDATE_SUB
%token FCOUNT
```

There are a few character tokens like ';' that aren't operators and so have no precedence that didn't have to be defined.

We finish the definition section with a list of nonterminals that have values. Because of the way we generate the RPN code in the parser, these values are either bitmasks where a nonterminal matches a set of options or else a count where the nonterminal matches a list of items of variable length.

```
%type <intval> select_opts select_expr_list
%type <intval> val_list opt_val_list case_list
%type <intval> groupby_list opt_with_rollup opt_asc_desc
%type <intval> table_references opt_inner_cross opt_outer
%type <intval> left_or_right opt_left_or_right_outer column_list
%type <intval> index_list opt_for_join

%type <intval> delete_opts delete_list
%type <intval> insert_opts insert_vals insert_vals_list
%type <intval> insert_asgn_list opt_if_not_exists update_opts update_asgn_list
%type <intval> opt_temporary opt_length opt_binary opt_uz enum_list
%type <intval> column_atts data_type opt_ignore_replace create_col_list

%start stmt_list

%%
```

The Top-Level Parsing Rules

```
stmt_list: stmt ';'
  | stmt_list stmt ';'
  ;
```

The top level is just a list of statements with each terminated by a semicolon, roughly the same as what the `mysql` command-line tool accepts. Each different statement will define an alternative, or several alternatives, for `stmt`.

SQL Expressions

Before we define the syntax for specific statements, we'll define the syntax of MySQL expressions, which are an extended version of the expressions familiar from languages like C and Fortran.

```
/**** expressions ****/

expr: NAME           { emit("NAME %s", $1); free($1); }
  | NAME '.' NAME  { emit("FIELDNAME %s.%s", $1, $3); free($1); free($3); }
  | USERVAR        { emit("USERVAR %s", $1); free($1); }
  | STRING         { emit("STRING %s", $1); free($1); }
  | INTNUM         { emit("NUMBER %d", $1); }
  | APPROXNUM      { emit("FLOAT %g", $1); }
  | BOOL           { emit("BOOL %d", $1); }
  ;
```

The simplest expressions are variable names and constants. Since a name in a SQL expression is usually a column name in a table, a name can also be qualified as `table.name` if there are several tables in the statement that use the same field name, which is quite common when the fields are used with common values to link tables together. Other simple expressions are user variables starting with an @ sign (dealt with in the lexer and not visible here) and constant strings, fixed and floating numbers, and boolean values. In each case, the code just emits an RPN statement for the item. For the items returned from the lexer as strings, it then frees the string created by the lexer to avoid storage leaks. In a more realistic parser, names would probably be entered into a symbol table rather than passed around as strings.

```
expr: expr '+' expr { emit("ADD"); }
    | expr '-' expr { emit("SUB"); }
    | expr '*' expr { emit("MUL"); }
    | expr '/' expr { emit("DIV"); }
    | expr '%' expr { emit("MOD"); }
    | expr MOD expr { emit("MOD"); }
    | '-' expr %prec UMINUS { emit("NEG"); }
    | expr ANDOP expr { emit("AND"); }
    | expr OR expr { emit("OR"); }
    | expr XOR expr { emit("XOR"); }
    | expr '|' expr { emit("BITOR"); }
    | expr '&' expr { emit("BITAND"); }
    | expr '^' expr { emit("BITXOR"); }
    | expr SHIFT expr { emit("SHIFT %s", $2==1?"left":"right"); }
    | NOT expr { emit("NOT"); }
    | '!' expr { emit("NOT"); }
    | expr COMPARISON expr { emit("CMP %d", $2); }

        /* recursive selects and comparisons thereto */
    | expr COMPARISON '(' select_stmt ')' { emit("CMPSELECT %d", $2); }
    | expr COMPARISON ANY '(' select_stmt ')' { emit("CMPANYSELECT %d", $2); }
    | expr COMPARISON SOME '(' select_stmt ')' { emit("CMPANYSELECT %d", $2); }
    | expr COMPARISON ALL '(' select_stmt ')' { emit("CMPALLSELECT %d", $2); }
    ;


expr:   expr IS NULLX     { emit("ISNULL"); }
    |   expr IS NOT NULLX { emit("ISNULL"); emit("NOT"); }
    |   expr IS BOOL      { emit("ISBOOL %d", $3); }
    |   expr IS NOT BOOL  { emit("ISBOOL %d", $4); emit("NOT"); }

    | USERVAR ASSIGN expr { emit("ASSIGN @%s", $1); free($1); }
    ;

expr: expr BETWEEN expr AND expr %prec BETWEEN { emit("BETWEEN"); }
    ;
```

Unary and binary expressions are straightforward and just emit the code for the appropriate operator. Comparisons also emit a subcode to tell what kind of comparison to do. (The subcodes are bit-encoded, where 1 means less than, 2 means greater than, and 4 means equal.)

SQL permits recursive SELECT statements where an internal SELECT returns a list of values that an external condition checks. If the internal SELECT can return multiple values, it can check whether ANY or ALL/SOME of the comparisons succeed. Although this can produce very complex statements, parsing it is simple since it just refers to select_stmt, defined later, for the internal SELECT. The RPN code emitted is the code for the expression to compare, then the code for the SELECT, and then an operator CMPSELECT, CMPANYSELECT, or CMPALLSELECT to say that this is a comparison of the preceding expression and SELECT.

SQL has some postfix operators including IS NULL, IS TRUE, and IS FALSE, as well as negated versions of them such as IS NOT FALSE. (Remember that BOOL is a boolean constant, TRUE, FALSE, or UNKNOWN.) Rather than coming up with RPN codes for the negated versions, we just emit a NOT operator to reverse the result of the test.

Next comes a MySQL extension to standard SQL: Internal assignments to user variables. These use a := assignment operator, returned from the lexer as an ASSIGN token, to avoid ambiguity with the equality comparison operator.

The syntactically unusual BETWEEN ... AND operator tests a value against two limits. It needed a lexical hack, described earlier, because of the ambiguity between the AND in this operator and the logical operation AND. (Like all hacks, this one isn't totally satisfactory, but it will do.) Since bison's precedence rules normally use the precedence of the rightmost token in a rule, we need a %prec to tell it to use BETWEEN's precedence.

```
val_list: expr { $$ = 1; }
   | expr ',' val_list { $$ = 1 + $3; }
   ;

opt_val_list: /* nil */ { $$ = 0 }
   | val_list
   ;

expr: expr IN '(' val_list ')'          { emit("ISIN %d", $4); }
   | expr NOT IN '(' val_list ')'       { emit("ISIN %d", $5); emit("NOT"); }
   | expr IN '(' select_stmt ')'        { emit("CMPANYSELECT 4"); }
   | expr NOT IN '(' select_stmt ')'    { emit("CMPALLSELECT 3"); }
   | EXISTS '(' select_stmt ')'         { emit("EXISTSSELECT"); if($1)emit("NOT"); }
   ;
```

The next set of operators uses variable-length lists of expressions (called *lists of values* or **val_lists** in the MySQL manual). In Chapter 3 we built trees to manage multiple expressions, but RPN makes the job considerably easier. Since an RPN interpreter evaluates each RPN value onto its internal stack, an operator that takes multiple values needs only to know how many values to pop off the stack. In our RPN code, such operators include an expression count.

This means the bison rules to parse the variable-length lists need only maintain a count of how many expressions they've parsed, which we keep as the value of the list's LHS symbol, in this case **val_list**. A single element list has length 1, and at each stage, a multi-element list has one more element than its sublist. There are some constructs where the list of values is optional, so an `opt_val_list` is either empty, with a count value of zero, or a `val_list` with a count value of whatever the `val_list` had. (Remember the default action `$$ = $1` for rules with no explicit action.)

Once we have the lists, we can parse the IN and NOT IN operators that test whether an expression is or isn't in a list of values. Note that the emitted code includes the count of values. SQL also has a variant form where the values come from a SELECT statement. For these statements, IN and NOT IN are equivalent to = ANY and != ALL, so we emit the same code.

Functions

SQL has a limited set of functions that MySQL greatly extends. Parsing normal function calls is very simple, since we can use the `opt_val_list` rule and the RPN is CALL with the number of arguments, but the parsing is made much more complex by several functions that have their own quirky optional syntax.

```
    /* regular functions */
expr: NAME '(' opt_val_list ')' {  emit("CALL %d %s", $3, $1); free($1); }
    ;

    /* functions with special syntax */
expr: FCOUNT '(' '*' ')' { emit("COUNTALL") }
    | FCOUNT '(' expr ')' { emit(" CALL 1 COUNT"); }

expr: FSUBSTRING '(' val_list ')'                  {  emit("CALL %d SUBSTR", $3); }
    | FSUBSTRING '(' expr FROM expr ')'            {  emit("CALL 2 SUBSTR"); }
    | FSUBSTRING '(' expr FROM expr FOR expr ')' {  emit("CALL 3 SUBSTR"); }

    | FTRIM '(' val_list ')'                      { emit("CALL %d TRIM", $3); }
    | FTRIM '(' trim_ltb expr FROM val_list ')'  { emit("CALL 3 TRIM"); }
    ;

trim_ltb: LEADING { emit("NUMBER 1"); }
    | TRAILING    { emit("NUMBER 2"); }
    | BOTH        { emit("NUMBER 3"); }
    ;

expr: FDATE_ADD '(' expr ',' interval_exp ')' { emit("CALL 3 DATE_ADD"); }
    | FDATE_SUB '(' expr ',' interval_exp ')' { emit("CALL 3 DATE_SUB"); }
    ;

interval_exp: INTERVAL expr DAY_HOUR { emit("NUMBER 1"); }
    | INTERVAL expr DAY_MICROSECOND   { emit("NUMBER 2"); }
    | INTERVAL expr DAY_MINUTE        { emit("NUMBER 3"); }
    | INTERVAL expr DAY_SECOND        { emit("NUMBER 4"); }
    | INTERVAL expr YEAR_MONTH        { emit("NUMBER 5"); }
    | INTERVAL expr YEAR              { emit("NUMBER 6"); }
    | INTERVAL expr HOUR_MICROSECOND  { emit("NUMBER 7"); }
    | INTERVAL expr HOUR_MINUTE       { emit("NUMBER 8"); }
    | INTERVAL expr HOUR_SECOND       { emit("NUMBER 9"); }
    ;
```

We handle five functions with special syntax here, COUNT, SUBSTRING, TRIM, DATE_ADD, and DATE_SUB. COUNT has a special form, COUNT(*), used to efficiently count the number of records returned by a SELECT statement, as well as a normal form that counts the number of different values of an expression. We have one rule for the special form, which emits a special COUNTALL operator, and a second rule for the regular form, which emits a regular function call. SUBSTRING is a normal substring operator taking the original string, where to start, and how many characters to take. It can either use the regular call syntax or use reserved words FROM and FOR to delimit the arguments. There's a rule for each form, all generating similar code since it's the same two or three arguments. TRIM similarly can use normal syntax or special syntax like TRIM(LEADING 'x' FROM a). Again, we parse each form and generate rules. The keywords LEADING, TRAILING, and BOTH turn into the integer values 1 through 3 passed as the first argument in a three-argument form. DATE_ADD and DATE_SUB add or subtract a scaled number of time periods to a date. The special syntax accepts a long list of scaling types, which again turn into integers passed to the functions.

Bison really shines when handling this kind of complex syntax for two reasons: one is that you can generally just write down rules like these as you need and they'll work, but more important, since bison will diagnose any ambiguous grammar, you know that if it doesn't report conflicts, you haven't accidentally broken some other part of the parser.

Other expressions

We wrap up the expression grammar with a grab bag of special cases.

```
expr: CASE expr case_list END          { emit("CASEVAL %d 0", $3); }
    | CASE expr case_list ELSE expr END { emit("CASEVAL %d 1", $3); }
    | CASE case_list END               { emit("CASE %d 0", $2); }
    | CASE case_list ELSE expr END      { emit("CASE %d 1", $2); }
    ;

case_list: WHEN expr THEN expr    { $$ = 1; }
         | case_list WHEN expr THEN expr { $$ = $1+1; }
    ;

expr: expr LIKE expr { emit("LIKE"); }
    | expr NOT LIKE expr { emit("LIKE"); emit("NOT"); }
    ;

expr: expr REGEXP expr { emit("REGEXP"); }
    | expr NOT REGEXP expr { emit("REGEXP"); emit("NOT"); }
    ;

expr: CURRENT_TIMESTAMP { emit("NOW") };
    | CURRENT_DATE      { emit("NOW") };
    | CURRENT_TIME      { emit("NOW") };
    ;
```

```
expr: BINARY expr %prec UMINUS { emit("STRTOBIN"); }
    ;
```

The CASE statement comes in two forms. In the first, CASE is followed by a value that is compared against a list of test values with an expression value for each test, and an optional ELSE default, as in CASE a WHEN 100 THEN 1 WHEN 200 THEN 2 ELSE 3 END. The other is just a list of conditional expressions, as in CASE WHEN a=100 THEN 1 WHEN a=200 THEN 2 END. We have a rule case_list that builds up a list of WHEN/THEN expression pairs and then uses it in four variants of CASE, each of the two versions with and without ELSE. The RPN is CASEVAL or CASE for the versions with or without an initial value, with a count of WHEN/THEN pairs and 1 or 0 if there's an ELSE value. The LIKE and REGEXP operators do forms of pattern matching. They're basically binary operators except that they permit a preceding NOT to reverse the sense of the test. Finally, there are three versions of the keyword for the current time, as well as a unary BINARY operator that coerces an expression to be treated as binary rather than text data.

Select Statements

By far the most complex statement in SQL is SELECT, which retrieves data from SQL tables and summaries and manipulates it. We deal with it first because it will use several subrules that we can reuse when parsing other statements.

```
    /* statements: select statement */

stmt: select_stmt { emit("STMT"); }
    ;

select_stmt: SELECT select_opts select_expr_list     simple select with no tables
                        { emit("SELECTNODATA %d %d", $2, $3); } ;

    | SELECT select_opts select_expr_list            select with tables
      FROM table_references
      opt_where opt_groupby opt_having opt_orderby opt_limit
      opt_into_list { emit("SELECT %d %d %d", $2, $3, $5); } ;
    ;
```

The first rule says that a select_stmt is a kind of statement, and it emits an RPN STMT as a delimiter between statements. The syntax of SELECT lists the expressions that SQL needs to calculate for each record (aka tuple) it retrieves, lists an optional (but usual) FROM with the tables containing the data for the expressions, and lists optional qualifiers such as WHERE, GROUP BY, and HAVING that limit, combine, and sort the records retrieved. Each qualifier has its own rules.

```
opt_where: /* nil */
    | WHERE expr { emit("WHERE"); };

opt_groupby: /* nil */
    | GROUP BY groupby_list opt_with_rollup
                        { emit("GROUPBYLIST %d %d", $3, $4); }
    ;
```

```
groupby_list: expr opt_asc_desc
                          { emit("GROUPBY %d", $2); $$ = 1; }
    | groupby_list ',' expr opt_asc_desc
                          { emit("GROUPBY %d", $4); $$ = $1 + 1; }
    ;

opt_asc_desc: /* nil */ { $$ = 0; }
    | ASC               { $$ = 0; }
    | DESC              { $$ = 1; }
    ;

opt_with_rollup: /* nil */  { $$ = 0; }
    | WITH ROLLUP  { $$ = 1; }
    ;

opt_having: /* nil */
    | HAVING expr { emit("HAVING"); };

opt_orderby: /* nil */
    | ORDER BY groupby_list { emit("ORDERBY %d", $3); }
    ;

opt_limit: /* nil */ | LIMIT expr { emit("LIMIT 1"); }
    | LIMIT expr ',' expr           { emit("LIMIT 2"); }
    ;

opt_into_list: /* nil */
    | INTO column_list { emit("INTO %d", $2); }
    ;

column_list: NAME { emit("COLUMN %s", $1); free($1); $$ = 1; }
    | column_list ',' NAME  { emit("COLUMN %s", $3); free($3); $$ = $1 + 1; }
    ;
```

Some of the options, WHERE, GROUPBY, and HAVING, take a fixed number of expressions, while LIMIT takes either one or two expressions. These each have straightforward rules to match the option and its expression(s), and they emit an RPN operator to say what to do with the expressions.

GROUP BY and ORDER BY take a list of expressions, usually column names, each optionally followed by ASC or DESC to set the sort order. The groupby_list rule makes a counted list of expressions, emitting a GROUPBY operator with an operand for the sort order. The GROUP BY and ORDER BY rules then emit GROUPBYLIST and ORDERBY operators with the count and, for GROUP BY, a flag to say whether to use the WITH ROLLUP option, which adds some extra summary fields to the result.

The INTO operator takes a plain list of names, which we call a column_list, that is a list of field names into which to store the selected data. INTO isn't used very often, but we'll reuse column_list several other places later where the syntax has a list of column names.

Select options and table references

Now we handle the initial options and the main list of expressions in a SELECT.

```
select_opts:                          { $$ = 0; }
| select_opts ALL
    { if($1 & 01) yyerror("duplicate ALL option"); $$ = $1 | 01; }
| select_opts DISTINCT
    { if($1 & 02) yyerror("duplicate DISTINCT option"); $$ = $1 | 02; }
| select_opts DISTINCTROW
    { if($1 & 04) yyerror("duplicate DISTINCTROW option"); $$ = $1 | 04; }
| select_opts HIGH_PRIORITY
    { if($1 & 010) yyerror("duplicate HIGH_PRIORITY option"); $$ = $1 | 010; }
| select_opts STRAIGHT_JOIN
    { if($1 & 020) yyerror("duplicate STRAIGHT_JOIN option"); $$ = $1 | 020; }
| select_opts SQL_SMALL_RESULT
    { if($1 & 040) yyerror("duplicate SQL_SMALL_RESULT option"); $$ = $1 | 040; }
| select_opts SQL_BIG_RESULT
    { if($1 & 0100) yyerror("duplicate SQL_BIG_RESULT option"); $$ = $1 | 0100; }
| select_opts SQL_CALC_FOUND_ROWS
    { if($1 & 0200) yyerror("duplicate SQL_CALC_FOUND_ROWS option"); $$ =
    $1 | 0200; }
    ;

select_expr_list: select_expr { $$ = 1; }
    | select_expr_list ',' select_expr {$$ = $1 + 1; }
    | '*' { emit("SELECTALL"); $$ = 1; }
    ;

select_expr: expr opt_as_alias ;

opt_as_alias: AS NAME { emit ("ALIAS %s", $2); free($2); }
    | NAME            { emit ("ALIAS %s", $1); free($1); }
    | /* nil */
    ;
```

The options are flags that affect the way that a SELECT is handled. The rules about what options are compatible with each other are too complex to encode into the grammar, so we just accept any set of options and build up a bitmask of them, which also lets us diagnose duplicate options. (When options can occur in any order, there's no good way to prevent duplicates in the grammar, and it's generally easy to detect them yourself as we do here.)

The SELECT expression list is a comma-separated list of expressions, each optionally followed by an AS clause to give the expression a name to use to refer to it elsewhere in the SELECT statement. We emit an ALIAS operator in the RPN. As a special case, * means all of the fields in the source records, for which we emit SELECTALL.

SELECT table references

The most complex and powerful part of SELECT, and the most powerful part of SQL, is the way it can refer to multiple tables. In a SELECT, you can tell it to create conceptual joined tables built from data stored in many actual tables, either by explicit joins or by recursive SELECT statements. Since tables can be rather large, there are also ways to give it hints about how to do the joining efficiently.

```
table_references:    table_reference { $$ = 1; }
    | table_references ',' table_reference { $$ = $1 + 1; }
    ;

table_reference:  table_factor
  | join_table
;

table_factor:
    NAME opt_as_alias index_hint { emit("TABLE %s", $1); free($1); }
  | NAME '.' NAME opt_as_alias index_hint { emit("TABLE %s.%s", $1, $3);
                             free($1); free($3); }
  | table_subquery opt_as NAME { emit("SUBQUERYAS %s", $3); free($3); }
  | '(' table_references ')' { emit("TABLEREFERENCES %d", $2); }
  ;

opt_as: AS
  | /* nil */
  ;

join_table:
    table_reference opt_inner_cross JOIN table_factor opt_join_condition
                { emit("JOIN %d", 100+$2); }
  | table_reference STRAIGHT_JOIN table_factor
                { emit("JOIN %d", 200); }
  | table_reference STRAIGHT_JOIN table_factor ON expr
                { emit("JOIN %d", 200); }
  | table_reference left_or_right opt_outer JOIN table_factor join_condition
                { emit("JOIN %d", 300+$2+$3); }
  | table_reference NATURAL opt_left_or_right_outer JOIN table_factor
                { emit("JOIN %d", 400+$3); }
  ;

opt_inner_cross: /* nil */ { $$ = 0; }
    | INNER { $$ = 1; }
    | CROSS  { $$ = 2; }
;

opt_outer: /* nil */  { $$ = 0; }
    | OUTER {$$ = 4; }
    ;

left_or_right: LEFT { $$ = 1; }
    | RIGHT { $$ = 2; }
    ;

opt_left_or_right_outer: LEFT opt_outer { $$ = 1 + $2; }
    | RIGHT opt_outer  { $$ = 2 + $2; }
    | /* nil */ { $$ = 0; }
    ;

opt_join_condition: /* nil */
    | join_condition ;

join_condition:
```

```
    ON expr { emit("ONEXPR"); }
    | USING '(' column_list ')' { emit("USING %d", $3); }
    ;

index_hint:
    USE KEY opt_for_join '(' index_list ')'
                  { emit("INDEXHINT %d %d", $5, 10+$3); }
    | IGNORE KEY opt_for_join '(' index_list ')'
                  { emit("INDEXHINT %d %d", $5, 20+$3); }
    | FORCE KEY opt_for_join '(' index_list ')'
                  { emit("INDEXHINT %d %d", $5, 30+$3); }
    | /* nil */
    ;

opt_for_join: FOR JOIN { $$ = 1; }
    | /* nil */ { $$ = 0; }
    ;

index_list: NAME  { emit("INDEX %s", $1); free($1); $$ = 1; }
    | index_list ',' NAME { emit("INDEX %s", $3); free($3); $$ = $1 + 1; }
    ;

table_subquery: '(' select_stmt ')' { emit("SUBQUERY"); }
    ;
```

Although the grammar for the table sublanguage is long, it's not all that complex, consisting mostly of lists of items and a lot of optional clauses. Each table_reference can be a table_factor (which is a plain table, a nested SELECT, or a parenthesized list) or else a join_table, an explicit join. A plain table reference is the name of the table, with or without the name of the database that contains it; an optional AS clause to give an alias name (a table can usefully appear more than once in the same SELECT, and this makes it possible to tell which instance an expression refers to); and an optional hint about which indexes to use, described in a moment.

A nested SELECT is a SELECT statement in parentheses, which must have a name assigned, although the AS before the name is optional. A table_factor can also be a parenthesized list of table_references, which can be useful when creating joins.

Each table_factor can also take an index hint. A SQL table can have indexes on any combination of fields, which makes it faster to do searches based on those fields. Each index has a name, typically something like foo_index for a field foo. Normally MySQL uses the appropriate indexes automatically, but you can also override its choice of indexes by USE KEY, FORCE KEY, or IGNORE KEY.

A join specifies the way to combine two groups of tables. Joins come in a variety of flavors that change the order in which the table are matched up, specify what to do with records in one group that don't match any records in the other group, and specify other details. Every join also explicitly or implicitly specifies the fields to use to match up the tables, in a variety of syntaxes, for example:

```
SELECT * FROM a JOIN b on a.foo=b.bar
SELECT * FROM a JOIN b USING (foo) a.foo=b.foo
```

In a NATURAL join, the join matches on fields with the same name, and in a regular join, if there are no fields listed, it creates a cross-product, joining every record in the first group with every record in the second group. In this latter case, the result is usually whittled down by a WHERE or HAVING clause. For all the various sorts of joins, we emit a JOIN operator with subfields describing the exact kind of join.

Note the separate rules table_factor and table_reference. They're separate to set the associativity of JOIN operators and resolve the ambiguity in an expression like a JOIN b JOIN c, which means (a JOIN b) JOIN c rather than a JOIN (b JOIN c). In the join_table rule, there's a table_reference on the left side of each join and table_factor on the right, making the syntax left associative. Since a table_factor can be a parenthesized table_reference, you can use parentheses if that's not what you want. In this case, we could have made everything a table_reference and used precedence to resolve the ambiguity, but this syntax comes directly from the SQL standard, and there seemed to be no reason to change it.

Delete Statement

Once we have the SELECT statement under control, the other data manipulation statements are easy to parse. DELETE deletes records from a table, with the records to delete chosen using a WHERE clause identical to the WHERE clause in a SELECT or chosen from a group of tables also specified the same as in a SELECT.

```
    /* statements: delete statement */

stmt: delete_stmt { emit("STMT"); }
    ;

    /* single table delete */
delete_stmt: DELETE delete_opts FROM NAME
    opt_where opt_orderby opt_limit
                    { emit("DELETEONE %d %s", $2, $4); free($4); }
    ;

delete_opts: delete_opts LOW_PRIORITY { $$ = $1 + 01; }
    | delete_opts QUICK { $$ = $1 + 02; }
    | delete_opts IGNORE { $$ = $1 + 04; }
    | /* nil */ { $$ = 0; }
    ;
```

The DELETE statement reuses several rules we wrote for SELECT: opt_where for an optional WHERE clause, opt_orderby for an optional ORDER BY clause, and opt_limit for an optional LIMIT clause. Since the rules for each of those clauses emits its own RPN, we only have to write rules for some keywords specific to DELETE, QUICK, and IGNORE, and for the DELETE statement itself.

```
    /* multitable delete, first version */
delete_stmt: DELETE delete_opts
    delete_list
    FROM table_references opt_where
```

```
                  { emit("DELETEMULTI %d %d %d", $2, $3, $5); }

  delete_list: NAME opt_dot_star { emit("TABLE %s", $1); free($1); $$ = 1; }
    | delete_list ',' NAME opt_dot_star
            { emit("TABLE %s", $3); free($3); $$ = $1 + 1; }
    ;

opt_dot_star: /* nil */ | '.' '*' ;

    /* multitable delete, second version */
delete_stmt: DELETE delete_opts
    FROM delete_list
    USING table_references opt_where
            { emit("DELETEMULTI %d %d %d", $2, $4, $6); }
    ;
```

There are two different syntaxes for multitable DELETEs, to be compatible with
various other implementations of SQL. One lists the tables followed by FROM and the
table_references; the other says FROM, the list of tables, USING, and the
table_references. Bison deals easily with these variants, and we emit the same RPN
for both. The delete_list has a little optional "syntactic sugar," letting you specify the
table from which records are to be deleted as name.*, as well as plain name, to remind
readers that all of the fields in each record are deleted.

Insert and Replace Statements

The INSERT and REPLACE statements add records to a table. The only difference between
them is that if the primary key fields in a new record have the same values as an existing
record, INSERT fails with an error unless there's an ON DUPLICATE KEY clause, while
REPLACE replaces the existing record. INSERT, like DELETE, has two equivalent variant
forms to insert new data, and it has a third form that inserts records created by a SELECT.

```
    INSERT INTO a(b,c) values (1,2),(3,DEFAULT)

    /* statements: insert statement */

stmt: insert_stmt { emit("STMT"); }
    ;

insert_stmt: INSERT insert_opts opt_into NAME
        opt_col_names
        VALUES insert_vals_list
        opt_ondupupdate { emit("INSERTVALS %d %d %s", $2, $7, $4); free($4) }
    ;

opt_ondupupdate: /* nil */
    | ONDUPLICATE KEY UPDATE insert_asgn_list { emit("DUPUPDATE %d", $4); }
    ;

insert_opts: /* nil */ { $$ = 0; }
    | insert_opts LOW_PRIORITY { $$ = $1 | 01 ; }
    | insert_opts DELAYED { $$ = $1 | 02 ; }
```

```
        | insert_opts HIGH_PRIORITY { $$ = $1 | 04 ; }
        | insert_opts IGNORE { $$ = $1 | 010 ; }
        ;

    opt_into: INTO | /* nil */
        ;

    opt_col_names: /* nil */
        | '(' column_list ')' { emit("INSERTCOLS %d", $2); }
        ;

    insert_vals_list: '(' insert_vals ')' { emit("VALUES %d", $2); $$ = 1; }
        | insert_vals_list ',' '(' insert_vals ')' { emit("VALUES %d", $4); $$ = $1 + 1; }

    insert_vals:
          expr { $$ = 1; }
        | DEFAULT { emit("DEFAULT"); $$ = 1; }
        | insert_vals ',' expr { $$ = $1 + 1; }
        | insert_vals ',' DEFAULT { emit("DEFAULT"); $$ = $1 + 1; }
        ;
```

The first form specifies the name of the table and the list of fields to be provided (all of them if not specified), then specifies VALUES, and finally specifies lists of values. This form can insert multiple records, so the rule insert_vals matches the fields for one record enclosed in parentheses and insert_vals_list matches multiple comma-separated sets of fields. Each field value can be an expression or the keyword DEFAULT. There are a few optional keywords to control the details of the insert.

The opt_ondupupdate rule handles the ON DUPLICATE clause, which gives a list of fields to change if an inserted record would have had a duplicate key. Since the syntax is SET field=value and = is scanned as a COMPARISON operator, we accept COMPARISON and check in our code to be sure that it's an equal sign and not something else.[4] Note that ONDUPLICATE is one token; in the lexer we treat the two words as one token to avoid ambiguity with ON clauses in nested SELECTs.

INSERT INTO a SET b=1, c=2

```
    insert_stmt: INSERT insert_opts opt_into NAME
        SET insert_asgn_list
        opt_ondupupdate
        { emit("INSERTASGN %d %d %s", $2, $6, $4); free($4) }
        ;

    insert_asgn_list:
        NAME COMPARISON expr
          { if ($2 != 4) { yyerror("bad insert assignment to %s", $1); YYERROR; }
            emit("ASSIGN %s", $1); free($1); $$ = 1; }
        | NAME COMPARISON DEFAULT
          { if ($2 != 4) { yyerror("bad insert assignment to %s", $1); YYERROR; }
```

---

4. This could fairly be considered a kludge, but the alternative would be to treat = separately from the other comparison operators and add an extra rule every place a comparison can occur, which would result in more code.

```
                emit("DEFAULT"); emit("ASSIGN %s", $1); free($1); $$ = 1; }
   | insert_asgn_list ',' NAME COMPARISON expr
       { if ($4 != 4) { yyerror("bad insert assignment to %s", $1); YYERROR; }
                emit("ASSIGN %s", $3); free($3); $$ = $1 + 1; }
   | insert_asgn_list ',' NAME COMPARISON DEFAULT
       { if ($4 != 4) { yyerror("bad insert assignment to %s", $1); YYERROR; }
                emit("DEFAULT"); emit("ASSIGN %s", $3); free($3); $$ = $1 + 1; }
   ;
```

The second form uses an assignment syntax similar to the one for ON DUPLICATE. We have to check that the COMPARISON is really an =. If not, we produce an error message by calling **yyerror()**, and then we tell the parser to start error recovery with YYERROR. (In this version of the parser there's no error recovery, but see Chapter 8.) This form uses same optional ON DUPLICATE syntax at the end of the statement, so we use the same rule.

```
       INSERT into a(b,c) SELECT x,y FROM z where x < 12
insert_stmt: INSERT insert_opts opt_into NAME opt_col_names
   select_stmt
   opt_ondupupdate { emit("INSERTSELECT %d %s", $2, $4); free($4); }
   ;
```

The third form of INSERT uses data from a SELECT statement to create new records. All of the pieces of this statement are the same as syntax we've seen before, so we write only the one rule and reuse subrules for the pieces.

Replace statement

The syntax of the REPLACE statement is just like INSERT, so the rules for it are the same too, changing INSERT to REPLACE and renaming the top-level rules.

```
   /** replace just like insert **/
stmt: replace_stmt { emit("STMT"); }
   ;

replace_stmt: REPLACE insert_opts opt_into NAME
       opt_col_names
       VALUES insert_vals_list
       opt_ondupupdate { emit("REPLACEVALS %d %d %s", $2, $7, $4); free($4) }
   ;

replace_stmt: REPLACE insert_opts opt_into NAME
       SET insert_asgn_list
       opt_ondupupdate
       { emit("REPLACEASGN %d %d %s", $2, $6, $4); free($4) }
   ;

replace_stmt: REPLACE insert_opts opt_into NAME opt_col_names
       select_stmt
       opt_ondupupdate { emit("REPLACESELECT %d %s", $2, $4); free($4); }
   ;
```

Update Statement

The UPDATE statement changes fields in existing records. Again, its syntax lets us reuse rules from previous statements.

```
/** update **/
stmt: update_stmt { emit("STMT"); }
   ;

update_stmt: UPDATE update_opts table_references
      SET update_asgn_list
      opt_where
      opt_orderby
opt_limit { emit("UPDATE %d %d %d", $2, $3, $5); }
   ;

update_opts: /* nil */ { $$ = 0; }
   | insert_opts LOW_PRIORITY { $$ = $1 | 01 ; }
   | insert_opts IGNORE { $$ = $1 | 010 ; }
   ;

update_asgn_list:
      NAME COMPARISON expr
      { if ($2 != 4) { yyerror("bad update assignment to %s", $1); YYERROR; }
      emit("ASSIGN %s", $1); free($1); $$ = 1; }
   | NAME '.' NAME COMPARISON expr
         { if ($4 != 4) { yyerror("bad update assignment to %s", $1); YYERROR; }
      emit("ASSIGN %s.%s", $1, $3); free($1); free($3); $$ = 1; }
   | update_asgn_list ',' NAME COMPARISON expr
         { if ($4 != 4) { yyerror("bad update assignment to %s", $3); YYERROR; }
      emit("ASSIGN %s.%s", $3); free($3); $$ = $1 + 1; }
   | update_asgn_list ',' NAME '.' NAME COMPARISON expr
         { if ($6 != 4) { yyerror("bad update  assignment to %s.$s", $3, $5);
            YYERROR; }
         emit("ASSIGN %s.%s", $3, $5); free($3); free($5); $$ = 1; }
   ;
```

UPDATE has its own set of options in the update_opts rule. The list of assignments after SET is similar to the one in INSERT, but it allows qualified table names since you can update more than one table at a time, and it doesn't have the default option in INSERT, so we have a similar but different update_asgn_list. INSERT uses the same opt_where and opt_orderby to limit and sort the records updated.

This ends the list of data manipulation statements in our SQL subset. MySQL has several more not covered here, but their syntax is straightforward to parse.

Create Database

Now we'll handle two of the many data definition statements that create and modify the structure of databases and tables.

```
/** create database **/
```

```
stmt: create_database_stmt { emit("STMT"); }
   ;

create_database_stmt:
     CREATE DATABASE opt_if_not_exists NAME
        { emit("CREATEDATABASE %d %s", $3, $4); free($4); }
   | CREATE SCHEMA opt_if_not_exists NAME
        { emit("CREATEDATABASE %d %s", $3, $4); free($4); }
   ;

opt_if_not_exists:  /* nil */ { $$ = 0; }
   | IF EXISTS
        { if(!$2) { yyerror("IF EXISTS doesn't exist"); YYERROR; }
                     $$ = $2; /* NOT EXISTS hack */ }
   ;
```

CREATE DATABASE, or the equivalent CREATE SCHEMA statement, makes a new database in which you can then create tables. It has one optional clause, IF NOT EXISTS, to prevent an error message if the database already exists. Recall that we did a lexical hack to treat IF NOT EXISTS and IF EXISTS as the same token in expressions. In this case, only IF NOT EXISTS is valid, so we test in the action code and complain and tell the parser it's a syntax error if it's the wrong one.

Create Table

The CREATE TABLE statement rivals SELECT in its length and number of options, but its syntax is much simpler since nearly all of the syntax is just declaring the type and attribute of each column in the table.

We start with six versions of create_table_statement. There are three pairs that differ only in NAME or NAME.NAME for the name of the table. The first pair is the normal version with an explicit list of columns in create_col_list. The other two create and populate a table from a SELECT statement, with one including a list of column names and the other defaulting to the column names from the SELECT.

```
   /** create table **/
stmt: create_table_stmt { emit("STMT"); }
   ;

create_table_stmt: CREATE opt_temporary TABLE opt_if_not_exists NAME
   '(' create_col_list ')' { emit("CREATE %d %d %d %s", $2, $4, $7, $5); free($5); }
   ;

create_table_stmt: CREATE opt_temporary TABLE opt_if_not_exists NAME '.' NAME
   '(' create_col_list ')' { emit("CREATE %d %d %d %s.%s", $2, $4, $9, $5, $7);
                         free($5); free($7); }
   ;

create_table_stmt: CREATE opt_temporary TABLE opt_if_not_exists NAME
   '(' create_col_list ')'
create_select_statement { emit("CREATESELECT %d %d %d %s", $2, $4, $7, $5); free($5); }
   ;
```

```
create_table_stmt: CREATE opt_temporary TABLE opt_if_not_exists NAME
    create_select_statement { emit("CREATESELECT %d %d 0 %s", $2, $4, $5); free($5); }
    ;

create_table_stmt: CREATE opt_temporary TABLE opt_if_not_exists NAME '.' NAME
    '(' create_col_list ')'
    create_select_statement  { emit("CREATESELECT %d %d 0 %s.%s", $2, $4, $5, $7);
                               free($5); free($7); }
    ;

create_table_stmt: CREATE opt_temporary TABLE opt_if_not_exists NAME '.' NAME
    create_select_statement { emit("CREATESELECT %d %d 0 %s.%s", $2, $4, $5, $7);
                              free($5); free($7); }
    ;

opt_temporary:   /* nil */ { $$ = 0; }
   | TEMPORARY { $$ = 1;}
   ;
```

The heart of a CREATE DATABASE statement is the list of columns, or more precisely the
list of create_definitions, which includes both columns and indexes. The indexes can
be the PRIMARY KEY, which means that it's unique for each record; a regular INDEX (also
called KEY); or a FULLTEXT index, which indexes individual words in the data. Each of
those takes a list of column names, for which we once again reuse the column_list rule
we defined for SELECT.

```
create_col_list: create_definition { $$ = 1; }
    | create_col_list ',' create_definition { $$ = $1 + 1; }
    ;

create_definition: PRIMARY KEY '(' column_list ')'    { emit("PRIKEY %d", $4); }
    | KEY '(' column_list ')'            { emit("KEY %d", $3); }
    | INDEX '(' column_list ')'          { emit("KEY %d", $3); }
    | FULLTEXT INDEX '(' column_list ')' { emit("TEXTINDEX %d", $4); }
    | FULLTEXT KEY '(' column_list ')'   { emit("TEXTINDEX %d", $4); }
    ;
```

Each definition is bracketed by an RPN STARTCOL operator since the set of per-column
options is large; this delimits each column's options. The column itself is the name of
the column, the data type, and the optional attributes, such as whether the column can
contain null values, what its default value is, and whether it's a key. (Declaring a column
to be a key is equivalent to creating an index on the column.) For the attributes, we
emit an ATTR operator for each one and count the number of attributes. The code here
doesn't check for duplicates, but we could do so by making the value of column_atts a
structure with both a count and a bitmask and checking the bitmask as we did earlier
in SELECT options.

```
create_definition: { emit("STARTCOL"); } NAME data_type column_atts
                  { emit("COLUMNDEF %d %s", $3, $2); free($2); }

column_atts: /* nil */ { $$ = 0; }
    | column_atts NOT NULLX            { emit("ATTR NOTNULL"); $$ = $1 + 1; }
```

```
    | column_atts NULLX
    | column_atts DEFAULT STRING
        { emit("ATTR DEFAULT STRING %s", $3); free($3); $$ = $1 + 1; }
    | column_atts DEFAULT INTNUM
        { emit("ATTR DEFAULT NUMBER %d", $3); $$ = $1 + 1; }
    | column_atts DEFAULT APPROXNUM
        { emit("ATTR DEFAULT FLOAT %g", $3); $$ = $1 + 1; }
    | column_atts DEFAULT BOOL
        { emit("ATTR DEFAULT BOOL %d", $3); $$ = $1 + 1; }
    | column_atts AUTO_INCREMENT
        { emit("ATTR AUTOINC"); $$ = $1 + 1; }
    | column_atts UNIQUE '(' column_list ')'
        { emit("ATTR UNIQUEKEY %d", $4); $$ = $1 + 1; }
    | column_atts UNIQUE KEY { emit("ATTR UNIQUEKEY"); $$ = $1 + 1; }
    | column_atts PRIMARY KEY { emit("ATTR PRIKEY"); $$ = $1 + 1; }
    | column_atts KEY { emit("ATTR PRIKEY"); $$ = $1 + 1; }
    | column_atts COMMENT STRING
        { emit("ATTR COMMENT %s", $3); free($3); $$ = $1 + 1; }
    ;
```

The syntax for the data type is long but not complicated. Many of the types allow the number of characters or digits to be specified, so there's an opt_length that takes one or two length values. (We encode them into one number here; a structure would have been more elegant.) Other options say whether a number is unsigned or displayed filled with zeros, whether a string is treated as binary data, and, for text, what character set and collation rule it uses. Those last two are specified as strings from a large set of language and collation systems, but for our purposes we just accept any string. With these auxiliary rules, we can now parse the long list of MySQL data types. Again we encode the data type into a number, and again a structure would be more elegant, but the number will do for our RPN.

The last two types, ENUM and SET, each take a list of strings that name the members of the enumeration or set, which we parse as enum_val.

```
opt_length: /* nil */ { $$ = 0; }
    | '(' INTNUM ')' { $$ = $2; }
    | '(' INTNUM ',' INTNUM ')' { $$ = $2 + 1000*$4; }
    ;

opt_binary: /* nil */ { $$ = 0; }
    | BINARY { $$ = 4000; }
    ;

opt_uz: /* nil */ { $$ = 0; }
    | opt_uz UNSIGNED { $$ = $1 | 1000; }
    | opt_uz ZEROFILL { $$ = $1 | 2000; }
    ;

opt_csc: /* nil */
    | opt_csc CHAR SET STRING { emit("COLCHARSET %s", $4); free($4); }
    | opt_csc COLLATE STRING { emit("COLCOLLATE %s", $3); free($3); }
    ;
```

```
data_type:
    BIT opt_length { $$ = 10000 + $2; }
    | TINYINT opt_length opt_uz { $$ = 10000 + $2; }
    | SMALLINT opt_length opt_uz { $$ = 20000 + $2 + $3; }
    | MEDIUMINT opt_length opt_uz { $$ = 30000 + $2 + $3; }
    | INT opt_length opt_uz { $$ = 40000 + $2 + $3; }
    | INTEGER opt_length opt_uz { $$ = 50000 + $2 + $3; }
    | BIGINT opt_length opt_uz { $$ = 60000 + $2 + $3; }
    | REAL opt_length opt_uz { $$ = 70000 + $2 + $3; }
    | DOUBLE opt_length opt_uz { $$ = 80000 + $2 + $3; }
    | FLOAT opt_length opt_uz { $$ = 90000 + $2 + $3; }
    | DECIMAL opt_length opt_uz { $$ = 110000 + $2 + $3; }
    | DATE { $$ = 100001; }
    | TIME { $$ = 100002; }
    | TIMESTAMP { $$ = 100003; }
    | DATETIME { $$ = 100004; }
    | YEAR { $$ = 100005; }
    | CHAR opt_length opt_csc { $$ = 120000 + $2; }
    | VARCHAR '(' INTNUM ')' opt_csc { $$ = 130000 + $3; }
    | BINARY opt_length { $$ = 140000 + $2; }
    | VARBINARY '(' INTNUM ')' { $$ = 150000 + $3; }
    | TINYBLOB { $$ = 160001; }
    | BLOB { $$ = 160002; }
    | MEDIUMBLOB { $$ = 160003; }
    | LONGBLOB { $$ = 160004; }
    | TINYTEXT opt_binary opt_csc { $$ = 170000 + $2; }
    | TEXT opt_binary opt_csc { $$ = 171000 + $2; }
    | MEDIUMTEXT opt_binary opt_csc { $$ = 172000 + $2; }
    | LONGTEXT opt_binary opt_csc { $$ = 173000 + $2; }
    | ENUM '(' enum_list ')' opt_csc { $$ = 200000 + $3; }
    | SET '(' enum_list ')' opt_csc { $$ = 210000 + $3; }
    ;

enum_list: STRING { emit("ENUMVAL %s", $1); free($1); $$ = 1; }
    | enum_list ',' STRING { emit("ENUMVAL %s", $3); free($3); $$ = $1 + 1; }
    ;
```

The other version of a CREATE uses a SELECT statement preceded by some optional key-words and an optional meaningless AS.

```
create_select_statement: opt_ignore_replace opt_as select_stmt { emit("CREATESELECT %d", $1) }
    ;

opt_ignore_replace: /* nil */ { $$ = 0; }
    | IGNORE { $$ = 1; }
    | REPLACE { $$ = 2; }
    ;
```

User Variables

The last statement we parse is a SET statement, which is a MySQL extension that sets user variables. The assignment can use either :=, which we call ASSIGN, or a plain = sign, checking as always to be sure it's not some other comparison operator.

```
    /**** set user variables ****/

stmt: set_stmt { emit("STMT"); }
    ;

set_stmt: SET set_list ;

set_list: set_expr | set_list ',' set_expr ;

set_expr:
      USERVAR COMPARISON expr { if ($2 != 4) { yyerror("bad set to @%s", $1); YYERROR; }
                  emit("SET %s", $1); free($1); }
    | USERVAR ASSIGN expr { emit("SET %s", $1); free($1); }
    ;
```

That ends our SQL syntax. MySQL has many, many other statements, but these give a reasonable idea of what's involved in parsing them.

The Parser Routines

Finally, we have a few support routines. The emit routine just prints out the RPN. In a more sophisticated compiler, it could act as a simpleminded assembler and emit a stream of bytecode operators for an RPN interpreter.

The yyerror and main routines should be familiar from the previous chapter. This main program accepts a -d switch to turn on parse-time debugging, a useful feature when debugging a grammar as complex as this one.

```
%%
void
emit(char *s, ...)
{
  extern yylineno;

  va_list ap;
  va_start(ap, s);

  printf("rpn: ");
  vfprintf(stdout, s, ap);
  printf("\n");
}

void
yyerror(char *s, ...)
{
  extern yylineno;

  va_list ap;
  va_start(ap, s);

  fprintf(stderr, "%d: error: ", yylineno);
  vfprintf(stderr, s, ap);
  fprintf(stderr, "\n");
}
```

```
main(int ac, char **av)
{
  extern FILE *yyin;

  if(ac > 1 && !strcmp(av[1], "-d")) {
    yydebug = 1; ac--; av++;
  }

  if(ac > 1 && (yyin = fopen(av[1], "r")) == NULL) {
    perror(av[1]);
    exit(1);
  }

  if(!yyparse())
    printf("SQL parse worked\n");
  else
    printf("SQL parse failed\n");
} /* main */
```

The Makefile for the SQL Parser

The Makefile runs the lexer and parser through flex and bison, respectively, and compiles them together. The dependencies take care of generating and compiling the scanner, including the bison-generated header file.

```
# Makefile for pmysql
CC = cc -g
LEX = flex
YACC = bison
CFLAGS = -DYYDEBUG=1

PROGRAMS5 = pmysql

all:    ${PROGRAMS5}

# chapter 5

pmysql: pmysql.tab.o pmysql.o
        ${CC} -o $@ pmysql.tab.o pmysql.o

pmysql.tab.c pmysql.tab.h:      pmysql.y
        ${YACC} -vd pmysql.y

pmysql.c:       pmysql.l
        ${LEX} -o $*.c $<

pmysql.o:       pmysql.c pmysql.tab.h

.SUFFIXES:      .pgm .l .y .c
```

Exercises

1. In several places, the SQL parser accepts more general syntax than SQL itself permits. For example, the parser accepts any expression as the left operand of a LIKE predicate, although that operand has to be a column reference. Fix the parser to diagnose these erroneous inputs. You can either change the syntax or add action code to check the expressions. Try both to see which is easier and which gives better diagnostics.

2. Turn the parser into a SQL cross-referencer, which reads a set of SQL statements and produces a report showing for each name where it is defined and where it is referenced.

3. (Term project.) Modify the embedded SQL translator to interface to a real database on your system.

A Reference for Flex Specifications

In this chapter we describe the syntax of flex programs, along with the various options and support functions available. POSIX lex is almost an exact subset of flex, so we note which parts of flex are extensions beyond what POSIX requires.

After the section on the structure of a lex program, the sections in this chapter are in alphabetical order by feature.

Structure of a Flex Specification

A flex program consists of three parts: the definition section, the rules section, and the user subroutines.

```
...definition section ...
%%

... rules section ...
%%
... user subroutines ...
```

The parts are separated by lines consisting of two percent signs. The first two parts are required, although a part may be empty. The third part and the preceding %% line may be omitted.

Definition Section

The definition section can include options, the literal block, definitions, start conditions, and translations. (There is a section on each in this reference.) Lines that start with whitespace are copied verbatim to the C file. Typically this is used to include comments enclosed in /* and */, preceded by whitespace.

Rules Section

The rules section contains pattern lines and C code. Lines that start with whitespace, or material enclosed in %{ and %}, are C code that is copied verbatim to yylex(). C code at the beginning of the rules section will be at the beginning of yylex() and can include declarations of variables used in the scanner, and code to run each time yylex() is called.

C code lines are copied verbatim to the generated C file. Lines at the beginning of the rules section are placed near the beginning of the generated yylex() function and should be declarations of variables used by code associated with the patterns and initialization code for the scanner. C code lines anywhere else should contain only comments, since it's unpredictable where in the scanner they'll be. (This is how you put comments in the rules section outside of actions.)

A line that starts with anything else is a pattern line. Pattern lines contain a pattern followed by some whitespace and C code to execute when the input matches the pattern. If the C code is more than one statement or spans multiple lines, it must be enclosed in braces ({ } or %{ %}).

When a flex scanner runs, it matches the input against the patterns in the rules section. Every time it finds a match (the matched input is called a *token*), it executes the C code associated with that pattern. If a pattern is followed by a single vertical bar, instead of C code, the pattern uses the same C code as the next pattern in the file. When an input character matches no pattern, the lexer acts as though it matched a pattern whose code is ECHO;, which writes a copy of the token to the output.

User Subroutines

The contents of the user subroutines section are copied verbatim by flex to the C file. This section typically includes routines called from the rules. If you redefine yywrap(), the new version or supporting subroutines might be here.

In a large program, it is often more convenient to put the supporting code in a separate source file to minimize the amount of material that is recompiled when you change the lex file.

BEGIN

The BEGIN macro switches among start states. You invoke it, usually in the action code for a pattern, as follows:

```
BEGIN statename;
```

The scanner starts in state 0 (zero), also known as INITIAL. All other states must be named in %s or %x lines in the definition section. (See "Start States" on page 136.)

Notice that even though BEGIN is a macro, the macro itself doesn't take any arguments, and the state name need not be enclosed in parentheses, although it is good style to do so.

C++ Scanners

Although flex has an option to create a C++ scanner, the manual says it's experimental, and the code is buggy and doesn't work very well.[1] All is not lost for C++ programmers, though. If you generate a C lexer, it will compile with a C++ compiler, and you can tell a C++ bison parser to call a C lexer.

Context Sensitivity

Flex provides several ways to make your patterns sensitive to left and right context, that is, to the text that precedes or follows the token.

Left Context

There are three ways to handle left context: the special beginning-of-line pattern character, start states, and explicit code.

The character ^ at the beginning of a pattern tells lex to match the pattern only at the beginning of the line. The ^ doesn't match any characters; it just specifies the context.

Start states can be used to require that one token precede another:

```
%s MYSTATE
%%
first { BEGIN MYSTATE; }
. . .
<MYSTATE>second  { BEGIN 0; }
```

In this lexer, the second token is recognized only after the first token. There may be intervening tokens between the first and second.

In some cases you can fake left context sensitivity by setting flags to pass context information from one token's routine to another:

```
%{
  int flag = 0;
%}
%%
a       { flag = 1; }
b       { flag = 2; }
zzz     {
            switch(flag) {
            case 1:     a_zzz_token(); break;
```

---

1. According to the guy who wrote it.

```
case 2:     b_zzz_token(); break;
default: plain_zzz_token(); break;
}
flag = 0;
}
```

Right Context

There are three ways to make token recognition depend on the text to the right of the token: the special end-of-line pattern character, the slash operator, and yyless().

The $ character at the end of a pattern makes the token match only at the end of a line, that is, immediately before a \n character. Like the ^ character, $ doesn't match any characters; it just specifies context. It is exactly equivalent to /\n and, therefore, can't be used with trailing context.

The / character in a pattern lets you include explicit trailing context. For instance, the pattern abc/de matches the token abc, but only if it is immediately followed by de. The / itself matches no characters. Lex counts trailing context characters when deciding which of several patterns has the longest match, but the characters do not appear in yytext, nor are they counted in yyleng.

The yyless() function tells lex to "push back" part of the token that was just read. The argument to yyless() is the number of token characters to keep. For example:

```
abcde { yyless(3); }
```

The previous has nearly the same effect as abc/de does because the call to yyless() keeps three characters of the token and puts back the other two. The only differences are that in this case the token in yytext contains all five characters and yyleng contains five instead of three.

Definitions (Substitutions)

Definitions (or substitutions) allow you to give a name to all or part of a regular expression and refer to it by name in the rules section. This can be useful to break up complex expressions and to document what your expressions are supposed to be doing. A definition takes this form:

```
NAME    expression
```

The name can contain letters, digits, hyphens, and underscores, and it must not start with a digit.

In the rules section, patterns may include references to substitutions with the name in braces, for example, {NAME}. The expression corresponding to the name is substituted into the pattern as though it were enclosed in parentheses. For example:

```
DIG     [0-9]
...
```

```
%%
{DIG}+                  process_integer();
{DIG}+\.{DIG}*          |
\.{DIG}+                process_real() ;
```

ECHO

In the C code associated with a pattern, the macro ECHO writes the token to the current output file yyout. It is equivalent to the following:

```
fprintf(yyout, "%s", yytext);
```

The default action in flex for input text that doesn't match any pattern is to write the text to the output, equivalent to ECHO. In flex, %option nodefault or the command-line flag -s or --nodefault makes the default action abort, which is useful in the common case that the scanner is supposed to include patterns to handle all possible input.

Input Management

Flex offers a variety of ways to manage the source of the text to be scanned. At the beginning of your program, you can assign any open stdio file to yyin to have the scanner read from that file. If that's not adequate, flex provides several different ways to change the input source.

Stdio File Chaining

You can tell the lexer to read from any stdio file by calling yyrestart(file). Also, when a lexer built with %option yywrap reaches the end of the input file, it calls yywrap(), which can switch to a different input file. See the sections "yyrestart()" and "yy-wrap()" on page 139 for more details.

Input Buffers

Flex scanners read input from an input buffer. An input buffer can be associated with a stdio file, in which case the lexer reads input from the file, or it can just be associated with a string in memory. The type YY_BUFFER_STATE is a pointer to a flex input buffer.

```
YY_BUFFER_STATE bp;
FILE *f;

f = fopen(..., "r");
bp = yy_create_buffer(f,YY_BUF_SIZE );   new buffer reading from f

yy_switch_to_buffer(bp);   use the buffer we just made
...
yy_flush_buffer(bp);   discard buffer contents
...
void yy_delete_buffer (bp);   free buffer
```

Call `yy_create_buffer` to make a new input buffer associated with an open stdio file. Its second argument is the size of the buffer, which should be `YY_BUF_SIZE`.

Call `yy_switch_to_buffer` to make the scanner read from a buffer. You can switch buffers as needed. The current buffer is `YY_CURRENT_BUFFER`. You can call `yy_flush_buffer` to discard whatever is in the buffer, which is occasionally useful in error recovery in interactive scanners to get back to a known state. Call `yy_delete_buffer` to free a buffer no longer in use.

Input from Strings

Normally flex reads from a file, but sometimes you want it to read from some other source, such as a string in memory.

```
bp = yy_scan_bytes(char *bytes, len);  scan a copy of bytes
bp = yy_scan_string("string");    scan a copy of null-terminated string

bp = yy_scan_buffer (char *base, yy_size_t size); scan (size-2) bytes in place
```

The routines `yy_scan_bytes` and `yy_scan_string` create a buffer with a copy of the text to be scanned. A slightly faster routine is `yy_scan_buffer`, which scans text in place, but the last two bytes of the buffer *must* be nulls (\0), which are not scanned. The type `yy_size_t` is flex's internal type used for sizes of objects.

Once a string buffer is created, use `yy_switch_to_buffer` to tell the scanner to read from it, and use `yy_delete_buffer` to free the buffer and (if appropriate) the copy of the text. The scanner treats the end of the buffer as an end-of-file.

File Nesting

Many input languages have features to allow input files to include other files, such as `#include` in C. Flex provides a pair of functions to manage a stack of input buffers:

```
void yypush_buffer_state(bp);  switch to bp, stack old buf

void yypop_buffer_state();  delete current buffer, return to previous
```

In practice, these functions are inadequate for any but the simplest input nesting, since they don't maintain any auxiliary information such as the line number or name of the current file. Maintaining your own stack of input files is not hard. See Example 2-3 for sample code.

Also helpful to maintain an input stack is the special token pattern `<<EOF>>`, which matches at the end of a file after the call to `yywrap()`.

input()

The input() function conceptually provides characters to the lexer. When the lexer matches characters, it conceptually calls input() to fetch each character. Flex bypasses input() for performance reasons, but the effect is the same.

The most likely place to call input() is in an action routine to do something special with the text that follows a particular token. For example, here is a way to handle C comments:

```
"/*" {   int c1 = 0, c2 = input ();

        for(;;) {
             if(c2 == EOF)
                 break;
             if(c1 == '*' && c2 == '/')
                 break;
             c1 = c2;
             c2 = input();
        }
    }
```

The calls to input() process the characters until either end-of-file or the characters */ occur. This approach is an alternative to exclusive start states (see "Start States" on page 136) to handle C-style comments. It is the best way to handle very long quoted strings and other tokens that might be too long for flex to buffer itself in its typical 16K input buffer.

If you use a C++ compiler, input is called yyinput instead to avoid name collisions with C++ libraries.

YY_INPUT

Flex scanners read input into a buffer using the macro YY_INPUT(buf,result, max_size). Whenever the scanner needs more input and the buffer is empty, it invokes YY_INPUT, where buf and maxsize are the buffer and its size, respectively, and result is where to put the actual amount read or zero at EOF. (Since this is a macro, it's result, not *result.) When the buffer is first set up, it calls isatty() to see whether the input source is the console and, if so, reads one character at a time rather than large chunks.

The main situation where redefining YY_INPUT is useful is when reading from an input source that is neither a string nor a stdio file.

Flex Library

Flex comes with a small library of helpful routines. You can link in the library by giving the -lfl flag at the end of the cc command line on Unix systems, or the equivalent on other systems. It contains versions of main() and yywrap().

Flex comes with a minimal `main` program, which can be useful for quickie programs and for testing, and comes with a stub `yywrap`. They're so simple we reproduce them here:

```
main(int ac,  char **av)
{
        return yylex();
}

int yywrap() { return 1; }
```

Interactive and Batch Scanners

A flex scanner sometimes needs to look ahead one character in the input to see whether the current token is done. (Think of a number that is a string of digits.) It turns out that the scanner runs a little faster if it always looks ahead even when it doesn't need to, but that would cause very unpleasant results when a scanner is reading directly from the console. For example, if the current token is a newline, \n, and it reads ahead, the scanner will wait until you type another new line before going ahead.

To minimize the unpleasantness, the scanner can run either in batch mode, where it always looks ahead, or in interactive mode, where it looks ahead only when it needs to do so (which is slightly slower). If you use the standard input routines, the scanner will check to see whether the input source is a terminal using `isatty()` and, if so, switch to interactive mode. You can use `%option batch` or `%option interactive` to force it always to use one or the other mode. Forcing batch mode can make sense if you know that your scanner will never need to be interactive, for example, if you read the input yourself or if it always reads from a file.

Line Numbers and yylineno

If you keep track of the line number in the input file, you can report it in error messages. If you set `%option yylineno`, flex defines `yylineno` to contain the current line number and automatically updates it each time it reads a \n character. The lexer does not initialize `yylineno`, so you need to set it to 1 each time you start reading a file. Lexers that handle nested include files have to save and restore the line number associated with each file if they want to track line numbers per file.

Literal Block

A literal block in the definition section is C code bracketed by the lines %{ and %}.

```
%{
... C code and declarations...
%}
```

The contents of each literal block are copied verbatim to the generated C source file. Literal blocks in the definition section are copied before the beginning of yylex(). The literal block usually contains declarations of variables and functions used by code in the rules section, as well as #include lines for header files.

If a literal block starts with %top{ rather than %{, it's copied near the front of the generated program, typically for #include files or #define lines to set YY_BUF_SIZE.

A literal block at the beginning of the rules section is copied near the beginning of yylex() after the declarations of local variables, so it can contain more declarations and setup code. A literal block elsewhere in the rules section is copied to an unspecified place in yylex, so it should contain only comments.

See also "YY_USER_ACTION" on page 139.

Multiple Lexers in One Program

You may want to have lexers for two partially or entirely different token syntaxes in the same program. For example, an interactive debugging interpreter might have one lexer for the programming language and use another for the debugger commands.

There are two basic approaches to handling two lexers in one program: combine them into a single lexer or put two complete lexers into the program.

Combined Lexers

You can combine two lexers into one by using start states. All of the patterns for each lexer are prefixed by a unique set of start states. When the lexer starts, you need a little code to put the lexer into the appropriate initial state for the particular lexer in use, for example, the following code (which will be copied at the front of yylex()):

```
%s INITA INITB INITC
%%
%{
    extern first_tok, first_lex;

    if(first_lex) {
        BEGIN first_lex;
        first_lex = 0;
    }
    if(first_tok) {
        int holdtok = first_tok;
        first_tok = 0;
        return holdtok;
    }
%}
```

In this case, before you call the lexer, you set first_lex to the initial state for the lexer. You will usually use a combined lexer in conjunction with a combined yacc parser, so you'll also usually have code to force an initial token to tell the parser which grammar to use. See "Variant and Multiple Grammars" on page 163.

The advantages of this approach are that the object code is somewhat smaller, since there is only one copy of the lexer code, and the different rule sets can share rules. The disadvantages are that you have to be careful to use the correct start states everywhere, you cannot have both lexers active at once (i.e., you can't call yylex() recursively unless you use the reentrant lexer option), and it is difficult to use different input sources for the different lexers.

Multiple Lexers

The other approach is to include two complete lexers in your program. The trick is to change the names that lex uses for its functions and variables so the two lexers can be generated separately by flex and then compiled together into one program.

Flex provides a command-line switch and program option to change the prefix used on the names in the scanner generated by lex. For example, these options tell flex to use the prefix "foo" rather than "yy" and to put the generated scanner in foolex.c.

```
%option prefix="foo"
%option outfile="foolex.c"
```

You can also set options on the command line:

```
$ flex --outfile=foolex.c --prefix=foo foo.l
```

Either way, the generated scanner has entry point foolex(), reads from stdio file fooin, and so forth. Somewhat confusingly, flex will generate a set of #define macros at the front of the lexer that redefine the standard "yy" names to the chosen prefix. This lets you write your lexer using the standard names, but the externally visible names will all use the chosen prefix.

```
#define yy_create_buffer foo_create_buffer
#define yy_delete_buffer foo_delete_buffer
#define yy_flex_debug foo_flex_debug
#define yy_init_buffer foo_init_buffer
#define yy_flush_buffer foo_flush_buffer
#define yy_load_buffer_state foo_load_buffer_state
#define yy_switch_to_buffer foo_switch_to_buffer
#define yyin fooin
#define yyleng fooleng
#define yylex foolex
#define yylineno foolineno
#define yyout fooout
#define yyrestart foorestart
#define yytext footext
#define yywrap foowrap
#define yyalloc fooalloc
#define yyrealloc foorealloc
#define yyfree foofree
```

Options When Building a Scanner

Flex offers several hundred options when building a scanner. Most can be written as

```
%option name
```

at the front of the scanner or as --name on the command line. To turn an option off, precede it with no, as in %option noyywrap or --noyywrap. In most cases, putting the options in %option lines is preferable to putting them on the command line, since a scanner typically won't work if the options are wrong. For a full list of options, see the section "Index of Scanner Options" in the info documentation that comes with flex.

Portability of Flex Lexers

Flex lexers are fairly portable among C implementations. There are two levels at which you can port a lexer: the original flex specification or the C source file generated by flex.

Porting Generated C Lexers

Flex generates portable C code, and you can usually move the code to any C compiler without trouble. Be sure to use %option noyywrap or to include your own version of yywrap() to avoid needing the flex library. For portability to very old C compilers, %option noansi-definitions and %option noansi-prototypes tell flex to generate K&R procedure definitions and prototypes, respectively.

Buffer sizes

You may want to adjust the size of some buffers. Flex uses two input buffers, each by default 16K, which may be too big for some microcomputer implementations. You can define the macro YY_BUF_SIZE in the definition section:

```
%{
#define YY_BUF_SIZE 4096
%}
```

If your lexer uses REJECT, it will also allocate a backup state buffer four times as large as YY_BUF_SIZE (eight times on 64-bit machines). Don't use REJECT if space is an issue.

Character sets

The knottiest portability problem involves character sets. The C code generated by every flex implementation uses character codes as indexes into tables in the lexer. If both the original and target machines use the same character code, such as ASCII, the ported lexer will work. You may have to deal with different line end conventions: Unix systems end a line with a plain \n, while Microsoft Windows and other systems use \r\n. You often can have lexers ignore \r and treat \n as the line end in either case.

When the original and target machines use different character sets, for example, ASCII and EBCDIC, the lexer won't work at all, since all of the character codes used as indexes will be wrong. Sophisticated users have sometimes been able to post-process the tables to rebuild them for other character sets, but in general the only reasonable approach is to find a version of flex that runs on the target machine or else to redefine the lexer's input routine to translate the input characters into the original character set. See "Input from Strings" on page 124 for how to change the input routine.

Reentrant Scanners

The normal code for a flex scanner places its state information in static variables so that each call to yylex() resumes where the previous one left off, using the existing input buffer, input file, start state, and so forth. In some situations, it can be useful to have multiple copies of the scanner active at once, typically in threaded programs that handle multiple independent input sources. For this situation, flex provides %option reentrant or --reentrant.

```
yyscan_t scanner;

if(yylex_init(&scanner)) { printf("no scanning today\n"); abort(); }
while((yylex(scanner))
    ... do something ...;
yylex_destroy(scanner);
```

In a reentrant scanner, all of the state information about the scan in progress is kept in a yyscan_t variable, which is actually a pointer to the structure with all the state. You create the scanner with yylex_init(), passing the address of the yyscan_t as an argument, and it returns 0 on success or 1 if it can't allocate the structure. Then you pass the yyscan_t to every call to yylex() and finally delete it with yylex_destroy. Each call to yylex_init creates a separate scanner, and several scanners can be active at once, passing the appropriate structure to each call to yylex().

In a reentrant scanner, some variables commonly used in yylex are redefined as macros, so you can use them the same as in an ordinary scanner. These variables are yyin, yyout, yyextra, yyleng, yytext, yylineno, yycolumn, and yy_flex_debug. The macros BEGIN, YY_START, YYSTATE, yymore(), unput(), and yyless() are also modified, so you can use them the same as in an ordinary scanner. All of the routines that create and manipulate input buffers take an additional yyscan_t argument, for example, yyrestart(file, scanner). The other routines that take a yyscan_t argument are yy_switch_to_buffer, yy_create_buffer, yy_delete_buffer, yy_flush_buffer, yypush_buffer_state, yypop_buffer_state, yy_scan_buffer, yy_scan_string, and yy_scan_bytes.

Extra Data for Reentrant Scanners

When using a reentrant scanner, you'll often have some other per-scanner data, such as a symbol table for the names the scanner has matched. You can use `yylex_init_extra` rather than `yylex_init`, passing it a pointer to your own per-scanner data. Within `yylex()`, your pointer is available as `yyextra`. The extra data is of type `YY_EXTRA_TYPE`, which is normally `void *`, but you can `#define` it to another type if you want.

```
yyscan_t scanner;
symbol *symp;

symp = symtabinit();   make per-scanner symbol table

if(yylex_init_extra(symp, &scanner)) { printf("no scanning today\n"); abort(); }
while((yylex(scanner))
    ... do something ...;
yylex_destroy(scanner);

... inside yylex ...
[a-z]+  { symlookup(yyextra, yylval); }
```

Access to Reentrant Scanner Data

In a normal scanner, code outside `yylex()` can refer directly to `yyin`, `yyout`, and other global variables, but in a reentrant scanner, they're part of the per-scanner data structure. Flex provides access routines to get and set the major variables.

```
YY_EXTRA_TYPE yyget_extra (yyscan_t yyscanner );   yyextra
void yyset_extra (YY_EXTRA_TYPE user_defined ,yyscan_t yyscanner );

FILE *yyget_in (yyscan_t yyscanner );   yyin
void yyset_in  (FILE * in_str ,yyscan_t yyscanner );

FILE *yyget_out (yyscan_t yyscanner );   yyout
void yyset_out  (FILE * out_str ,yyscan_t yyscanner );

int yyget_lineno (yyscan_t yyscanner );
void yyset_lineno (int line_number ,yyscan_t yyscanner );

int yyget_leng(yyscan_t yyscanner);   yyleng, read only

char *yyget_text(yyscan_t yyscanner);   yytext
```

These functions are all available in nonreentrant scanners, without the `yyscanner` argument, although there's little need for them since they are entirely equivalent to reading or setting the appropriate variable.

Reentrant Scanners, Nested Files, and Multiple Scanners

Reentrant scanners, nested files, and multiple scanners all address sort of the same issue, more than one scanner in the same program, but they each do very different things.

- Reentrant scanners allow you to have multiple instances simultaneously active that are applying the same set of patterns to separate input sources.
- Nested files (using `yy_switch_to_buffer` and related routines) allow you to have a single scanner that reads from one file, then another, and then perhaps returns to the first file.
- Multiple scanners allow you to apply different sets of patterns to different input sources.

You can combine all three of these as needed. For example, you can call `yy_switch_to_buffer` in a reentrant scanner to change the input source for a particular instance. You can say `%option reentrant prefix="foo"` to create a scanner that can be invoked multiple times (call `foolex_init` to get started) and can be linked into the same program with other reentrant or nonreentrant scanners.

Using Reentrant Scanners with Bison

Bison has its own option to create a reentrant parser, known as `pure-parser`, which can, with some effort, be used along with a reentrant scanner. A pure parser normally gets tokens by calling `yylex`, with a pointer to the place to put the token value, but without the `yyscan_t` value that flex needs. (Flex and bison developers don't always talk to each other.) Flex provides `%option reentrant bison-bridge`, which changes the declaration of `yylex` to be

```
int yylex (YYSTYPE * yylval_param ,yyscan_t yyscanner);
```

and also sets `yylval` automatically from the argument. One important difference from normal scanners is that `yylval` is now a pointer to a union rather than a union, so a reference that was `yylval.member` is now `yylval->member`. See "Pure Scanners and Parsers" on page 209 for an example of a pure bison parser calling a reentrant scanner.

Regular Expression Syntax

Flex patterns are an extended version of the regular expressions used by editors and utilities such as grep. Regular expressions are composed of normal characters, which represent themselves, and metacharacters, which have special meaning in a pattern. All characters other than those listed in the following section are regular characters. Whitespace (spaces and tabs) separate the pattern from the action and so must be quoted to include them in a pattern.

Metacharacters

The metacharacters in a flex expression include the following:

.

Matches any single character except the newline character \n.

[ ]

Match any one of the characters within the brackets. A range of characters is indicated with the - (dash), for example, [0-9] for any of the 10 digits. If the first character after the open bracket is a dash or close bracket, it is not interpreted as a metacharacter. If the first character is a circumflex ^, it changes the meaning to match any character except those within the brackets. (Such a character class will match a newline unless you explicitly exclude it.) Other metacharacters have no special meaning within square brackets except that C escape sequences starting with \ are recognized. POSIX added more special square bracket patterns for internationalization. See the last few items in this list for details.

[a-z]{-}[jv] [a-f]{+}[0-9]

Set difference or union of character classes. The pattern matches characters that are in the first class, with the characters in the second class omitted (for {-}) or added (for {+}).

*

Matches zero or more of the preceding expression. For example, the pattern a.*z matches any string that starts with *a* and ends with *z*, such as *az*, *abz* or *alcatraz*.

+

Matches one or more occurrence of the preceding regular expression. For example, x+ matches *x*, *xxx*, or *xxxxxx*, but not an empty string, and (ab)+ matches *ab*, *abab*, *ababab*, and so forth.

?

Matches zero or one occurrence of the preceding regular expression. For example, -?[0-9]+ indicates a number with an optional leading unary minus.

{}

Mean different things depending on what is inside. A single number {n} means n repetitions of the preceding pattern; for example, [A-Z]{3} matches any three uppercase letters. If the braces contain two numbers separated by a comma, {n,m}, they are the minimum and maximum numbers of repetitions of the preceding pattern. For example, A{1,3} matches one to three occurrences of the letter *A*. If the second number is missing, it is taken to be infinite, so *{1,}* means the same as +, and *{0,}* is the same as *. If the braces contain a name, it refers to the substitution by that name.

****

If the following character is a lowercase letter, then it is a C escape sequence such as \t for tab. Some implementations also allow octal and hex characters in the form \123 and \x3f. Otherwise, \ quotes the following character, so * matches an asterisk.

()

Group a series of regular expressions together. Each of *, +, and [] affects only the expression immediately to its left, and | normally affects everything to its left and right. Parentheses can change this; for example, (ab|cd)?ef matches *abef*, *cdef*, or just *ef*.

|

Matches either the preceding regular expression or the subsequent regular expression. For example, twelve|12 matches either *twelve* or *12*.

"..."

Match everything within the quotation marks literally. Metacharacters other than \ lose their meaning. For example, "/*" matches the two characters /*.

/

Matches the preceding regular expression but only if followed by the following regular expression. For example, 0/1 matches "0" in the string "01" but does not match anything in the strings "0" or "02". Only one slash is permitted per pattern, and a pattern cannot contain both a slash and a trailing $.

^

As the first character of a regular expression, it matches the beginning of a line; it is also used for negation within square brackets. Otherwise, it's not special.

$

As the last character of a regular expression, it matches the end of a line—otherwise not special. This has the same meaning as /\n at the end of an expression.

<>

A name or list of names in angle brackets at the beginning of a pattern makes that pattern apply only in the given start states.

<<EOF>>

The special pattern <<EOF>> matches the end of file.

(?# comment)

Perl-style expression comments.

(?a:pattern) or (?a-x:pattern)

Perl-style pattern modifiers. Interpret the pattern using modifier a, but without modifier x. The modifiers are i for case insensitive, s to match as though everything is a single line (in particular, make the . match a \n character), and x to ignore whitespace and C-style comments. The pattern can extend over more than one line.

```
(?i:xyz) [Xx][Yy][Zz]
(?i:x(?-i:y)z) [Xx]y[Zz]
(?s:a.b) a(.|\n)b
(?x:a /* hi */ b) ab
```

Flex also allows a limited set of POSIX character classes inside character class expressions:

```
[:alnum:]  [:alpha:]  [:blank:]  [:cntrl:]  [:digit:]  [:graph:]  [:lower:]
[:print:] [:punct:] [:space:] [:upper:] [:xdigit:]
```

A character class expression stands for any character of a named type handled by the ctype macros, with the types being `alnum`, `alpha`, `blank`, `cntrl`, `digit`, `graph`, `lower`, `print`, `punct`, `space`, `upper`, and `xdigit`. The class name is enclosed in square brackets and colons and must itself be inside a character class. For example, `[[:digit:]]` would be equivalent to `[0123456789]`, and `[x[:xdigit:]]`, equivalent to `[x0123456789AaBbCcDdEeFf]`.

REJECT

Usually lex separates the input into nonoverlapping tokens. But sometimes you want all occurrences of a token even if it overlaps with other tokens. The special action `REJECT` lets you do this. If an action executes `REJECT`, flex conceptually puts back the text matched by the pattern and finds the next best match for it. The example finds all occurrences of the words *pink*, *pin*, and *ink* in a file, even when they overlap:

```
...
%%
pink    { npink++; REJECT;  }
ink     { nink++; REJECT; }
pin     { npin++; REJECT; }
.       |
\n      ;    /* discard other characters */
```

If the input contains the word *pink*, all three patterns will match. Without the `REJECT` statements, only *pink* would match.

Scanners that use `REJECT` are much larger and slower than those that don't, since they need considerable extra information to allow backtracking and re-lexing.

Returning Values from yylex()

The C code executed when a pattern matches a token can contain a return statement that returns a value from `yylex()` to its caller, typically a parser generated by yacc. The next time `yylex()` is called, the scanner picks up where it left off. When a scanner matches a token of interest to the parser (e.g., a keyword, variable name, or operator), it returns to pass the token back to the parser. When it matches a token not of interest to the parser (e.g., whitespace or a comment), it does not return, and the scanner immediately proceeds to match another token.

This means that you cannot restart a lexer just by calling `yylex()`. You have to reset it into the default state using `BEGIN INITIAL` and reset the input state so that the next call to `input()` will start reading the new input. A call to `yyrestart(file)`, where `file` is a standard I/O file pointer, arranges to start reading from that file.

Start States

You can declare start states, also called *start conditions* or *start rules*, in the definition section. Start states are used to limit the scope of certain rules or to change the way the lexer treats part of the file. Start states come in two versions, inclusive declared with %s and exclusive declared with %x. For example, suppose we want to scan the following C preprocessor directive:

```
#include <somefile.h>
```

Normally, the angle brackets and the filename would be scanned as the five tokens <, somefile, ., h, and >, but after #include, they are a single filename token. You can use a start state to apply a set of rules only at certain times. Be warned that those rules that do not have start states can apply in any inclusive state! The BEGIN statement (see "BEGIN" on page 120) in an action sets the current start state. For example:

```
%s INCLMODE
%%
^"#include" { BEGIN INCLMODE; }
<INCLMODE>"<" [^>\n]+">" { ... do something with the name ... }
<INCLMODE>\n     { BEGIN INITIAL;  /* return to normal */ }
```

You declare a start state with a %s or %x line. For example:

```
%s  PREPROC
```

The previous code creates the inclusive start state PREPROC. In the rules section, then, a rule that has <PREPROC> prepended to it will apply only in state PREPROC. The standard state in which lex starts is state zero, also known as INITIAL. The current start state can be found in YY_START (also called YYSTATE for compatibility with older versions of lex), which is useful when you have a state that wants to switch back to whatever the previous state was, for example:

```
%s A B C X
 int savevar;
%%
<A,B,C>start { save = YY_START; BEGIN X; }
<X>end       { BEGIN save;
```

Flex also has exclusive start states declared with %x. The difference between regular and exclusive start states is that a rule with no start state is not matched when an exclusive state is active. In practice, exclusive states are a lot more useful than regular states, and you will probably want to use them.

Exclusive start states make it easy to do things like recognize C language comments:

```
%x COMMENT
%%
"/*"                { BEGIN COMMENT;  /* switch to comment mode */ }
```

```
<COMMENT>.          |
<COMMENT>\n ;                        /* throw away comment text */
<COMMENT>"*/"    { BEGIN INITIAL;  /* return to regular mode */ }
```

This wouldn't work using regular start states since all of the regular token patterns would still be active in COMMENT state.

unput()

The macro unput(c) returns the character c to the input stream. Unlike the analogous stdio routine unputc(), you can call unput() several times in a row to put several characters back in the input. The limit of data "pushed back" by unput() varies, but it is always at least as great as the longest token the lexer recognizes.

For example, when expanding macros such as C's #define, you need to insert the text of the macro in place of the macro call. One way to do this is to call unput() to push back the text, for example:

```
... in lexer action code...
char *p = macro_contents () ;
char *q = p + strlen(p);

while(q > p)
    unput(*--q);    /* push back right-to-left */
```

yyinput() yyunput()

In C++ scanners, the macros input() and unput() are called yyinput() and yyunput() to avoid colliding with C++ library names.

yyleng

Whenever a scanner matches a token, the text of the token is stored in the null-terminated string yytext, and its length is in yyleng. The length in yyleng is the same as the value that would be returned by strlen(yytext).

yyless()

You can call yyless(n) from the code associated with a rule to "push back" all but the first n characters of the token. This can be useful when the rule to determine the boundary between tokens is inconvenient to express as a regular expression. For example, consider a pattern to match quoted strings, but where a quotation mark within a string can be escaped with a backslash:

```
\" [^"]*\"    { /* is the char before close quote a \ ? */
                if(yytext[yyleng-2]   ==   '\\') {
                    yyless(yyleng-1); /* return last quote */
```

```
            yymore();          /* append next string */
        } else {
        ...  /* process string */
        }
    }
```

If the quoted string ends with a backslash before the closing quotation mark, it uses yyless() to push back the closing quote, and it uses yymore() to tell lex to append the next token to this one (see "yymore()" on page 139). The next token will be the rest of the quoted string starting with the pushed back quote, so the entire string will end up in yytext.

A call to yyless() has the same effect as calling unput() with the characters to be pushed back, but yyless() is often much faster because it can take advantage of the fact that the characters pushed back are the same ones just fetched from the input.

Another use of yyless() is to reprocess a token using rules for a different start state:

```
sometoken  { BEGIN OTHER_STATE; yyless(0); }
```

BEGIN tells lex to use another start state, and the call to yyless() pushes back all of the token's characters so they can be reread using the new start state. If the new start state doesn't enable different patterns that take precedence over the current one, yyless(0) will cause an infinite loop in the scanner because the same token is repeatedly recognized and pushed back. (This is similar to the function of REJECT but is considerably faster.) Unlike REJECT, it will loop and match the same pattern unless you use BEGIN to change what patterns are active.

yylex() and YY_DECL

Normally, yylex is called with no arguments and interacts with the rest of the program primarily through global variables. The macro YY_DECL declares its calling sequence, and you can redefine it to add whatever arguments you want.

```
%{
#define YY_DECL int yylex(int *fruitp)
%}

%%

apple|orange   { (*fruitp)++; }
```

Note that there is no semicolon in YY_DECL, since it is expanded immediately before the open brace at the beginning of the body of yylex.

When using a reentrant or bison-bridge parser, you can still redefine YY_DECL, but you must be sure to include the parameters that the reentrant code in the lexer is expecting. In a bison-bridge scanner, the normal definition is as follows:

```
#define YY_DECL int yylex (YYSTYPE * yylval_param , yyscan_t yyscanner)
```

In a plain reentrant scanner there's no yylval_param.

---

yymore()

You can call yymore() from the code associated with a rule to tell lex to append the next token to this one. For example:

```
%%
hyper  yymore ();
text    printf("Token is %s\n", yytext);
```

If the input string is hypertext, the output will be "Token is hypertext."

Using yymore() is most often useful where it is inconvenient or impractical to define token boundaries with regular expressions. See "yyless()" on page 137 for an example.

yyrestart()

You can call yyrestart(f) to make your scanner read from open stdio file f. See "Stdio File Chaining" on page 123.

yy_scan_string and yy_scan_buffer

These functions prepare to take the scanner's input from a string or buffer in memory. See "Input from Strings" on page 124.

YY_USER_ACTION

This macro is expanded just before the code for each scanner action, after yytext and yyleng are set up. Its most common use is to set bison token locations. See Chapter 8.

yywrap()

When a lexer encounters an end of file, it optionally calls the routine yywrap() to find out what to do next. If yywrap() returns 0, the scanner continues scanning, while if it returns 1, the scanner returns a zero token to report the end-of-file. If your lexer doesn't use yywrap() to switch files, the option %option noyywrap removes the calls to yywrap(). The special token <<EOF>> is usually a better way to handle end-of-file situations.

The standard version of yywrap() in the flex library always returns 1, but if you use yywrap(), you should replace it with one of your own. If yywrap() returns 0 to indicate that there is more input, it needs first to adjust yyin to point to a new file, probably using fopen().

# CHAPTER 6

A Reference for Bison Specifications

In this chapter we describe the syntax of bison programs, along with the various options and support functions available. POSIX yacc is almost an exact subset of bison, so we note which parts of bison are extensions beyond what POSIX requires.

After the section on the structure of a bison grammar, the sections in this chapter are in alphabetical order by feature.

Structure of a Bison Grammar

A bison grammar consists of three sections: the definition section, the rules section, and the user subroutines section.

```
... definition section ...
%%
... rules section ...
%%
... user subroutines section ...
```

The sections are separated by lines consisting of two percent signs. The first two sections are required, although a section may be empty. The third section and the preceding %% line may be omitted.

Symbols

A bison grammar is constructed from symbols, which are the "words" of the grammar. Symbols are strings of letters, digits, periods, and underscores that do not start with a digit. The symbol **error** is reserved for error recovery; otherwise, bison attaches no fixed meaning to any symbol. (Since bison defines a C preprocessor symbol for each token, you also need to be sure token names don't collide with C reserved words or bison's own symbols such as **yyparse**, or strange errors will ensue.)

Symbols produced by the lexer are called *terminal symbols* or *tokens*. Those that are defined on the left-hand side of rules are called *nonterminal symbols* or *nonterminals*.

Tokens may also be literal quoted characters. (See "Literal Tokens" on page 151.) A widely followed convention makes token names all uppercase and nonterminals lowercase. We follow that convention throughout the book.

Definition Section

The definition section can include a literal block, which is C code copied verbatim to the beginning of the generated C file, usually containing declaration and #include lines in %{ %} or %code blocks. There may be %union, %start, %token, %type, %left, %right, and %nonassoc declarations. (See "%union Declaration" on page 163, "%start Declaration" on page 159, "Tokens" on page 161, "%type Declaration" on page 162, and "Precedence and Associativity Declarations" on page 154.) The definition section can also contain comments in the usual C format, surrounded by /* and */. All of these are optional, so in a very simple parser the definition section may be completely empty.

Rules Section

The rules section contains grammar rules and actions containing C code. See "Actions" below and "Rules" on page 157 for details.

User Subroutines Section

Bison copies the contents of the user subroutines section verbatim to the C file. This section typically includes routines called from the actions.

In a large program, it is usually more convenient to put the supporting code in a separate source file to minimize the amount of material recompiled when you change the bison file.

Actions

An *action* is C code executed when bison matches a rule in the grammar. The action must be a C compound statement, for example:

```
date: month '/' day '/' year { printf("date found"); } ;
```

The action can refer to the values associated with the symbols in the rule by using a dollar sign followed by a number, with the first symbol after the colon being 1, for example:

```
date: month '/' day '/' year { printf("date %d-%d-%d found", $1, $3, $5); }
    ;
```

The name $$ refers to the value for the left-hand side (LHS) symbol, the one to the left of the colon. Symbol values can have different C types. See "Tokens" on page 161, "%type Declaration" on page 162, and "%union Declaration" on page 163 for details.

For rules with no action, bison uses a default of the following:

```
{ $$ = $1; }
```

If you have a rule with no RHS symbols and the LHS symbol has a declared type, you *must* write an action to set its value.

Embedded Actions

Even though bison's parsing technique allows actions only at the end of a rule, bison can simulate actions embedded within a rule. If you write an action within a rule, bison invents a rule with an empty right-hand side and a made-up name on the left, makes the embedded action into the action for that rule, and replaces the action in the original rule with the made-up name. For example, these are equivalent:

```
thing:          A { printf("seen an A"); } B ;

thing:          A fakename B ;
fakename:       /* empty */ { printf("seen an A"); } ;
```

Although this feature is quite useful, it can have some surprising consequences. The embedded action turns into a symbol in the rule, so its value (whatever it assigns to $$) is available to an end-of-rule action like any other symbol:

```
thing:          A { $$ = 17; } B C
                { printf("%d", $2); }
        ;
```

This example prints "17". Either action can refer to the value of A as $1, and the end-of-rule action can refer to the value of the embedded action as $2 and can refer to the values of B and C as $3 and $4.

Embedded actions can cause shift/reduce or reduce/reduce conflicts in otherwise acceptable grammars. For example, this grammar causes no problem:

```
%%
thing:      abcd | abcz ;

abcd: 'A' 'B' 'C' 'D' ;
abcz: 'A' 'B' 'C' 'Z' ;
```

But if you add an embedded action, it has a shift/reduce conflict:

```
%%
thing:      abcd | abcz ;

abcd: 'A' 'B' { somefunc(); } 'C' 'D' ;
abcz: 'A' 'B' 'C' 'Z' ;
```

In the first case, the parser doesn't need to decide whether it's parsing an abcd or an abcz until it's seen all four tokens, when it can tell which it's found. In the second case, it needs to decide after it parses the B, but at that point it hasn't seen enough of the input to decide which rule it is parsing. If the embedded action came after the C, there would be no problem, since bison could use its one-token lookahead to see whether a D or a Z is next.

Symbol Types for Embedded Actions

Since embedded actions aren't associated with grammar symbols, there is no way to declare the type of the value returned by an embedded action. If you are using %union and typed symbol values, you have to put the value in angle brackets when referring to the action's value, for example, $<*type*>$ when you set it in the embedded action and $<*type*>3 (using the appropriate number) when you refer to it in the action at the end of the rule. See "Symbol Values" on page 160. If you have a simple parser that uses all *int* values, as in the previous example, you don't need to give a type.

Ambiguity and Conflicts

Bison may report conflicts when it translates a grammar into a parser. In some cases, the grammar is truly ambiguous; that is, there are two possible parses for a single input string, and bison cannot handle that. In others, the grammar is unambiguous, but the standard parsing technique that bison uses is not powerful enough to parse the grammar. The problem in an unambiguous grammar with conflicts is that the parser would need to look more than one token ahead to decide which of two possible parses to use. Usually you can rewrite the grammar so that one token of lookahead is enough, but bison also offers a more powerful technique, GLR, that provides lookahead of unlimited length.

See "Precedence and Associativity Declarations" on page 154 and Chapter 7 for more details and suggestions on how to fix these problems, and see "GLR Parsing" on page 230 for details on GLR parsing.

Types of Conflicts

There are two kinds of conflicts that can occur when bison tries to create a parser: shift/reduce and reduce/reduce.

Shift/Reduce Conflicts

A *shift/reduce* conflict occurs when there are two possible parses for an input string and one of the parses completes a rule (the reduce option) and one doesn't (the shift option). For example, this grammar has one shift/reduce conflict:

```
%%
e:        'X'
    |   e '+' e
    ;
```

For the input string X+X+X there are two possible parses, (X+X)+X or X+(X+X). Taking the reduce option makes the parser use the first parse, and taking the shift option makes the parser take the second. Bison chooses the shift unless the user puts in operator precedence declarations. See "Precedence and Associativity Declarations" on page 154 for more information.

Reduce/Reduce Conflicts

A *reduce/reduce* conflict occurs when the same token could complete two different rules. For example:

```
%%
prog: proga | progb ;

proga:      'X' ;
progb:      'X' ;
```

An X could either be a proga or be a progb. Most reduce/reduce conflicts are less obvious than this, but they usually indicate mistakes in the grammar. See Chapter 8 for details on handling conflicts.

%expect

Occasionally you may have a grammar that has a few conflicts, you are confident that bison will resolve them the way you want, and it's too much hassle to rewrite the grammar to get rid of them. (If/then/else-style constructs are the most common place this happens.) The declaration %expect N tells bison that your parser should have N shift/reduce conflicts, so bison reports a compile-time error if the number is different.

You can also use %expect-rr N to tell it how many reduce/reduce conflicts to expect; unless you are using a GLR parser, do not use this feature since reduce/reduce conflicts almost always indicate an error in the grammar.

GLR Parsers

Sometimes a grammar is truly too hard for bison's normal LALR parsing algorithm to handle. In that case, you can tell bison to create a Generalized LR (GLR) parser instead, by including a %glr-parser declaration. When a GLR parser encounters a conflict, it conceptually splits and continues both possible parses in parallel, with each one consuming each token. If there are several conflicts, it can create a tree of partial parses, splitting each time there is a conflict. At the end of the parse, either there will be only one surviving parse, the rest having been abandoned because they didn't match the rest of the input, or, if the grammar is truly ambiguous, there may be several parses, and it is up to you to decide what to do with them.

See "GLR Parsing" on page 230 for examples and more details.

Bugs in Bison Programs

Bison itself is pretty robust, but there are a few common programming mistakes that can cause serious failures in your bison parser.

Infinite Recursion

A common error in bison grammars is to create a recursive rule with no way to terminate the recursion. Bison will diagnose this grammar with the somewhat mysterious "start symbol xlist does not derive any sentence."

```
%%
xlist:    xlist 'X' ;
```

Interchanging Precedence

People occasionally try to use %prec to swap the precedence of two tokens:

```
%token  NUMBER
%left PLUS
%left MUL
%%
expr  :    expr PLUS expr %prec MUL
      |    expr MUL expr %prec PLUS
      |    NUMBER
      ;
```

This example seems to give PLUS higher precedence than MUL, but in fact it makes them the same. The precedence mechanism resolves shift/reduce conflicts by comparing the precedence of the token to be shifted to the precedence of the rule. In this case, there are several conflicts. A typical conflict arises when the parser has seen "expr PLUS expr" and the next token is a MUL. In the absence of a %prec, the rule would have the precedence of PLUS, which is lower than that of MUL, and bison takes the shift. But with %prec, both the rule and the token have the precedence of MUL, so it reduces because MUL is left associative.

One possibility would be to introduce pseudotokens, for example, XPLUS and XMUL, with their own precedence levels to use with %prec. A far better solution is to rewrite the grammar to say what it means, in this case exchanging the %left lines (see "Precedence and Associativity Declarations" on page 154).

Embedded Actions

When you write an action in the middle of a rule rather than at the end, bison has to invent an anonymous rule to trigger the embedded action. Occasionally the anonymous rule causes unexpected shift/reduce conflicts. See "Actions" on page 142 for more details.

C++ Parsers

Bison can produce a C++ parsers. If your bison file is called `comp.yxx`, it will create the C++ source `comp.tab.cxx` and header `comp.tab.hxx` files. (You can change the output filenames with the -o flag, perhaps as `-o comp.c++`, which will also rename the header to `comp.h++`.) It also creates the header files `stack.hh`, `location.hh`, and `position.hh`, which define three classes used in the parser. The contents of these three files are always the same unless you use `-p` or `%name-prefix` to change the namespace of the parser from "yy" to something else.

Bison defines a class called `yy::parser` (unless you change its name) with a main `parse` routine and some minor routines for error reporting and debugging. See "C++ Parsers" on page 234 for more details.

%code Blocks

Bison has always accepted C code in the declaration section surrounded by `%{ ... %}` brackets. Sometimes the code has to go in a particular place in the generated program, before or after particular parts of the standard parser skeleton code. The `%code` directive allows more specific placement of the code.

```
%code [place] {
    ... code here ...
}
```

The optional *place*, which the bison manual calls the *qualifier*, says where in the generated program to put the code. Current places in C language programs are `top`, `provides`, and `requires`. They put the code at the top of the file, before the definitions of `YYSTYPE` and `YYLTYPE`, and after those definitions. This feature is considered experimental, so the places are likely to change; therefore, check the current bison manual to see what the current options are. The use of `%code` without a place will definitely remain and is intended to replace `%{ %}`.

End Marker

Each bison grammar includes a pseudotoken called the *end marker*, which marks the end of input. In bison listings, the end marker is usually indicated as `$end`.

The lexer must return a zero token to indicate the end of input.

Error Token and Error Recovery

Bison parsers will always detect syntax errors as early as possible, that is, as soon as they read a token for which there is no potential parse. When bison detects a syntax error, that is, when it receives an input token that it cannot parse, it attempts to recover from the error using this procedure:

1. It calls yyerror("syntax error"). This usually reports the error to the user.
2. It discards any partially parsed rules until it returns to a state in which it could shift the special error symbol.
3. It resumes parsing, starting by shifting an error.
4. If another error occurs before three tokens have been shifted successfully, bison does not report another error but returns to step 2.

See Chapter 8 for more details on error recovery. Also, see "yyerror()" on page 167, "YYRECOVERING()" on page 171, "yyclearin" on page 169, and "yyerrok" on page 169 for details on features that help control error recovery.

%destructor

When bison is trying to recover from a parse error, it discards symbols and their values from the parse stack. If the value is a pointer to dynamically allocated memory, or otherwise needs special treatment when it's discarded, the **%destructor** directive lets you get control when particular symbols, or symbols with values of particular types, are deleted. It also will handle the value of the start symbol after a successful parse. See Chapter 8 for more details.

Inherited Attributes ($0)

Bison symbol values can act as *inherited attributes* or *synthesized attributes*. (What bison calls *values* are usually referred to in compiler literature as *attributes*.) The usual synthesized attributes start as token values, which are the leaves of the parse tree. Information conceptually moves up the parse tree each time a rule is reduced, and each action synthesizes the value of its resulting symbol ($$) from the values of the symbols on the right-hand side of the rule.

Sometimes you need to pass information the other way, from the root of the parse tree toward the leaves. Consider this example:

```
declaration:    class type namelist ;

class:      GLOBAL      { $$ = 1; }
        |   LOCAL       { $$ = 2; }
        ;

type:       REAL        { $$ = 1; }
        |   INTEGER     { $$ = 2; }
        ;

namelist:   NAME        { mksymbol($0, $-1, $1); }
```

```
        |    namelist NAME { mksymbol($0, $-1, $2); }
        ;
```

It would be useful to have the class and type available in the actions for `namelist`, both for error checking and for entering into the symbol table. Bison makes this possible by allowing access to symbols on its internal stack to the left of the current rule, via `$0`, `$-1`, etc. In the example, the `$0` in the call to `mksymbol()` refers to the value of the `type`, which is stacked just before the symbol(s) for the `namelist` production, and it will have the value 1 or 2 depending on whether the type was `REAL` or `INTEGER`. `$-1` refers to the class, which will have the value 1 or 2 if the class was `GLOBAL` or `LOCAL`.

Although inherited attributes can be useful, they can also be a source of hard-to-find bugs. An action that uses inherited attributes has to take into account every place in the grammar where its rule is used. In this example, if you changed the grammar to use a `namelist` somewhere else, you'd have to make sure that, in the new place where the `namelist` occurs, appropriate symbols precede it so that `$0` and `$-1` will get the right values:

```
        declaration:    STRING namelist ; /* won't work! */
```

Inherited attributes can occasionally be very useful, particularly for syntactically complex constructs such as C language variable declarations. But it's usually safer and easier to use a global variable for the value that would have been fetched from a synthesized attribute. Or it's often nearly as easy to use synthesized attributes. In the previous example, the `namelist` rules could create a linked list of references to the names to be declared and return a pointer to that list as its value. The action for declaration could take the class, type, and `namelist` values and at that point assign the class and type to the names in the `namelist`.

Symbol Types for Inherited Attributes

When you use the value of an inherited attribute, the usual value declaration techniques (e.g., `%type`) don't work. Since the symbol corresponding to the value doesn't appear in the rule, bison cannot tell what the correct type is. You have to supply type names in the action code using an explicit type. In the previous example, if the types of `class` and `type` were `cval` and `tval`, the last two lines would actually read like this:

```
        namelist:    NAME       { mksymbol($<tval>0, $<cval>-1, $1); }
        |    namelist NAME       { mksymbol($<tval>0, $<cval>-1, $2); }
```

See "Symbol Values" on page 160 for additional information.

%initial-action

If you need to initialize something when your parser starts up, you can use `%initial-action { some-code }` to tell bison to copy `some-code` near the beginning of `yyparse`. The place where the code is copied comes after the standard initialization code, so you cannot usefully put variable declarations in the code. (They'll be accepted, but they won't be accessible in your actions.) If you need to define your own parse-time variables, you have to either use static globals or pass them as arguments via %parse-param.

Lexical Feedback

Parsers can sometimes feed information back to the lexer to handle otherwise difficult situations. For example, consider an input syntax like this:

```
message (any characters)
```

where in this particular context the parentheses are acting as string quotes. You can't just decide to parse a string any time you see an open parenthesis, because open parentheses might be used differently elsewhere in the grammar.

A straightforward way to handle this situation is to feed context information from the parser back to the lexer, for example, set a flag in the parser when a context-dependent construct is expected:

```
/* parser */
%{
int parenstring = 0;
}%
. . .
%%
statement: MESSAGE { parenstring = 1; } '(' STRING ')' ;
```

and look for it in the lexer:

```
%{
extern int parenstring;
%}
%s PSTRING
%%
. . .
"message"  return MESSAGE;
"("    {    if(parenstring)
                BEGIN PSTRING;
            return '(';
        }
<PSTRING>[^)]*    {
                yylval.svalue = strdup(yytext);    /* pass string to parser */
                BEGIN INITIAL;
                return STRING;
                }
```

This code is not bulletproof, because if there is some other rule that starts with MESSAGE, bison might have to use a lookahead token, in which case the in-line action wouldn't be executed until after the open parenthesis had been scanned. In most real cases that isn't a problem because the syntax tends to be simple. If the parser does error recovery, the error code needs to reset parenstring.

In this example, you could also handle the special case in the lexer by setting `parenstring` in the lexer, for example:

```
"message("  { parenstring = 1; return MESSAGE; }
```

This could cause problems, however, if the token MESSAGE is used elsewhere in the grammar and is not always followed by a parenthesized string. You usually have the choice of doing lexical feedback entirely in the lexer or doing it partly in the parser, with the best solution depending on how complex the grammar is. If the grammar is simple and tokens do not appear in multiple contexts, you can do all of your lexical hackery in the lexer, while if the grammar is more complex, it is easier to identify the special situations in the parser.

This approach can be taken to extremes—I wrote a complete Fortran 77 parser in yacc, bison's predecessor (but, not lex, since tokenizing Fortran is just too strange), and the parser needed to feed a dozen special context states back to the lexer. It was messy, but it was far easier than writing the whole parser and lexer in C.

Literal Block

The literal block in the definition section is bracketed by the lines %{ and %}.

```
%{
... C code and declarations ...
%}
```

The contents of the literal block are copied verbatim to the generated C source file near the beginning, before the beginning of **yyparse()**. The literal block usually contains declarations of variables and functions used by code in the rules section, as well as #include lines for any necessary header files.

Bison also provides an experimental %code POS { ... } where POS is a keyword to suggest where in the generated parser the code should go. See "%code Blocks" on page 147 for current details.

Literal Tokens

Bison treats a character in single quotes as a token. In this example,

```
expr: '(' expr ')' ;
```

the open and close parentheses are literal tokens. The token number of a literal token is the numeric value in the local character set, usually ASCII, and is the same as the C value of the quoted character.

The lexer usually generates these tokens from the corresponding single characters in the input, but as with any other token, the correspondence between the input characters and the generated tokens is entirely up to the lexer. A common technique is to have the lexer treat all otherwise unrecognized characters as literal tokens. For example, in a flex scanner:

```
.        return yytext[0];
```

this covers all of the single-character operators in a language and lets bison catch all unrecognized characters in the input with parse errors.

Bison also allows you to declare strings as aliases for tokens, for example:

```
%token NE "!="
%%
...
exp: exp "!=" exp ;
```

This defines the token NE and lets you use NE and != interchangeably in the parser. The lexer must still return the internal token value for NE when the token is read, not a string.

Locations

To aid in error reporting, bison offers locations, a feature to track the source line and column range for every symbol in the parser. Locations are enabled explicitly with %locations or implicitly by referring to a location in the action code. The lexer has to track the current line and column and set the location range for each token in yylloc before returning the token. (Flex lexers will automatically track the line number, but tracking the column number is up to you.) A default rule in the parser invoked every time a rule is reduced sets the location range of the LHS symbol from the beginning line and column of the first RHS symbol to the ending line and column of the last RHS symbol.

Within action code, the location for each symbol is referred to as @$ for the LHS and as @1, and so forth, for the RHS symbols. Each location is actually a structure, with references to fields like @3.first_column.

Locations are overkill for the error-reporting needs of many, perhaps most, parsers. Parse errors still just report the single token where the parse failed, so the only time a location range is visible to the user is if your action code reports it. The most likely place to use them is in an integrated development environment that could use them to highlight the source code responsible for semantic errors. For some examples, see Chapter 8.

%parse-param

Normally, you call yyparse() with no arguments. If the parser needs to import information from the surrounding program, it can use global variables, or you can add parameters to its definition:

```
%parse-param {char *modulename}
%parse-param {int intensity}
```

This allows you to call `yyparse("mymodule", 42)` and refer to `modulename` and `intensity` in action code in the parser. Note that there are no semicolons and no trailing punctuation, since the parameters are just placed between the parentheses in the definition of `yyparse`.

In normal parsers, there's little reason to use parse parameters rather than global variables, but if you generate a pure parser that can be called multiple times, either recursively or in multiple threads, parameters are the easiest way to provide the parameters to each instance of the parser.

Portability of Bison Parsers

There are two levels at which you can port a parser: the original bison grammar or the generated C source file.

Porting Bison Grammars

For the most part, you can write bison parsers and expect anyone's version of bison to handle them, since the core features bison have changed very little in the past 15 years. If you know that your parser requires features added in recent years, you can declare the minimum version of bison needed to compile it:

```
%require "2.4"
```

Porting Generated C Parsers

Bison parsers are in general very portable among reasonably modern C or C++ implementations, C89 or later, or ANSI/ISO C++.

Libraries

The only routines in the bison library are usually `main()` and `yyerror()`. Any nontrivial parser has its own version of those two routines, so the library usually isn't necessary.

Character Codes

Moving a generated parser between machines that use different character codes can be tricky. In particular, you must avoid literal tokens like `'0'` since the parser uses the character code as an index into internal tables; so, a parser generated on an ASCII machine where the code for `'0'` is 48 will fail on an EBCDIC machine where the code is 240.

Bison assigns its own numeric values to symbolic tokens, so a parser that uses only symbolic tokens should port successfully.

Precedence and Associativity Declarations

Normally, all bison grammars have to be unambiguous. That is, there is only one possible way to parse any legal input using the rules in the grammar.

Sometimes, an ambiguous grammar is easier to use. Ambiguous grammars cause *conflicts*, situations where there are two possible parses and hence two different ways that bison can process a token. When bison processes an ambiguous grammar, it uses default rules to decide which way to parse an ambiguous sequence. Often these rules do not produce the desired result, so bison includes operator declarations that let you change the way it handles shift/reduce conflicts that result from ambiguous grammars. (See also "Ambiguity and Conflicts" on page 144.)

Most programming languages have complicated rules that control the interpretation of arithmetic expressions. For example, the C expression:

```
a = b = c + d / e / f
```

is treated as follows:

```
a = (b = (c + ((d / e) / f))))
```

The rules for determining what operands group with which operators are known as *precedence* and *associativity*.

Precedence

Precedence assigns each operator a precedence "level." Operators at higher levels bind more tightly; for example, if * has higher precedence than +, A+B*C is treated as A+(B*C), while D*E+F is (D*E)+F.

Associativity

Associativity controls how the grammar groups expressions using the same operator or different operators with the same precedence. They can group from the left, from the right, or not at all. If - were left associative, the expression A-B-C would mean (A-B)-C, while if it were right associative, it would mean A-(B-C).

Some operators such as Fortran .GE. are not associative either way; that is, A .GE. B .GE. C is not a valid expression.

Precedence Declarations

Precedence declarations appear in the definition section. The possible declarations are %left, %right, and %nonassoc. The %left and %right declarations make an operator left or right associative, respectively. You declare nonassociative operators with %nonassoc.

Operators are declared in increasing order of precedence. All operators declared on the same line are at the same precedence level. For example, a Fortran grammar might include the following:

```
%left '+' '-'
%left '*' '/'
%right POW
```

The lowest precedence operators here are + and -, the middle predecence operators are * and /, and the highest is POW, which represents the ** power operator.

Using Precedence and Associativity to Resolve Conflicts

Every token in a grammar can have a precedence and an associativity assigned by a precedence declaration. Every rule can also have a precedence and an associativity, which is taken from a %prec clause in the rule or, failing that, the rightmost token in the rule that has a precedence assigned.

Whenever there is a shift/reduce conflict, bison compares the precedence of the token that might be shifted to that of the rule that might be reduced. It shifts if the token's precedence is higher or reduces if the rule's precedence is higher. If both have the same precedence, bison checks the associativity. If they are left associative, it reduces; if they are right associative, it shifts; and if they are nonassociative, bison generates an error.

Typical Uses of Precedence

Although you can in theory use precedence to resolve any kind of shift/reduce conflict, you should use precedence only for a few well-understood situations and rewrite the grammar otherwise. Precedence declarations were designed to handle expression grammars, with large numbers of rules like this:

```
expr OP expr
```

Expression grammars are almost always written using precedence.

The only other common use is if/then/else, where you can resolve the "dangling else" problem more easily with precedence than by rewriting the grammar.

See Chapter 7 for details. Also see "Bugs in Bison Programs" on page 146 for a common pitfall using %prec.

Recursive Rules

To parse a list of items of indefinite length, you write a *recursive* rule, one that is defined in terms of itself. For example, this parses a possibly empty list of numbers:

```
numberlist: /* empty */
        | numberlist NUMBER
        ;
```

The details of the recursive rule vary depending on the exact syntax to be parsed. The next example parses a nonempty list of expressions separated by commas, with the symbol `expr` being defined elsewhere in the grammar:

```
exprlist:     expr
        |     exprlist ',' expr
        ;
```

It's also possible to have mutually recursive rules that refer to each other:

```
exp:      term
    |     term '+' term
    ;
term:     '(' exp ')'
    |     VARIABLE
    ;
```

Any recursive rule and each rule in a group of mutually recursive rules must have at least one nonrecursive alternative (one that does not refer to itself). Otherwise, there is no way to terminate the string that it matches, which is an error.

Left and Right Recursion

When you write a recursive rule, you can put the recursive reference at the left end or the right end of the right-hand side of the rule, for example:

```
exprlist:     exprlist ',' expr ;    /* left recursion */

exprlist:     expr ',' exprlist ;    /* right recursion */
```

In most cases, you can write the grammar either way. Bison handles left recursion much more efficiently than right recursion. This is because its internal stack keeps track of all symbols seen so far for all partially parsed rules. If you use the right-recursive version of `exprlist` and have an expression with 10 expressions in it, by the time the 10th expression is read, there will be 20 entries on the stack: an `expr` and a comma for each of the 10 expressions. When the list ends, all of the nested `exprlist`s will be reduced, starting from right to left. On the other hand, if you use the left-recursive version, the `exprlist` rule is reduced after each `expr`, so the list will never have more than three entries on the internal stack.

A 10-element expression list poses no problems in a parser, but grammars often parse lists that are hundreds or thousands of items long, particularly when a program is defined as a list of statements:

```
%start program
%%
program:    statementlist ;

statementlist :    statement
              | statementlist ';' statement
              ;
statement: . . .
```

In this case, a 5,000-statement program is parsed as a 10,000-element list of statements and semicolons, and a right-recursive list of 10,000 elements is too large for most bison parsers.

Right-recursive grammars can be useful for a list of items that you know will be short and that you want to make into a linked list of values:

```
thinglist:   THING { $$ = $1; }
         |   THING thinglist { $1->next = $2; $$ = $1; }
         ;
```

With a left-recursive grammar, either you end up with the list linked in reverse order with a reversal step at the end or you need extra code to search for the end of the list at each stage in order to add the next thing to the end.

You can control the size of the parser stack by defining YYINITDEPTH, which is the initial stack size that is normally 200, and YYMAXDEPTH, which is the maximum stack size that is normally 10,000. For example:

```
%{
#define YYMAXDEPTH 50000
%}
```

Each stack entry is the size of a semantic value (the largest size in the %union entries) plus two bytes for the token number plus, if you are using locations, 16 bytes for the location. On a workstation with a gigabyte of virtual memory, a stack of 100,000 entries would be a manageable 2 or 3 megabytes, but on a smaller embedded system, you'd probably want to rewrite your grammar to limit the stack size.

Rules

A bison grammar consists of a set of *rules*. Each rule starts with a nonterminal symbol and a colon and is followed by a possibly empty list of symbols, literal tokens, and actions. Rules by convention end with a semicolon, although the semicolon is technically optional. For example,

```
date: month '/' day '/' year ;
```

says that a date is a month, a slash, a day, another slash, and a year. (The symbols month, day, and year must be defined elsewhere in the grammar.) The initial symbol and colon are called the *left-hand side (LHS)* of the rule, and the rest of the rule is the *right-hand side (RHS)*. The right-hand side may be empty.

If several consecutive rules in a grammar have the same LHS, the second and subsequent rules may start with a vertical bar rather than the name and the colon. These two fragments are equivalent:

```
declaration:   EXTERNAL name ;
declaration:   ARRAY name '(' size ')' ;
```

```
declaration:    EXTERNAL name
        |    ARRAY name '(' size ')' ;
```

The form with the vertical bar is better style. The semicolon must be omitted before a vertical bar. Multiple rules with the same LHS need not occur together. See the SQL grammar in Chapter 4 where there are multiple rules defining the term **sql** throughout the grammar.

An *action* is a C compound statement that is executed whenever the parser reaches the point in the grammar where the action occurs:

```
date: month '/' day '/' year
                    { printf("Date recognized.\n"); }
        ;
```

The C code in actions may have some special constructs starting with $ or @ that are specially treated by bison. (See "Actions" on page 142 and "Locations" on page 152 for details.) Actions that occur anywhere except at the end of a rule are treated specially. (See "Embedded Actions" on page 143 for details.)

A rule may have an explicit precedence at the end:

```
expr: expr '*' expr
    | expr '-' expr
    | '-' expr %prec UMINUS ;
```

The precedence is used only to resolve otherwise ambiguous parses. See "Precedence and Associativity Declarations" on page 154 for details. In a GLR parser, a rule can also have a **%dprec** precedence to resolve ambiguous parses.

Special Characters

Since bison deals with symbolic tokens rather than literal text, its input character set is considerably simpler than lex's. Here is a list of the special characters that it uses:

%

> A line with two percent signs separates the parts of a bison grammar (see "Structure of a Bison Grammar" on page 141). All of the declarations in the definition section start with %, including %{ %}, %start, %token, %type, %left, %right, %nonassoc, and %union. See "Literal Block" on page 151, "%start Declaration" on page 159, "%type Declaration" on page 162, "Precedence and Associativity Declarations" on page 154, and "%union Declaration" on page 163.

$

> In actions, a dollar sign introduces a value reference, for example, $3 for the value of the third symbol in the rule's right-hand side. See "Symbol Values" on page 160.

@

> In actions, an @ sign introduces a location reference, such as @2 for the location of the second symbol in the RHS.

'
    Literal tokens are enclosed in single quotes, for example, `'Z'`. See "Literal To-kens" on page 151.

"
    Bison lets you declare quoted strings as parser aliases for tokens. See "Literal To-kens" on page 151.

< >
    In a value reference in an action, you can override the value's default type by en-closing the type name in angle brackets, for example, `$<xtype>3`. See "Declaring Symbol Types" on page 160.

{ }
    The C code in actions is enclosed in curly braces. (See "Actions" on page 142.) C code in the literal block declarations section is enclosed in `%{` and `%}`. See "Literal Block" on page 151.

;
    Each rule in the rules section should end with a semicolon, except those that are immediately followed by a rule that starts with a vertical bar. The semicolons are optional, but they are always a good idea. See "Rules" on page 157.

|
    When two consecutive rules have the same left-hand side, the second rule may replace the symbol and colon with a vertical bar. See "Rules" on page 157.

:
    In each rule, a colon follows the symbol on the rule's left-hand side. See "Rules" on page 157.

_
    Symbols may include underscores along with letters, digits, and periods.

.
    Symbols may include periods along with letters, digits, and underscores. This can cause trouble because C identifiers cannot include periods. In particular, do not use tokens whose names contain periods, since the token names are all `#define`'d as C preprocessor symbols.

%start Declaration

Normally, the start rule, the one that the parser starts trying to parse, is the one named in the first rule. If you want to start with some other rule, in the declaration section you can write the following:

    %start *somename*

to start with rule *somename*.

In most cases, the clearest way to present the grammar is top-down, with the start rule first, so no %start is needed.

Symbol Values

Every symbol in a bison parser, both tokens and nonterminals, can have a value associated with it. If the token were NUMBER, the value might be the particular number; if it were STRING, the value might be a pointer to a copy of the string; and if it were SYMBOL, the value might be a pointer to an entry in the symbol table that describes the symbol. Each of these kinds of value corresponds to a different C type: int or double for the number, char * for the string, and a pointer to a structure for the symbol. Bison makes it easy to assign types to symbols so that it automatically uses the correct type for each symbol.

Declaring Symbol Types

Internally, bison declares each value as a C union that includes all of the types. You list all of the types in %union declarations. Bison turns them into a typedef for a union type called YYSTYPE. Then for each symbol whose value is set or used in action code, you have to declare its type. Use %type for nonterminals. Use %token, %left, %right, or %nonassoc for tokens to give the name of the union field corresponding to its type.

Then, whenever you refer to a value using $$, $1, etc., bison automatically uses the appropriate field of the union.

Bison doesn't understand any C, so any symbol typing mistakes you make, such as using a type name that isn't in the union or using a field in a way that C doesn't allow, will cause errors in the generated C program.

Explicit Symbol Types

Bison allows you to declare an explicit type for a symbol value reference by putting the type name in angle brackets between the dollar sign and the symbol number or between the two dollar signs, for example, $<xxx>3 or $<zzz>$.

The feature is rarely used, since in nearly all cases it is easier and more readable to declare the symbols. The most plausible uses are when referring to inherited attributes and when setting and referring to the value returned by an embedded action. See "Inherited Attributes ($0)" on page 148 and "Actions" on page 142 for details.

Tokens

Tokens or *terminal symbols* are symbols that the lexer passes to the parser. Whenever a bison parser needs another token, it calls `yylex()`, which returns the next token from the input. At the end of input, `yylex()` returns zero.

Tokens may be either symbols defined by `%token` or individual characters in single quotes. (See "Literal Tokens" on page 151.) All symbols used as tokens must be defined explicitly in the definition section, for example:

```
%token UP DOWN LEFT RIGHT
```

Tokens can also be declared by `%left`, `%right`, or `%nonassoc` declarations, each of which has exactly the same syntax options as `%token` has. See "Precedence and Associativity Declarations" on page 154.

Token Numbers

Within the lexer and parser, tokens are identified by small integers. The token number of a literal token is the numeric value in the local character set, usually ASCII, and is the same as the C value of the quoted character.

Symbolic tokens usually have values assigned by bison, which gives them numbers higher than any possible character's code, so they will not conflict with any literal tokens. You can assign token numbers yourself by following the token name by its number in `%token`:

```
%token UP 50 DOWN 60 LEFT 17 RIGHT 25
```

It is an error to assign two tokens the same number. In most cases it is easier and more reliable to let bison choose its own token numbers.

The lexer needs to know the token numbers in order to return the appropriate values to the parser. For literal tokens, it uses the corresponding C character constant. For symbolic tokens, you can tell bison with the `-d` command-line flag to create a C header file with definitions of all the token numbers. If you `#include` that header file in your lexer, you can use the symbols, for example, UP, DOWN, LEFT, and RIGHT, in its C code. The header file is normally called `xxx.tab.h` if your source file was `xxx.y`, or you can rename it with the `%defines` declaration or the `--defines=`*filename* command-line option.

```
%defines "xxxsyms.h"
```

Token Values

Each symbol in a bison parser can have an associated value. (See "Symbol Values" on page 160.) Since tokens can have values, you need to set the values as the lexer returns tokens to the parser. The token value is always stored in the variable `yylval`. In the simplest parsers, `yylval` is a plain `int` variable, and you might set it like this in a flex scanner:

```
[0-9]+     { yylval = atoi(yytext); return NUMBER; }
```

In most cases, though, different symbols have different value types. See "%union Declaration" on page 163, "Symbol Values" on page 160, and "%type Declaration" below.

In the parser you must declare the value types of all tokens that have values. Put the name of the appropriate union tag in angle brackets in the `%token` or precedence declaration. You might define your values types like this:

```
%union {
        enum optype opval;
        double dval;
}

%nonassoc <opval> RELOP
%token <dval> REAL

%union { char *sval; }
. . .
%token <sval> STRING
```

In this case `RELOP` might be a relational operator such as `==` or `>`, and the token value says which operator it is.

You set the appropriate field of `yylval` when you return the token. In this case, you'd do something like this in lex:

```
%{
#include "parser.tab.h"
%}
. . .
[0-9]+\.[0-9]*   { yylval.dval = atof(yytext); return REAL; }
\"[^"]*\"  { yylval.sval = strdup(yytext); return STRING; }
"=="       { yyval.opval = OPEQUAL; return RELOP; }
```

The value for `REAL` is a `double`, so it goes into `yylval.dval`, while the value for `STRING` is a `char *`, so it goes into `yylval.sval`.

%type Declaration

You declare the types of nonterminals using `%type`. Each declaration has the following form:

```
%type <type> name, name, . . .
```

Each `type` name must have been defined by a `%union`. (See "%union Declaration" on page 163.) Each `name` is the name of a nonterminal symbol. See "Declaring Symbol Types" on page 160 for details and an example.

Use %type to declare nonterminals. To declare tokens, you can also use %token, %left, %right, or %nonassoc. See "Tokens" on page 161 and "Precedence and Associativity Declarations" on page 154 for details.

%union Declaration

The %union declaration identifies all of the possible C types that a symbol value can have. (See "Symbol Values" on page 160.) The declaration takes this form:

```
%union {
  ... field declarations...
}
```

The field declarations are copied verbatim into a C union declaration of the type YYSTYPE in the output file. Bison does not check to see whether the contents of the %union are valid C. If you have more than one %union declaration, their contents are concatenated to create the C or C++ union declaration.

In the absence of a %union declaration, bison defines YYSTYPE to be int, so all of the symbol values are integers.

You associate the types declared in %union with particular symbols using the %type declaration.

Bison puts the generated C union declaration both in the generated C file and in the optional generated header file (called *name*.tab.h unless you tell it otherwise), so you can use YYSTYPE in other source files by including the generated header file. Conversely, you can put your own declaration of YYSTYPE in an include file that you reference with #include in the definition section. In this case, there must be at least one %type or other declaration that specifies a symbol type to warn bison that you are using explicit symbol types.

Variant and Multiple Grammars

You may want to have parsers for two partially or entirely different grammars in the same program. For example, an interactive debugging interpreter might have one parser for the programming language and another for debugger commands. A one-pass C compiler might need one parser for the preprocessor syntax and another for the C language itself.

There are two ways to handle two grammars in one program: combine them into a single parser or put two complete parsers into the program.

Combined Parsers

If you have several similar grammars, you can combine them into one by adding a new start rule that depends on the first token read. For example:

```
%token CSTART PPSTART
%%
combined:   CSTART cgrammar
        |   PPSTART ppgrammar
        ;

cgrammar:   . . .

ppgrammar: . . .
```

In this case, if the first token is CSTART, it parses the grammar whose start rule is cgrammar, while if the first token is PPSTART, it parses the grammar whose start rule is ppgrammar.

You also need to put code in the lexer that returns the appropriate special token the first time that the parser asks the lexer for a token:

```
%%
%{
        extern first_tok;

        if(first_tok) {
                int holdtok = first_tok;

                first_tok = 0;
                return holdtok;
        }
%}
. . . <the rest of the lexer>
```

In this case, you set first_tok to the appropriate token before calling **yyparse()**.

One advantage of this approach is that the program is smaller than it would be with multiple parsers, since there is only one copy of the parsing code. Another is that if you are parsing related grammars, for example, C preprocessor expressions and C itself, you should be able to share some parts of the grammar. The disadvantages are that you cannot call one parser while the other is active unless you create a pure parser and that you have to use different symbols in the two grammars except where they deliberately share rules, and the possibilities for hard-to-find errors are rife if you accidentally use the same symbol in the two grammars.

In practice, this approach is useful when you want to parse slightly different versions of a single language, for example, a full language that is compiled and an interactive subset that you interpret in a debugger. If one language is actually a subset of the other, a better approach would be to use a single parser for both, check in the action code in the rules excluded from the subset for which version is being parsed, and if it's the subset, report an error to the user.

Multiple Parsers

The other approach is to include two complete parsers in a single program. Every bison parser normally has the same entry point, yyparse(), and calls the same lexer, yylex(), which uses the same token value variable yylval. Also, the parse tables and parser stack are in global variables with names like yyact and yyv. If you just translate two grammars and compile and link the two resulting files, you get a long list of multiply defined symbols. The trick is to change the names that bison uses for its functions and variables.

Using %name-prefix or the -p Flag

You can use a declaration in the bison source code to change the prefix used on the names in the parser generated by bison.

```
%name-prefix "pdq"
```

This produces a parser with the entry point pdqparse(), which calls the lexer pdqlex(), and so forth.

Specifically, the names affected are yyparse(), yylex(), yyerror(), yylval, yychar, and yydebug. (The variable yychar holds the most recently read token, which is sometimes useful when printing error messages.) The other variables used in the parser may be renamed or may be made static or auto; in any event, they are guaranteed not to collide. There is also a -p flag to specify the prefix on the command line rather than in the source file, and there is a a -b flag to specify the prefix of the generated C file; for example,

```
bison -d -p pdq -b pref mygram.y
```

would produce pref.tab.c and pref.tab.h with a parser whose entry point is pdqparse.

You have to provide properly named versions of yyerror() and yylex().

Lexers for Multiple Parsers

If you use a flex lexer with your multiple parsers, you need to make adjustments to the lexer to correspond to the changes to the parser. (See "Multiple Lexers in One Program" on page 127.) You will usually want to use a combined lexer with a combined parser and use multiple lexers with multiple parsers.

Pure Parsers

A slightly different problem is that of recursive parsing, calling yyparse() a second time while the original call to yyparse() is still active. This can be an issue when you have combined parsers. If you have a combined C language and C preprocessor parser, you can call yyparse() in C language mode once to parse the whole program, and you can call it recursively whenever you see a #if to parse a preprocessor expression.

Pure parsers are also useful in threaded programs, where each thread might be parsing input from a separate source. See "Pure Scanners and Parsers" on page 209 in Chapter 9 for the details on pure parsers.

y.output Files

Bison can create a log file, traditionally named *y.output* or now more often *name*.output, that shows all of the states in the parser and the transitions from one state to another. Use the *--report=all* flag to generate a log file.

Here's part of the log for the bison grammar in Chapter 1:

```
state 3

    10 term: NUMBER .

     $default  reduce using rule 10 (term)

state 4

    11 term: ABS . term

     NUMBER  shift, and go to state 3
     ABS     shift, and go to state 4

     term  go to state 9


state 5

    2 calclist: calclist calc . EOL

    EOL  shift, and go to state 10
```

The dot in each state shows how far the parser has gotten parsing a rule when it gets to that state. When the parser is in state 4, for example, if the parser sees a NUMBER token, it shifts the NUMBER onto the stack and switches to state 3. If it sees an ABS, it shifts and switches back to state 4, and any other token is an error. If a subsequent reduction returns to this state with a term on the top of the stack, it switches to state 9. In state 3, it always reduces rule 10. (Rules are numbered in the order they appear in the input file.) After the reduction, the NUMBER is replaced on the parse stack by a term, and the parser pops back to state 4, at which point the term makes it go to state 9.

When there are conflicts, the states with conflicts show the conflicting shift and reduce actions.

```
State 19 conflicts: 3 shift/reduce

state 19

    5 exp: exp . ADD exp
    5    | exp ADD exp .
```

```
6      | exp . SUB factor
7      | exp . ABS factor

ADD  shift, and go to state 12
SUB  shift, and go to state 13
ABS  shift, and go to state 14

ADD          [reduce using rule 5 (exp)]
SUB          [reduce using rule 5 (exp)]
ABS          [reduce using rule 5 (exp)]
$default  reduce using rule 5 (exp)
```

In this case, there is a shift/reduce conflict when bison sees a plus sign. You could fix it either by rewriting the grammar or by adding an operator declaration for the plus sign. See "Precedence and Associativity Declarations" on page 154.

Bison Library

Bison inherits a library of helpful routines from its predecessor yacc. You can include the library by giving the -ly flag at the end of the cc command line. The library contains main() and yyerror().

main()

The library has a minimal main program that is sometimes useful for quickie programs and for testing. It's so simple we can reproduce it here:

```
main(ac, av)
{
      yyparse();
      return 0;
}
```

As with any library routine, you can provide your own main(). In nearly any useful application you will want to provide a main() that accepts command-line arguments and flags, opens files, and checks for errors.

yyerror()

Bison also provides a simple error-reporting routine. It's also simple enough to list in its entirety:

```
yyerror(char *errmsg)
{
      fprintf(stderr, "%s\n", errmsg);
}
```

This sometimes suffices, but a better error routine that reports at least the line number and the most recent token (available in yytext if your lexer is written with lex) will make your parser much more usable.

YYABORT

The special statement

```
YYABORT;
```

in an action makes the parser routine **yyparse()** return immediately with a nonzero value, indicating failure.

It can be useful when an action routine detects an error so severe that there is no point in continuing the parse.

Since the parser may have a one-token lookahead, the rule action containing the YYABORT may not be reduced until the parser has read another token.

YYACCEPT

The special statement

```
YYACCEPT;
```

in an action makes the parser routine **yyparse()** return immediately with a value 0, indicating success.

It can be useful in a situation where the lexer cannot tell when the input data ends but the parser can.

Since the parser may have a one-token lookahead, the rule action containing the YYACCEPT may not be reduced until the parser has read another token.

YYBACKUP

The macro YYBACKUP lets you unshift the current token and replace it with something else. The syntax is as follows:

```
sym:    TOKEN  { YYBACKUP(newtok, newval); }
```

It discards the symbol **sym** that would have been substituted by the reduction and pretends that the lexer just read the token **newtok** with the value **newval**. If there is a lookahead token or the rule has more than one symbol on the right side, the rule fails with a call to **yyerror()**.

It is extremely difficult to use **YYBACKUP()** correctly, so you're best off not using it. (It's documented here in case you come across an existing grammar that does use it.)

yyclearin

The macro `yyclearin` in an action discards a lookahead token if one has been read. It is most often useful in error recovery in an interactive parser to put the parser into a known state after an error:

```
stmtlist: stmt | stmtlist stmt ;

stmt: error   { reset_input(); yyclearin; } ;
```

After an error, this calls the user routine `reset_input()`, which presumably puts the input into a known state, and then uses `yyclearin` to prepare to start reading tokens anew.

See "YYRECOVERING()" on page 171 and "yyerrok" below for more information.

yydebug and YYDEBUG

Bison can optionally compile in trace code that reports everything that the parser does. These reports are extremely verbose but are often the only way to figure out what a recalcitrant parser is doing.

YYDEBUG

Since the trace code is large and slow, it is not automatically compiled into the object program. To include the trace code, either use the `-t` flag on the bison command line or else define the C preprocessor symbol YYDEBUG to be nonzero either on the C compiler command line or by including something like this in the definition section:

```
%{
#define YYDEBUG 1
%}
```

yydebug

The integer variable `yydebug` in the running parser controls whether the parser actually produces debug output. If it is nonzero, the parser produces debugging reports, while if it is zero, it doesn't. You can set `yydebug` nonzero in any way you want, for instance, in response to a flag on the program's command line or by patching it at runtime with a debugger.

yyerrok

After bison detects a syntax error, it normally refrains from reporting another error until it has shifted three consecutive tokens without another error. This somewhat alleviates the problem of multiple error messages resulting from a single mistake as the parser gets resynchronized.

If you know when the parser is back in sync, you can return to the normal state in which all errors are reported. The macro **yyerrok** tells the parser to return to the normal state.

For example, assume you have a command interpreter in which all commands are on separate lines. No matter how badly the user botches a command, you know the next line is a new command.

```
cmdlist: cmd | cmdlist cmd ;

cmd:  error '\n' { yyerrok; } ;
```

The rule with **error** skips input after an error up to a newline, and **yyerrok** tells the parser that error recovery is complete.

See also "YYRECOVERING()" on page 171 and "yyclearin" on page 169.

YYERROR

Sometimes your action code can detect context-sensitive syntax errors that the parser itself cannot. If your code detects a syntax error, you can call the macro YYERROR to produce exactly the same effect as if the parser had read a token forbidden by the grammar. As soon as you invoke YYERROR, the parser goes into error recovery mode looking for a state where it can shift an **error** token. See "Error Token and Error Recovery" on page 147 for details. If you want to produce an error message, you have to call **yyerror** yourself.

yyerror()

Whenever a bison parser detects a syntax error, it calls **yyerror()** to report the error to the user, passing it a single argument: a string describing the error. (Unless you have calls to **yyerror()** in your own code, usually the only error you ever get is "syntax error.") The default version of **yyerror** in the bison library merely prints its argument on the standard output. Here is a slightly more informative version:

```
yyerror(const char *msg)
{
      printf("%d: %s at '%s'\n", yylineno, msg, yytext);
}
```

We assume **yylineno** is the current line number. (See "Line Numbers and yylineno" on page 126.) **yytext** is the flex token buffer that contains the current token.

Since bison doggedly tries to recover from errors and parse its entire input, no matter how badly garbled, you may want to have **yyerror()** count the number of times it's called and exit after 10 errors, on the theory that the parser is probably hopelessly confused by the errors that have already been reported.

You can and probably should call yyerror() yourself when your action routines detect other sorts of errors.

yyparse()

The entry point to a bison-generated parser is yyparse(). When your program calls yyparse(), the parser attempts to parse an input stream. The parser returns a value of zero if the parse succeeds and nonzero if not. The parser normally takes no arguments, but see "%parse-param" on page 152 for more information.

Every time you call yyparse(), the parser starts parsing anew, forgetting whatever state it might have been in the last time it returned. This is quite unlike the scanner yylex() generated by lex, which picks up where it left off each time you call it.

See also "YYACCEPT" on page 168 and "YYABORT" on page 168.

YYRECOVERING()

After bison detects a syntax error, it normally enters a recovery mode in which it refrains from reporting another error until it has shifted three consecutive tokens without another error. This somewhat alleviates the problem of multiple error messages resulting from a single mistake as the parser gets resynchronized.

The macro YYRECOVERING() returns nonzero if the parser is currently in the error recovery mode and zero if it is not. It is sometimes convenient to test YYRECOVERING() to decide whether to report errors discovered in an action routine.

See also "yyclearin" on page 169 and "yyerrok" on page 169.

# CHAPTER 7

Ambiguities and Conflicts

This chapter focuses on finding and correcting *conflicts* within a bison grammar. Conflicts occur when bison reports shift/reduce and reduce/reduce errors. Bison lists any errors in the listing file *name*.output, which we will describe in this chapter, but it can still be a challenge to figure out what's wrong with the grammar and how to fix it. Before reading this chapter, you should understand the general way that bison parsers work, described in Chapter 3.

The Pointer Model and Conflicts

To describe what a conflict is in terms of the bison grammar, we introduce a model of bison's operation. In this model, a *pointer* moves through the bison grammar as each individual token is read. When you start, there is one pointer (represented here as an up arrow, ↑) at the beginning of the start rule:

```
%token A B C
%%
start:     ↑ A B C;
```

As the bison parser reads tokens, the pointer moves. Say it reads A and B:

```
%token A B C
%%
start:     A B ↑ C;
```

At times, there may be more than one pointer because of the alternatives in your bison grammar. For example, suppose with the following grammar it reads A and B:

```
%token A B C D E F
%%
start:     x
    |      y;
x:    A B ↑ C D;
y:    A B ↑ E F;
```

(For the rest of the examples in this chapter, all capital letters are tokens, so we will leave out the %token and the %%.) There are two ways for pointers to disappear. One happens when a subsequent token doesn't match a partially matched rule. If the next token that the parser reads is C, the second pointer will disappear, and the first pointer advances:

```
start:      x
        |     y;
x:      A B C ↑ D;
y:      A B E F;
```

The other way for pointers to disappear is for them to merge in a common subrule. In this example, z appears in both x and y:

```
start:      x
        |     y;
x:      A B z R;
y:      A B z S;
z:      C D
```

After reading A, there are two pointers:

```
start:      x
        |     y;
x:      A ↑ B z R;
y:      A ↑ B z S;
z:      C D
```

After A B C, there is only one pointer, in rule z:

```
start:      x
        |     y;
x:      A B z R;
y:      A B z S;
z:      C ↑ D;
```

And after A B C D, the parser has completed rule z, and there again are two:

```
start:      x
        |     y;
x:      A B z ↑ R;
y:      A B z ↑ S;
z:      C D;
```

When a pointer reaches the end of a rule, the rule is *reduced*. Rule z was reduced when the pointer got to the end of it after the parser read D. Then the pointer returns to the rule from which the reduced rule was called, or as in the earlier case, the pointer splits up into the rules from which the reduced rule was called.

There is a conflict if a rule is reduced when there is more than one pointer. Here is an example of reductions with only one pointer:

```
start:      x
        |     y;
x:      A ↑ ;
y:      B ;
```

After A, there is only one pointer—in rule x—and rule x is reduced. Similarly, after B, there is only one pointer—in rule y—and rule y is reduced.

Here is an example of a conflict:

```
start:     x
     |       y;
x:     A ↑ ;
y:     A ↑ ;
```

After A, there are two pointers, at the ends of rules x and y. They both want to reduce, so it is a *reduce/reduce* conflict.

There is no conflict if there is only one pointer, even if it is the result of merging pointers into a common subrule and even if the reduction will result in more than one pointer:

```
start:     x
     |       y;
x:     z R ;
y:     z S ;
z:     A B↑ ;
```

After A B, there is one pointer, at the end of rule z, and that rule is reduced, resulting in two pointers:

```
start:     x
     |       y;
x:     z ↑ R;
y:     z ↑ S;
z:     A B;
```

But at the time of the reduction, there is only one pointer, so it is *not* a conflict.

Kinds of Conflicts

There are two kinds of conflicts, reduce/reduce and shift/reduce. Conflicts are categorized based upon what is happening with the other pointer when one pointer is reducing. If the other rule is also reducing, it is a reduce/reduce conflict. The following example has a *reduce/reduce* conflict in rules x and y:

```
start:     x
     |       y;
x:     A ↑ ;
y:     A ↑ ;
```

If the other pointer is not reducing, then it is shifting, and the conflict is a *shift/reduce* conflict. The following example has a shift/reduce conflict in rules x and y:

```
start:     x
     |       y R;
x:     A ↑ R;
y:     A ↑ ;
```

After the parser reads A, rule y needs to reduce to rule start, where R can then be accepted, while rule x can accept R immediately.

If there are more than two pointers at the time of a reduce, bison lists the conflicts. The following example has a reduce/reduce conflict in rules x and y and another reduce/reduce conflict in rules x and z:

```
start:      x
     |      y
     |      z;
x:     A ↑ ;
y:     A ↑ ;
z:     A ↑ ;
```

Let's define exactly when the reduction takes place with respect to token *lookahead* and pointers disappearing so we can keep our simple definition of conflicts correct. Here is a reduce/reduce conflict:

```
start:      x B
     |      y B;
x:     A ↑ ;
y:     A ↑ ;
```

But there is no conflict here:

```
start:      x B
     |      y C;
x:     A ↑ ;
y:     A ↑ ;
```

The reason the second example has no conflict is that a bison parser can look ahead one token beyond the A. If it sees a B, the pointer in rule y disappears before rule x is reduced. Similarly, if it sees a C, the pointer in rule x disappears before rule y is reduced.

A bison parser can look ahead only one token. The following would not be a conflict in a parser that could look ahead two tokens, but in a bison parser, it is a reduce/reduce conflict:

```
start:      x B C
     |      y B D;
x:     A ↑ ;
y:     A ↑ ;
```

A GLR parser can resolve this kind of conflict in situations where it's impractical to rewrite the grammar to avoid the conflict. See Chapter 9.

Parser States

Bison tells you about your grammar's conflicts in *name*.output, which is a description of the state machine it is generating. We will discuss what the states are, describe the contents of *name*.output, and then discuss how to find the problem in your bison grammar given a conflict described in *name*.output. You can generate *name*.output by running bison with the -v (verbose) option.

Each state corresponds to a unique combination of possible pointers in your bison grammar. Every nonempty bison grammar has at least three unique possible states: one at the beginning when no input has been accepted, one when a complete valid input has been accepted, and a third after the $end token has been accepted. The following simple example has two more states:

```
start:    A <one here> B <another here> C;
```

For future examples, we will number the states as a clear means of identification. Bison assigns a number to each state, but the particular numbers are not significant. Different versions of bison may number the states differently.

```
start:    A <state 1> B <state 2> C;
```

When a given stream of input tokens can correspond to more than one possible pointer position, then all the pointers for a given token stream correspond to one state:

```
start:        a
    |         b;
a:    X <state 1> Y <state 2> Z;
b:    X <state 1> Y <state 2> Q;
```

Different input streams can correspond to the same state when they correspond to the same pointer:

```
start:        threeAs;
threeAs: /* empty */
        | threeAs A <state 1> A <state2> A <state3>;
```

The previous grammar accepts some multiple of three As. State 1 corresponds to 1, 4, 7, ... As; state 2 corresponds to 2, 5, 8, ... As; and state 3 corresponds to 3, 6, 9, ... As. We rewrite this as a right-recursive grammar to illustrate the next point.

```
start:        threeAs;
threeAs:  /* empty */
        | A A A threeAs;
```

A position in a rule does not necessarily correspond to only one state. A given pointer in one rule can correspond to different pointers in another rule, making several states:

```
start:        threeAs X
    |         twoAs Y;
threeAs: /* empty */
        | A A A threeAs;
twoAs: /* empty */
        | A A twoAs;
```

The grammar above accepts multiples of 2 or 3 As, followed by an X for multiples of 3, or a Y for multiples of 2. Without the X or Y, the grammar would have a conflict, not knowing whether a multiple of 6 As satisfied threeAs or twoAs. It would also have a conflict if we'd used left recursion, since it would have to reduce twoAs or threeAs before it saw a final X or Y. If we number the states as follows:

```
state 1: 1, 7, ... A's accepted
state 2: 2, 8, ... A's accepted
```

```
    ...
    state 6: 6, 12, ... A's accepted
```

then the corresponding pointer positions are as follows:

```
start:      threeAs X
      |     twoAs Y;
threeAs: /* empty */
      | A <1,4> A <2,5> A <3,6> threeAs;
twoAs: /* empty */
      | A <1,3,5> A <2,4,6> twoAs;
```

That is, after the first A in threeAs, the parser could have accepted 6i+1 or 6i+4 As, where i is 0, 1, etc. Similarly, after the first A in twoAs, the parser could have accepted 6i+1, 6i+3, or 6i+5 As.

Contents of name.output

Now that we have defined states, we can look at the conflicts described in *name*.output. The format of the file has varied among versions of bison, but it always includes a listing of all the rules in the grammar and all the parser states. It usually has a summary of conflicts and other errors at the beginning, including rules that are never used, typically because of conflicts. For each state, it lists the rules and positions that correspond to the state, the shifts and reductions the parser will do when it reads various tokens in that state, and what state it will switch to after a reduction produces a non-terminal in that state. We'll show some ambiguous grammars and the *name*.output reports that identify the ambiguities. The files that bison produces show the cursor as a dot, but we'll show it as an up arrow (↑) to make it easier to read and to be consistent with the examples so far.

Reduce/Reduce Conflicts

Consider the following ambiguous grammar:

```
start:      a Y
      |      b Y ;
a:    X ;
b:    X ;
```

When we run it through bison, a typical state description is as follows:

```
state 3

    1 start: a ↑ Y

    Y  shift, and go to state 6
```

In this state, the parser has already reduced an a. If it sees a Y, it shifts the Y and moves to state 6. Anything else would be an error. The ambiguity produces a reduce/reduce conflict in state 1:

```
state 1

    3 a: X ↑
    4 b: X ↑

    Y          reduce using rule 3 (a)
    Y          [reduce using rule 4 (b)]
    $default   reduce using rule 3 (a)
```

The fourth and fifth lines show a conflict between rule 3 and rule 4 when token Y is read. In this state, it's reading an X, which may be an a or a b. They show the two rules that might be reduced. The dot shows where in the rule you are before receiving the next token. This corresponds to the pointer in the bison grammar. For reduce conflicts, the pointer is always at the end of the rule. In a conflict, the rule not used is shown in brackets; in this case bison chose to reduce rule 3, since it resolves reduce/reduce conflicts by reducing the rule that appears earlier in the grammar.

The rules may have tokens or nonterminals in them. The following ambiguous grammar:

```
    start:     a Z
         |     b Z;
    a:    X y;
    b:    X y;
    y:    Y;
```

produces a parser with this state:

```
state 6

    3 a: X y .
    4 b: X y .

    Z          reduce using rule 3 (a)
    Z          [reduce using rule 4 (b)]
    $default   reduce using rule 3 (a)
```

In this state, the parser has already reduced a Y to a y, but the y could complete either an a or a b. Transitions on nonterminals can lead to reduce/reduce conflicts just as tokens can. It's easy to tell the difference if you use uppercase token names, as we have.

The rules that conflict do not have to be identical. This grammar:

```
    start:     A B x Z
         |     y Z;
    x:    C;
    y:    A B C;
```

when processed by bison, produces a grammar containing this state:

```
state 7

    3 x: C .
    4 y: A B C .

    Z          reduce using rule 3 (x)
```

```
Z          [reduce using rule 4 (y)]
$default  reduce using rule 3 (x)
```

In state 7, the parser has already accepted A B C. Rule x has only C in it, because in the start rule from which x is called, A B is accepted before reaching x. The C could complete either an x or a y. Bison again resolves the conflict by reducing the earlier rule in the grammar, in this case rule 3.

Shift/Reduce Conflicts

Identifying a shift/reduce conflict is a little harder. To identify the conflict, we will do the following:

- Find the shift/reduce error in *name*.output.
- Identify the reduce rule.
- Identify the relevant shift rule(s).
- See what state the reduce rule reduces to.
- Deduce the token stream that will produce the conflict.

This grammar contains a shift/reduce conflict:

```
start:     x
    |      y R;
x:     A R;
y:     A;
```

Bison produces this complaint:

```
state 1

    3 x: A . R
    4 y: A .

    R  shift, and go to state 5

    R  [reduce using rule 4 (y)]
```

State 1 has a shift/reduce conflict between shifting token R, which moves to state 5, and reducing rule 4 when it reads an R. Rule 4 is rule y, as shown in this line:

```
    4 y: A .
```

You can find the reduce rule in a shift/reduce conflict the same way you find both rules in a reduce/reduce conflict. The reduction number is listed in the reduce using line. In the previous case, the rule with the shift conflict is the only rule left in the state:

```
    3 x: A . R
```

The parser is in rule x, having read A and about to accept R. The shift conflict rule was easy to find in this case, because it is the only rule left, and it shows that the next token

---

is R. Bison resolves shift/reduce conflicts in favor of the shift, so in this case if it receives an R, it shifts to state 5.

The next thing showing may be a rule instead of a token:

```
start:      x1
       |    x2
       |    y R;
x1:    A R;
x2:    A z;
y:     A;
z:     R;
```

Bison reports several conflicts, including this one:

```
state 1

    4 x1: A ↑ R
    5 x2: A ↑ z
    6 y: A ↑

    R  shift, and go to state 6

    R  [reduce using rule 6 (y)]

    z  go to state 7
```

In the previous example, the reduction rule is as follows:

```
    6 y: A ↑
```

so that leaves two candidates for the shift conflict:

```
    4 x1: A ↑ R
    5 x2: A ↑ z
```

Rule x1 uses the next token, R, so you know it is part of the shift conflict, but rule x2 shows the next symbol (not token). You have to look at the rule for z to find out whether it starts with an R. In this case it does, so there is a conflict for an A followed by an R: it could be an x1, an x2 that includes a z, or a y followed by an R.

There could be more rules in a conflicting state, and they may not all accept an R. Consider this extended version of the grammar:

```
start:      x1
       |    x2
       |    x3
       |    y R;
x1:    A R;
x2:    A z1;
x3:    A z2
y:     A;
z1:    R;
z2:    S;
```

Bison produces a listing with this state:

```
state 1

    5 x1: A ↑ R
    6 x2: A ↑ z1
    7 x3: A ↑ z2
    8 y: A ↑

    R  shift, and go to state 7
    S  shift, and go to state 8

    R  [reduce using rule 8 (y)]

    z1  go to state 9
    z2  go to state 10
```

The conflict is between shifting to state 7 and reducing rule 8. The reduce problem, rule 8, is the rule for y. The rule for x1 has a shift problem, because the next token after the dot is R. It is not immediately obvious whether x2 or x3 caused conflicts, because they show rules z1 and z2 following the dots. When you look at rules z1 and z2, you find that z1 contains an R next and z2 contains an S next, so x2 that uses z1 is part of the shift conflict and x3 is not.

In each of our last two shift/reduce conflict examples, can you also see a reduce/reduce conflict? Run bison, and look in *name*.output to check your answer.

Review of Conflicts in name.output

We'll review the relationship among our pointer model, conflicts, and *name*.output. First, here is a reduce/reduce conflict:

```
start:      A B x Z
    |         y Z;
x:    C;
y:    A B C;
```

The bison listing contains the following:

```
state 7

    3 x: C ↑
    4 y: A B C ↑

    Z          reduce using rule 3 (x)
    Z          [reduce using rule 4 (y)]
    $default   reduce using rule 3 (x)
```

There is a conflict because if the next token is Z, bison wants to reduce rules 3 and 4, which are the rules for both x and y. Or using our pointer model, there are two pointers, and both are reducing:

```
start:      A B x z
    |         y Z;
```

```
x:    c ↑ ;
y:    A B C ↑ ;
```

Here is a shift/reduce conflict example:

```
start:    x
    |     y R;
x:        A R;
y:        A;
```

Bison reports this conflict:

```
state 1

    3 x: A ↑ R
    4 y: A ↑

    R  shift, and go to state 5

    R  [reduce using rule 4 (y)]
```

If the next token is R, bison wants both to reduce the rule for y and to shift an R in the rule for x, causing a conflict. Or there are two pointers, and one is reducing:

```
start:    x
    |     y R;
x:    A ↑ R;
y:    A ↑ ;
```

Common Examples of Conflicts

The three most common situations that produce shift/reduce conflicts are expression grammars, if/then/else, and nested lists of items. After we see how to identify these three situations, we'll look at ways to get rid of the conflicts.

Expression Grammars

Our first example is adapted from the original 1975 Unix yacc manual.

```
expr: TERMINAL
    | expr '-' expr ;
```

The state with a conflict is as follows:

```
state 5

    2 expr: expr ↑ '-' expr
    2     | expr '-' expr ↑

    '-'  shift, and go to state 4

    '-'      [reduce using rule 2 (expr)]
    $default  reduce using rule 2 (expr)
```

Bison tells us that there is a shift/reduce conflict when it reads the minus token. We can add our pointers to get the following:

```
expr: expr ↑ - expr ;
expr: expr - expr ↑ ;
```

These are in the same rule, not even different alternatives with the same LHS. You can have a state where your pointers can be in two different places in the same rule, because the grammar is recursive. (In fact, all of the examples in this section are recursive. Most tricky bison problems turn out to involve recursive rules.)

After accepting two exprs and -, the pointer is at the end of rule expr, as shown in the second line of the earlier pointer example. But expr - expr is also an expr, so the pointer can also be just after the first expr, as shown in the first line of the earlier example. If the next token is not -, then the pointer in the first line disappears because it wants - next, so you are back to one pointer. But if the next token is -, then the second line wants to reduce, and the first line wants to shift, causing a conflict.

To solve this conflict, look at *name*.output, shown earlier, to find the source of the conflict. Get rid of irrelevant rules in the state (there are not any in this tiny example), and you get the two pointers we just discussed. It becomes clear that the problem is as follows:

```
expr - expr - expr
```

The middle expr might be the second expr of an expr - expr, in which case the input is interpreted as follows:

```
(expr - expr) - expr
```

which is left associative, or might be the first expr, in which case the input is interpreted as follows:

```
expr - (expr - expr)
```

which is right associative. After reading expr - expr, the parser could reduce if using left associativity or shift using right associativity. If not instructed to prefer one or the other, this ambiguity causes a shift/reduce conflict, which bison resolves by choosing the shift. Figure 7-1 shows the two possible parses.

Later in this chapter, we cover the ways to handle this kind of conflict.

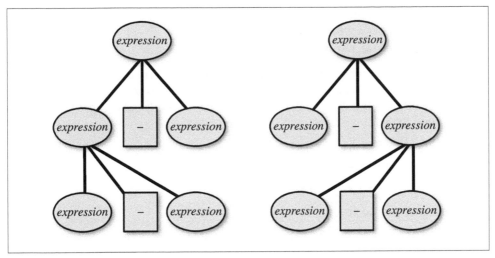

Figure 7-1. Two parses of expr - expr - expr

IF/THEN/ELSE

Our next example is also from the Unix yacc manual. Again, we have added a terminal symbol for completeness:

```
stmt:   IF '(' cond ')' stmt
    |   IF '(' cond ')' stmt ELSE stmt
    |   TERMINAL;
cond:   TERMINAL;
```

Bison complains:

```
State 9 conflicts: 1 shift/reduce
  ...

state 9

    1 stmt: IF '(' cond ')' stmt ↑
    2     | IF '(' cond ')' stmt ↑ ELSE stmt

    ELSE  shift, and go to state 10

    ELSE     [reduce using rule 1 (stmt)]
    $default  reduce using rule 1 (stmt)
```

In terms of pointers this is as follows:

```
stmt: IF ( cond ) stmt ↑ ;
stmt: IF ( cond ) stmt ↑ ELSE stmt ;
```

The first line is the reduce part of the conflict, and the second is the shift part. This time they are different rules with the same LHS. To figure out what is going wrong, we check to see where the first line reduces to. It has to be a call to stmt, followed by an ELSE. There is only one place where that happens:

> stmt: IF (cond) stmt *<return to here>* ELSE stmt ;

After the reduction, the pointer returns to the same spot where it is for the shift part of the conflict. This problem is very similar to the one with expr - expr - expr in the previous example. And using similar logic, in order to reduce IF (cond) stmt into stmt and end up here:

> stmt: IF (cond) stmt *<here>* ELSE stmt ;

you have to have this token stream:

> IF (cond) IF (cond) stmt ELSE

Again, do you want to group it like this:

> IF (cond) { IF (cond) stmt } ELSE stmt

or like this?

> IF (cond) { IF (cond) stmt ELSE stmt }

The next section explains what to do about this kind of conflict.

Nested List Grammar

Our final example is a simple version of a problem that novice bison programmers often encounter:

```
start:          outerList Z ;
outerList:  /* empty */
        |       outerList outerListItem ;

outerListItem:      innerList ;

innerList:  /* empty */
        |       innerList innerListItem ;

innerListItem:      I ;
```

Bison reports this conflict:

```
state 2

    1 start: outerList ↑ Z
    3 outerList: outerList ↑ outerListItem

    Z  shift, and go to state 4

    Z          [reduce using rule 5 (innerList)]
    $default   reduce using rule 5 (innerList)

    outerListItem  go to state 5
    innerList      go to state 6
```

Once again we can analyze the problem step by step. The reduce rule is the empty alternative of innerList. That leaves two candidates for the shift problem. Rule start is one, because it explicitly takes Z as the next token. The nonempty alternative of outerList might be a candidate, if it takes Z next. We see that outerList includes an outerListItem, which is an innerList. In this situation, innerList can't include an innerListItem, because that includes an I, and this conflict occurs only when the next token is a Z. But an innerList can be empty, so the outerListItem involves no tokens, so we might actually be at the end of the outerList as well, since as the first line in the conflict report told us, an outerList can be followed by a Z.

This all boils down to this state: We have just finished an innerList, possibly empty, or an outerList, possibly empty. How can it not know which list it has just finished? Look at the two list expressions. They can both be empty, and the inner one sits in the outer one without any token to say it is starting or finishing the inner loop. Assume the input stream consists solely of a Z. Is it an empty outerList, or is it an outerList with one item, an empty innerList? That's ambiguous.

The problem with this grammar is that it is redundant. It has to have a loop within a loop, with nothing to separate them. Since this grammar actually accepts a possibly empty list of Is followed by a Z, it can easily be rewritten using only one recursive rule:

```
start:              outerList Z ;
outerList:      /* empty */
    |           outerList outerListItem ;
outerListItem:      I ;
```

But rewriting it this way is rarely the right thing to do. More likely there really are supposed to be two nested lists, but you forgot to include punctuation in outerListItem to delimit the inner from the outer loop. We offer some suggestions later in this chapter.

How Do You Fix the Conflict?

The rest of this chapter describes what to do with a conflict once you've figured out what it is. We'll discuss how to fix classes of conflicts that have commonly caused trouble for bison users.

When trying to resolve conflicts, start with the rules that are involved in the most conflicts, and work your way down the list. More often than not, when you resolve the major conflicts, many of the minor ones will go away, too.

If you're writing a parser for a language you're inventing, conflicts in the parser often indicate ambiguities or inconsistencies in the language's definition. First figure out what's causing the conflict, and then decide whether the language is OK and you just need to adjust the grammar to describe the language correctly or whether the language is ambiguous, in which case you may want to change both the language and the grammar to be unambiguous. Languages that bison has trouble parsing are often hard for people to parse in their heads; you'll often end up with a better language design if you change your language to remove the conflicts.

IF/THEN/ELSE (Shift/Reduce)

We saw this conflict earlier in this chapter. Here we describe what to do with the shift/ reduce conflict once you've tracked it down. It turns out that the default way that bison resolves this particular conflict is usually what you want it to do anyway. How do you know it's doing what you want it to do? Your choices are to (1) be good enough at reading bison descriptions, (2) be masochistic enough to decode the *name*.output listing, or (3) test the generated code to death. Once you've verified that you're getting what you want, you ought to make bison quit complaining. Conflict warnings may confuse or annoy anyone trying to maintain your code, and if there are other conflicts in the grammar that indicate genuine errors, it's hard to tell the real problems from the false alarms.

The standard way to resolve this conflict is to have separate rules for matched and unmatched IF/THEN statements and to rewrite the grammar this way:

```
stmt:       matched
    |       unmatched
    ;
matched:    other_stmt
    |       IF expr THEN matched ELSE matched
    ;
unmatched:  IF expr THEN stmt
    |       IF expr THEN matched ELSE unmatched
    ;
other_stmt: /* rules for other kinds of statement */  ...
```

The nonterminal other_stmt represents all of the other possible statements in the language.

It's also possible to use explicit precedence to tell bison which way to resolve the conflict and to keep it from issuing a warning. If your language uses a THEN keyword (as Pascal does), you can do this:

```
%nonassoc THEN
%nonassoc ELSE

%%

stmt:     IF expr THEN stmt
    |     IF expr stmt ELSE stmt
    ;
```

In languages that don't have a THEN keyword, you can use a fake token and %prec to accomplish the same result:

```
%nonassoc LOWER_THAN_ELSE
%nonassoc ELSE
```

```
%%

stmt:     IF expr stmt           %prec LOWER_THAN_ELSE ;
      |   IF expr stmt ELSE stmt;
```

The shift/reduce conflict here is a conflict between shifting an ELSE token and reducing a stmt rule. You need to assign a precedence to the token (%nonassoc ELSE) and to the rule, with %nonassoc THEN or %nonassoc LOWER_THAN_ELSE and %prec LOWER_THAN_ELSE. The precedence of the token to shift must be higher than the precedence of the rule to reduce, so %nonassoc ELSE must come after %nonassoc THEN or %nonassoc LOWER_THAN_ELSE. It makes no difference for this application if you use %nonassoc, %left, or %right, since there's no situation with a conflict that involves shifting a token and reducing a rule containing the same token.

The goal here is to hide a conflict you know about and understand, *not* to hide any others. When you're trying to mute bison's warnings about other shift/reduce conflicts, the further you get from the previous example, the more careful you should be. Use %nonassoc, so if you accidentally do add other rules that create such a conflict, bison will still report it. Other shift/reduce conflicts may be amenable to a simple change in the bison description. And, as we mentioned, *any* conflict can be fixed by changing the language. For example, the IF/THEN/ELSE conflict can be eliminated by insisting on BEGIN-END or braces around the stmt.

What would happen if you swapped the precedence of the token to shift and the rule to reduce? The normal IF-ELSE handling makes the following two equivalent:

```
if expr if expr stmt else stmt
if expr { if expr stmt else stmt }
```

It seems only fair that swapping the precedence would make the following two equivalent, right?

```
if expr if expr stmt else stmt
if expr { if expr stmt } else stmt
```

Nope. That's not what it does. Having higher precedence on the shift (normal IF-ELSE) makes it always shift the ELSE. Swapping the precedence makes it *never* shift the ELSE, so your IF-ELSE can no longer have an else.

Normal IF-ELSE processing associates the ELSE with the most recent IF. Suppose you want it some other way. One possibility is that you allow only one ELSE with a sequence of IFs, and the ELSE is associated with the first IF. This would require a two-level statement definition, as follows:

```
%nonassoc LOWER_THAN_ELSE
%nonassoc ELSE

%%

stmt:     IF expr stmt2 %prec LOWER_THAN_ELSE
      |   IF expr stmt2 ELSE stmt;
```

```
stmt2:   IF expr stmt2;
```

But don't do that, since a language is extremely counterintuitive.

Loop Within a Loop (Shift/Reduce)

This conflict occurs when the grammar has two nested list-creating loops, with no punctuation to say where the boundaries between entries in the outer list are.

```
start:            outerList Z ;
outerList: /* empty */
        |    outerList outerListItem ;

outerListItem:   innerList ;
innerList: /* empty */
        |    innerList innerListItem ;

innerListItem:   I ;
```

Assuming that's really what you want, the resolution of this conflict depends on whether you want repetitions to be treated as one outer loop and many inner loops or as many outer loops of one inner loop each. The difference is whether the code associated with outerListItem gets executed once for each repetition or once for each set of repetitions. If it makes no difference, choose one or the other arbitrarily. If you want many outer loops, remove the inner loop:

```
start:            outerList Z ;

outerList:    /* empty */
        |        outerList innerListItem ;

innerListItem:    I ;
```

If you want many inner loops, remove the outer loop:

```
start:            innerList Z ;

innerList:    /* empty */
        |        innerList innerListItem ;

innerListItem:  I ;
```

In practice, it's pretty rare to have a pair of nested lists with no punctuation. It's confusing to bison, and it's confusing to us humans, too. If the outer list is something like a list of statements in a programming language, if you change the language and put a semicolon after each outerListItem, the conflicts go away:

```
start:            outerList Z ;
outerList: /* empty */
        |    outerList outerListItem ';' ;

outerListItem:   innerList ;
innerList: /* empty */
```

```
     |     innerList innerListItem ;

innerListItem:   I ;
```

Expression Precedence (Shift/Reduce)

```
expr:        expr  '+'  expr
     |       expr  '-'  expr
     |       expr  '*'  expr
     |       ...
     ;
```

If you describe an expression grammar but forget to define the precedence with %left and %right, you get a truckload of shift/reduce conflicts. Assigning precedence to all of the operators should resolve the conflicts. Keep in mind that if you use any of the operators in other ways, for example, using a - to indicate a range of values, the precedence can also mask conflicts in the other contexts.

Limited Lookahead (Shift/Reduce or Reduce/Reduce)

Most shift/reduce conflicts are because of bison's limited lookahead. That is, a parser that could look further ahead would not have a conflict. For example:

```
statement: command optional_keyword '('  identifier_list ')'
     ;

optional_keyword: /* blank */
     |      '(' keyword ')'
     ;
```

The example describes a command line that starts with a required command, ends with a required identifier list in parentheses, and has in the middle an optional keyword in parentheses. Bison gets a shift/reduce conflict with this when it gets to the first parenthesis in the input stream, because it can't tell whether it is part of the optional keyword or the identifier list. In the first case, the parser would shift the parenthesis within the optional_keyword rule, and in the second, it would reduce an empty optional_keyword and move on to the identifier list. If a bison parser could look further ahead, it could tell the difference between the two. But a parser using the regular bison parsing algorithm can't.

The default is for bison to choose the shift, which means it always assumes the optional keyword is there. (You can't really call it optional in that case.) If you apply precedence, you could get the conflict to resolve in favor of the reduction, which would mean you could never have the optional keyword.

We can *flatten* the description, expanding the optional_keyword rule where it occurs in statement:

```
statement:     command '(' keyword ')' '(' identifier_list ')'
         |  command '(' identifier_list ')'
         ;
```

By flattening the list, we allow the parser to scan ahead with multiple possible pointers until it sees a keyword or identifier, at which point it can tell which rule to use.

Flattening is a practical solution in this example, but when more rules are involved, it rapidly becomes impractical because of the exponential expansion of the bison description. You may run into a shift/reduce conflict from limited lookahead for which your only practical solution is to change the language or use a GLR parser.

It's also possible to get a reduce/reduce conflict because of limited lookahead. One way is to have an overlap of alternatives:

```
statement:  command_type_1 ':' '[' ...
         |  command_type_2 ':' '(' ...

command_type_1:  CMD_1  | CMD_2 | CMD_COMMON  ;

command_type_2:  CMD_A  | CMD_B | CMD_COMMON  ;
```

If the input includes CMD_COMMON, the parser can't tell whether it's parsing a command_type_1 or command_type_2 until it sees the bracket or parenthesis, but that's two tokens ahead. The solution for this is flattening, as we did earlier, or making the alternatives disjoint, as described in the following section.

You can also get a reduce/reduce conflict from limited lookahead because actions in the middle of a rule are really anonymous rules that must be reduced:

```
statement: command_list { <action for '['form> }':' '[' ...
         |  command_list { <action for '('form> }':' '(' ...
```

This is already flattened, so there's nothing you can do to get it to work without using a GLR parser. It simply needs a two-token lookahead, and LALR(1) parsers don't have that. Unless you're doing some sort of exotic communication between the parser and lexer, you can just move the action over:

```
statement:  command_list ':' '[' { <action for '[' form> } ...
         |  command_list ':' '(' { <action for '(' form> } ...
```

Overlap of Alternatives (Reduce/Reduce)

In this case, you have two alternative rules with the same LHS, and the inputs accepted by them overlap partially. The easiest way to make this work in a regular bison parser is to make the two input sets disjoint. For example:

```
person:     girls
       |    boys
       ;

girls:      ALICE
       |    BETTY
```

```
            |       CHRIS
            |       DARRYL
      ;

boys:       ALLEN
            |       BOB
            |       CHRIS
            |       DARRYL
      ;
```

You will get a reduce/reduce conflict on CHRIS and DARRYL because bison can't tell
whether they're intended to be girls or boys. There are several ways to resolve the
conflict. One is as follows:

```
person:     girls  | boys | either;

girls:      ALICE
            |       BETTY
      ;

boys:       ALLEN
            |       BOB
      ;

either:     CHRIS
            |       DARRYL
      ;
```

But what if these lists were really long or were complex rules rather than just lists of
keywords? What would you do if you wanted to minimize duplication and girls and
boys were referenced many other places in the bison description? Here's one possibility:

```
person:     just_girls
            |       just_boys
            |       either
      ;

girls:      just_girls
            |       either
      ;

boys:       just_boys
            |       either
      ;

just_girls: ALICE
            |       BETTY
      ;

just_boys:  ALLEN
            |       BOB
      ;

either:     CHRIS
```

```
    |   DARRYL
    ;
```

All references to **boys | girls** have to be fixed. GLR doesn't help much here since the original grammar is ambiguous, so you'd still have to deal with the ambiguity.

But what if it's impractical to make the alternatives disjoint? If you just can't figure out a clean way to break up the overlap, then you'll have to leave the reduce/reduce conflict, use a GLR parser, and deal explicitly with the ambiguity using the techniques discussed in Chapter 9.

If you don't use a GLR parser, bison will use its default disambiguating rule for reduce/reduce, which is to choose the first definition in the bison description. So in the first **girls | boys** example earlier, CHRIS and DARRYL would always be **girls**. Swap the positions of the **boys** and **girls** lists, and CHRIS and DARRYL are always **boys**. You'll still get the reduce/reduce warning, and bison will make the alternatives disjoint for you, exactly what you were trying to avoid.

Summary

Ambiguities and conflicts within the bison grammar are just one type of coding error, one that is problematic to find and correct. This chapter has presented some techniques for correcting these errors. In the chapter that follows, we will look at other sources of errors.

Our goal in this chapter has been for you understand the problem at a high enough level that you can fix it. To review how to get to that point:

- Find the shift/reduce error in *name*.output.
- Identify the reduce rule.
- Identify the relevant shift rule(s).
- See where the reduce rule will reduce back to.
- With this much information, you should be able to identify the token stream leading up to the conflict.

Seeing where the reduce rule reduces to is typically straightforward, as we have shown. Sometimes a grammar is so complicated that it is not practical to use our "hunt-around" method, and you will need to learn the detailed operation of the state machine to find the states to which you reduce.

Exercises

1. All reduce/reduce conflicts and many shift/reduce conflicts are caused by ambiguous grammars. Beyond the fact that bison doesn't like them, why are ambiguous grammars usually a bad idea?

2. Find a grammar for a substantial programming language like C, C++, or Fortran, and run it through bison. Does the grammar have conflicts? (Nearly all of them do.) Go through the *name*.output listing, and determine what causes the conflicts. How hard would they be to fix?

3. After doing the previous exercise, opine about why languages are usually defined and implemented with ambiguous grammars.

# CHAPTER 8

Error Reporting and Recovery

The previous chapters discussed techniques for finding errors within bison grammars. In this chapter, we turn our attention to the other side of error detection—how the parser and lexical analyzer detect errors. This chapter presents some techniques to incorporate error detection and reporting into a parser. We'll make a modified version of the SQL parser from Chapter 4 that demonstrates them.

Bison provides the **error** token and the **yyerror()** routine, which are typically sufficient for early versions of a tool. However, as any program begins to mature, especially a programming tool, it becomes important to provide better error recovery, which allows for detection of errors in later portions of the file, and to provide better error reporting.

Error Reporting

Error reporting should give as much detail about the error as possible. The default bison error declares only that it found a syntax error and stops parsing. In our examples, we used **yylineno** to report the line number. This provides the location of the error but does not report any other errors within the file or where in the specified line the error occurs. The bison locations feature, described later in this chapter, is an easy way to pinpoint the location of an error, down to the exact line and character numbers. In our example, we print out the locations, but precise location information would also allow a visual interface to highlight the relevant text.

It is often useful to categorize the possible errors, perhaps building an array of error types and defining symbolic constants to identify the errors. For example, in many languages a common error is to fail to terminate a string. Another error might be using the wrong type of string (a quoted string instead of an identifier, or vice versa). A parser might detect the following:

- General syntactic errors (e.g., a line that makes no sense)
- A nonterminated string
- The wrong type of string (quoted instead of unquoted, or vice versa)

- A premature end-of-file within a comment or other item that should have a terminator
- Names with multiple definitions, or names used but not defined

The duty for error detection does not lie with bison alone, however. Many fundamental errors are better detected by the lexer. For instance, the normal quoted string matching pattern is as follows:

```
\"[^\"\n]*\"
```

We would like to detect an unterminated quoted string. One potential solution is to add a new rule to catch unterminated strings as we did in the SQL parser in Chapter 4. If a quoted string runs all the way to the end of the line without a closing quote, we print an error:

```
\"[^\"\n]*\"  {
                yylval.string = yytext;
                return QSTRING;
             }
\"[^\"\n]*$ {
                warning("Unterminated string");
                yylval.string = yytext;
                return QSTRING;
             }
```

This technique of accepting not quite valid input and then reporting it with an error or warning is a powerful one that can be used to improve the error reporting of the compiler. If we had not added this rule, the compiler would have reported the generic "syntax error" message; by reporting the specific error, we can tell the user precisely what to fix. Later in this chapter, we will describe ways to resynchronize and attempt to continue operation after such errors.

The bison equivalent of accepting erroneous input is demonstrated by testing for the improper use of a quoted string for an identifier. For example, in MySQL it can be easy to confuse a quoted string in single forward quotes, `'string'`, with a quoted name in back quotes, `` `name` ``. In contexts where only one is valid, you can add a rule for the other and diagnose it in detail. Here's a version of the column_list rule that is used as the target of SELECT ... INTO:

```
column_list: NAME { emit("COLUMN %s", $1); free($1); $$ = 1; }
    | STRING        { yyerror("Column name %s cannot be a string", $1);
                      emit("COLUMN %s", $1); free($1); $$ = 1; }
    | column_list ',' NAME   { emit("COLUMN %s", $3); free($3); $$ = $1 + 1; }
    | column_list ',' STRING { yyerror("Column name %s cannot be a string", $3);
                               emit("COLUMN %s", $3); free($3); $$ = $1 + 1; }
    ;
```

If the user types a string rather than a name, it calls yyerror() to report it, and then it goes ahead pretending the string was a name.

Some simple flex hackery can let you produce better error reports than the rather dull defaults. A very simple technique that we used in the SQL parser reports the line number and current token. The `yylineno` option automatically increments the line number on each \n character, and the current token is always available in `yytext`, so a simple but useful error routine would be the following:

```
void yyerror(char *s)
{
        printf("%d: %s at %s\n", yylineno, s, yytext);
}
```

A slightly more complex trick saves the input a line at a time:

```
%code {
char linebuf[500];
%}
%%
\n.*  { strncpy(linebuf, yytext+1, sizeof(linebuf)); /* save the next line */
        yyless(1);      /* give back all but the \n to rescan */
      }
%%

void yyerror(char *s)
{
        printf("%d: %s at %s in this line:\n%s\n",
              lineno, s, yytext, linebuf);
}
```

The pattern \n.* matches a newline character and the entire next line. The action code saves the line, and then it gives it back to the scanner with `yyless()`.

To pinpoint the exact position of an erroneous token in the input line, we need to use locations.

Locations

The bison *locations* feature associates a section of the input file identified by line and column numbers with every symbol in the parser. Locations are stored in YYLTYPE structures, which by default are declared as follows:

```
typedef struct YYLTYPE
{
  int first_line;
  int first_column;
  int last_line;
  int last_column;
} YYLTYPE;
```

Later we'll see how to override this if, for example, you want to add a filename or other extra information to each location.

The lexer sets the location for each token it returns, and every time it reduces a rule, the parser automatically sets the location of the newly created LHS symbol to run from the beginning of the first RHS symbol to the end of the last RHS symbol. Within action code in the parser, you can refer to the location of the LHS symbol as @$ and the RHS symbols as @1, @2, and so forth. The lexer has to put the location information for each token into yylloc, which the parser defines each time it returns a token. Fortunately, we can do this without having to add code to each lexer action.

Adding Locations to the Parser

Bison automatically adds the location code to the parser if it sees a reference to an @N location in the action code, or you can put the %locations declaration in the declaration part of the program.

We also need to change the error routines to use the location information. In our SQL example, we have both yyerror(), which uses the current location in yylloc, and a new routine lyyerror(), which takes an extra argument, which is the location of the error. In both cases, it prints out the location information (if any) before the error report.

```
/* in code section at the end of the parser */
void
yyerror(char *s, ...)
{
  va_list ap;
  va_start(ap, s);

  if(yylloc.first_line)
    fprintf(stderr, "%d.%d-%d.%d: error: ", yylloc.first_line, yylloc.first_column,
        yylloc.last_line, yylloc.last_column);
  vfprintf(stderr, s, ap);
  fprintf(stderr, "\n");

}

void
lyyerror(YYLTYPE t, char *s, ...)
{
  va_list ap;
  va_start(ap, s);

  if(t.first_line)
    fprintf(stderr, "%d.%d-%d.%d: error: ", t.first_line, t.first_column,
        t.last_line, t.last_column);
  vfprintf(stderr, s, ap);
  fprintf(stderr, "\n");
}
```

Note the defensive check for a nonzero first_line value; a rule with an empty RHS uses the location information of the previous item in the parse stack.

Within the parser proper, we change all the yyerror calls to lyyerror to report the appropriate token. For example:

```
column_list: NAME          { emit("COLUMN %s", $1); free($1); $$ = 1; }
    | STRING               { lyyerror(@1, "string %s found where name required", $1);
                             emit("COLUMN %s", $1); free($1); $$ = 1; }

    ...
```

```
select_opts:                    { $$ = 0; }
 | select_opts ALL              { if($$ & 01) lyyerror(@2,"duplicate ALL option"); $$ = $1 | 01; }
   ...
insert_asgn_list:
     NAME COMPARISON expr  { if ($2 != 4) {
                               lyyerror(@2,"bad insert assignment to %s", $1); YYERROR;
                            }
                            emit("ASSIGN %s", $1); free($1); $$ = 1;
                          }
```

That's all we need to do to the parser, since the default location update code does the right thing for us.

Adding Locations to the Lexer

Since locations need to report the line and column range for errors, the lexer needs to track the current line and column each time it scans a token and return that information to the parser in yylloc. Fortunately, a little-known feature called *YY_USER_ACTION* makes that very simple. If you define the macro YY_USER_ACTION in the first part of your lexer, it will be invoked for each token recognized by yylex, before calling the action code. We define a new variable, yycolumn, to remember the current column number, and we define YY_USER_ACTION as follows in the definition section of the lexer:

```
%code {
/* handle locations */
int yycolumn = 1;

#define YY_USER_ACTION yylloc.first_line = yyloc.last_line = yylineno; \
    yylloc.first_column = yycolumn; yylloc.last_column = yycolumn+yyleng-1; \
    yycolumn += yyleng;
%}
```

Since yyleng, the length of the token, is already set, we can use that to fill in yylloc and update yycolumn. In a few cases (comments and whitespace), the token isn't returned to the parser and the lexer keeps going, but it doesn't hurt to fill in yylloc anyway. This takes care of the vast majority of location bookkeeping.

The last thing we have to do is to reset yycolumn to 1 whenever there's a newline. (Flex already handles yylineno for us.)

```
NOT[ \t]+EXISTS      { yylval.subtok = 1; return EXISTS; }

ON[ \t]+DUPLICATE { return ONDUPLICATE; } /* hack due to limited lookahead */

<COMMENT>\n      { yycolumn = 1; }
<COMMENT><<EOF>> { yyerror("unclosed comment"); }

[ \t]            /* whitespace */
\n               { yycolumn = 1; }
```

In each pattern that can match a newline, we've separated out the \n into a separate pattern and set yycolumn to 1. We've also simplified the patterns for NOT EXISTS and

ON DUPLICATE so they don't allow newlines. The alternative would be to manually rescan the tokens to check for newlines and set yycolumn to the number of characters after the newline.

That's enough to report errors with the exact line and column numbers. Since it's so easy to do, there's little reason not to use locations in your bison parsers even if you don't need the exact column numbers of each token and rule.

More Sophisticated Locations with Filenames

Most of the parsers we've written can handle more than one input file. How hard would it be to include the filename in the location data? Not very, it turns out. We have to define our own YYLTYPE that includes a pointer to the filename. We redefine the parser macro YYLLOC_DEFAULT that combines the location information when the parser reduces a rule, change the code in YY_USER_ACTION in the lexer to put the filename into yylloc for each token, and make a few other small changes to remember the name of the file the parser is reading. We add this section to the definition section of the parser:

```
%code requires {

char *filename; /* current filename here for the lexer */

typedef struct YYLTYPE {
  int first_line;
  int first_column;
  int last_line;
  int last_column;
  char *filename;
} YYLTYPE;
# define YYLTYPE_IS_DECLARED 1 /* alert the parser that we have our own definition */

# define YYLLOC_DEFAULT(Current, Rhs, N)                            \
    do                                                              \
      if (N)                                                        \
        {                                                           \
          (Current).first_line   = YYRHSLOC (Rhs, 1).first_line;    \
          (Current).first_column = YYRHSLOC (Rhs, 1).first_column;  \
          (Current).last_line    = YYRHSLOC (Rhs, N).last_line;     \
          (Current).last_column  = YYRHSLOC (Rhs, N).last_column;   \
          (Current).filename     = YYRHSLOC (Rhs, 1).filename;      \
        }                                                           \
      else                                                          \
        { /* empty RHS */                                           \
          (Current).first_line   = (Current).last_line    =         \
            YYRHSLOC (Rhs, 0).last_line;                             \
          (Current).first_column = (Current).last_column =          \
            YYRHSLOC (Rhs, 0).last_column;                          \
          (Current).filename  = NULL;                   /* new */ \
        }                                                           \
    while (0)
}
```

Rather than try to write the structure and macro from scratch, I looked at the generated C code for the first version of the parser with locations, copied the definitions of YYLTYPE and YYLLOC_DEFAULT, and modified them a little. The default declaration of YYLTYPE is enclosed in #if !YYLTYPE_IS_DECLARED, and the default declaration of YYLLOC_DEFAULT is enclosed in #ifndef YYLLOC_DEFAULT, so our new versions have to define them to turn off the default versions.

This code is enclosed in a %code requires { } block. The normal %code { %} block puts the code after the default definition of YYLTYPE, which is too late in the generated C program, and doesn't put a copy on the generated header file. The requires tells bison to copy the code ahead of the default versions and also into the header file.

This version of YYLTYPE includes the four standard fields, as well as a pointer to the filename. Then comes a definition of YYLTYPE_IS_DECLARED to prevent the standard version of YYLTYPE.

The long YYLLOC_DEFAULT macro copies location information from the RHS of a rule to the new LHS symbol. The three arguments to the macro are Current, the location information for the LHS; Rhs, the address of the first RHS location structure; and N, the number of symbols on the RHS. The internal macro YYRHSLOC returns the location structure for a particular RHS symbol. If N is nonzero, that is, there's at least one RHS symbol, it copies the relevant information from the first and Nth symbols. The do ... while(0) is a C idiom to make the macro expansion a statement that will parse correctly when the macro is followed by a semicolon. (Remember that there's no semicolon after the } at the end of a block such as the else clause here.) Only the two lines marked new are new; the rest is copied from the default YYLLOC_DEFAULT.

Having added the filename to the YYLTYPE structure, we add small amounts of code to yyerror and lyyerror to report the filename and to main() to set filename to the filename or the string (stdin) before starting the parser.

```
void
yyerror(char *s, ...)
{
  va_list ap;
  va_start(ap, s);

  if(yylloc.first_line)
    fprintf(stderr, "%s:%d.%d-%d.%d: error: ", yylloc.filename, yylloc.first_line,
    yylloc.first_column, yylloc.last_line, yylloc.last_column);
  vfprintf(stderr, s, ap);
  fprintf(stderr, "\n");

}

void
lyyerror(YYLTYPE t, char *s, ...)
{
  va_list ap;
  va_start(ap, s);
```

```
    if(t.first_line)
      fprintf(stderr, "%s:%d.%d-%d.%d: error: ", t.filename, t.first_line,
        t.first_column, t.last_line, t.last_column);
    vfprintf(stderr, s, ap);
    fprintf(stderr, "\n");
}

main(int ac, char **av)
{
  extern FILE *yyin;

  if(ac > 1 && !strcmp(av[1], "-d")) {
    yydebug = 1; ac--; av++;
  }

  if(ac > 1) {
    if((yyin = fopen(av[1], "r")) == NULL) {
      perror(av[1]);
      exit(1);
    }
    filename = av[1];
  } else
    filename = "(stdin)";

  if(!yyparse())
    printf("SQL parse worked\n");
  else
    printf("SQL parse failed\n");
} /* main */
```

The change to the lexer adds just one line—just copy `filename` into `yylloc.filename` in the YY_USER_ACTION macro:

```
#define YY_USER_ACTION yylloc.filename = filename; \
    yylloc.first_line = yylloc.last_line = yylineno; \
    yylloc.first_column = yycolumn; yylloc.last_column = yycolumn+yyleng-1; \
    yycolumn += yyleng;
```

Now our compiler reports the filename and the line and column. In a compiler with `include` statements that switch files within a single parse, the reports with this technique wouldn't be completely accurate, since they would report the first filename only if an error spanned input from two files, but the additional code to remember two filenames in YYLTYPE should be obvious.

Error Recovery

We concentrated on error reporting in the previous section; in this section, we discuss the problem of error recovery. When an error is detected, the bison parser is left in an ambiguous position. It is unlikely that meaningful processing can continue without some adjustment to the existing parser stack.

Depending on the environment in which you'll be using your parser, error recovery may not always be necessary if the environment makes it easy to correct the error and rerun the parser. In other environments such as a compiler, it may be possible to recover from the error enough to continue parsing and look for additional errors, stopping the compiler at the end of the parse stage. This technique can improve the productivity of the programmer by shortening the edit-compile-test cycle, since several errors can be repaired in each iteration of the cycle.

Bison Error Recovery

Bison has some provisions for error recovery, which are available by using the special-purpose **error** token. Essentially, the **error** token is used to find a *synchronization point* in the grammar from which it is likely that processing can continue. That's *likely*, not certain. Sometimes attempts at recovery will not remove enough of the erroneous state to continue, and the error messages will cascade. Either the parser will reach a point from which processing *can* continue or the entire parser will abort.

After reporting a syntax error, a bison parser discards symbols from the parse stack until it finds a state in which it can shift an **error** token. It then reads and discards input tokens until it finds one that can follow the **error** token in the grammar. This latter process is called *resynchronizing*. It then resumes parsing in a *recovering* state, which doesn't report subsequent parse errors. Once it has shifted three tokens successfully, it presumes that recovery is complete, leaves the recovering state, and resumes normal parsing.

This is the basic "trick" to bison error recovery—attempting to move forward in the input stream far enough that the new input is not adversely affected by the older input.

Error recovery is easier with proper language design. Modern programming languages use statement terminators, which serve as convenient synchronization points. For instance, when parsing a C grammar, a logical synchronizing character is the semicolon. Error recovery can introduce other problems, such as missed declarations if the parser skips over a declaration looking for a semicolon, but these can also be included in the overall error recovery scheme.

In the SQL parser, the simplest place to resynchronize is at the semicolon at the end of each SQL statement. These rules added to the parser resynchronize at the semicolon that terminates each statement:

```
stmt_list: error ';'       error in the first statement
    | stmt_list error ';'  error in a subsequent statement
    ;
```

The potential for cascading errors caused by lost state (e.g., discarded variable declarations) can make a strategy that throws away large portions of the input stream ineffective. One mechanism for counteracting the problem of cascading errors is to count the number of error messages reported and abort the compilation process when the count exceeds some arbitrary number. For example, some C compilers abort after reporting 10 errors within a file.

Like any other bison rule, one that contains **error** can be followed with action code. One could clean up after the error, reinitialize data state, or otherwise recover to a point where processing can continue. For example, the previous error recovery fragment might say the following:

```
stmt_list: error ';'    { yyerror("First statement discarded, try again"); }
    | stmt_list error ';' { yyerror("Current statement discarded, try again"); }
    ;
```

Freeing Discarded Symbols

Bison's error recovery involves popping symbols off the internal parse stack. Each symbol can have a semantic value, and if those semantic values contain pointers to allocated storage or data structures, storage leaks and data corruption can occur. The **%destructor** declaration tells bison what to do when it pops a symbol with a semantic value. Its syntax is as follows:

```
%destructor { ... code ... } symbols or <types>
```

This tells the parser to execute the code each time it pops one of the named symbols or a symbol whose value is of the given type. There can be as many **%destructor** declarations as there are different treatments of discarded symbols. The type **<*>** is a catch-all for any type of symbol with a defined type but no other destructor.

In our SQL parser, the only symbols that need special treatment are the ones with **<strval>** values, which are just strings that need to be freed:

```
/* free discarded tokens */
%destructor { printf ("free at %d %s\n",@$.first_line, $$); free($$); } <strval>
```

This code reports what it's doing, including the location reference, which is useful for debugging but perhaps overkill for a production parser.

Error Recovery in Interactive Parsers

When a bison parser is designed to read directly from the console, a few tricks can smooth the error recovery. A typical parser reads a sequence of commands:

```
commands:       /* empty */
    |       commands command
    ;

command:       . . .
    |       error {
                yyclearin /* discard lookahead */
                yyerrok;
                printf("Enter another command\n");
                }
    ;
```

The macro `yyclearin` discards any lookahead token, and `yyerrok` tells the parser to resume normal parsing, so it will start anew with the next command the user types.

If your code reports its own errors, your error routines can use the bison macro `YYRECOVERING()` to test whether the parser is trying to resynchronize, in which case you shouldn't print any more errors, for example:

```
warning(char *err1, char *err2)
{
        if (YYRECOVERING() )
                return;    /* no report at this time */
        . . .
}
```

Where to Put Error Tokens

The proper placement of error tokens in a grammar is a black art with two conflicting goals. You want make it likely that the resynchronization will succeed, so you want error tokens in the highest-level rules in the grammar, maybe even the start rule, so there will always be a rule to which the parser can recover. On the other hand, you want to discard as little input as possible before recovering, so you want the error tokens in the lowest-level rules to minimize the number of partially matched rules the parser has to discard during recovery. The most practical recovery points are places where punctuation delimits elements of a list.

If your top-level rule matches a list (e.g., the list of statements in the SQL parser) or a list of declarations and definitions in a C compiler, you can make one of the alternatives for a list entry contain `error`, as in the previous command and SQL examples. This applies equally for relatively high-level lists such as the list of statements in a C function.

For example, since C statements are punctuated by semicolons and braces, in a C compiler you might write this:

```
stmt:           . . .
        |       RETURN expr ';'
        |       '{' opt_decls stmt_list '}'
        |       error ';'
        |       error '}'
        ;
```

The two `error` rules tell the parser that it should start looking for the next statement after a ; or }.

You can also put error rules at lower levels, for example, as a rule for an expression, but unless the language provides punctuation or keywords that make it easy to tell where the expression ends, the parser can rarely recover at such a low level.

Compiler Error Recovery

In the previous section we described the mechanisms bison provides for error recovery. In this section we discuss external recovery mechanisms provided by the programmer.

Error recovery depends upon semantic knowledge of the grammar rather than just syntactic knowledge. This greatly complicates complex recovery within the grammar.

It may be desirable for the recovery routine to scan the input and, using a heuristic, perform appropriate error recovery. For instance, a C compiler writer might decide that errors encountered during the declaration section of a code block are best recovered from by skipping the entire block rather than continuing to report additional errors. She might also decide that an error encountered during the code section of the code block need only skip to the next semicolon. A truly ambitious writer of compilers or interpreters might want to report the error and attempt to describe potential correct solutions. Some recovery schemes have tried to insert new tokens into the input stream, based on what the parser would have been able to accept at the point where the error was detected. They might do some trial parses to see whether the proposed correction does indeed allow the parser to keep reading from the input.

There is a great deal of literature on error correction and recovery, most dating from the era of batch computation when the time between program runs might be measured in hours or days, and compiler developers tried to guess what sorts of errors programmers might make and how to fix them. I can report from experience that they didn't guess very well, and errors other than the most trivial invariably baffled the correction schemes. On today's computers, the interval is more likely to be seconds, so rather than trying to guess the programmer's intentions and continue after severe errors, it makes more sense to recover as quickly as possible to a state where the programmer can revise the input and rerun the compiler.

Exercises

1. Add error recovery to the calculator in Chapter 3. The most likely place to recover is at the EOL token at the end of each statement. Don't forget destructors to free up ASTs, symbols, and symbol lists.

2. (Term project.) Bison's error recovery works by discarding input tokens until it comes up with something that is syntactically correct. Another approach inserts rather than discards tokens, because in many cases it is easy to predict what token must come next. For example, in a C program, every break and continue must be followed by a semicolon, and every case must be preceded by a semicolon or a close brace. How hard would it be to augment a bison parser so that in the case of an input error it can suggest appropriate tokens to insert? You'll need to know more about the insides of bison for this exercise. The bison parser skeleton has some undocumented code that tries to suggest valid tokens you can start with.

# CHAPTER 9

Advanced Flex and Bison

Bison was originally a version of yacc, the original Unix parser generator that generated LALR parsers in C. In recent years it's grown a lot of new features. We discuss some of the most useful ones here.

Pure Scanners and Parsers

A flex scanner and bison parser built in the usual way is not reentrant and can parse only one input stream at a time. That's because both the scanner and the parser use static data structures to keep track of what they're doing and to communicate with each other and with the calling program. Both flex and bison can create "pure" reentrant code, which replaces the static data structures with one passed as an argument to each routine in the scanner and parser. This both allows recursive calls to the scanner and parser, which is occasionally useful, and allows scanners and parsers to be used in multithreaded programs where there may be several parses going on at once in different threads.

As a demonstration, we'll take the calculator from Chapter 3 and modify it to use a pure scanner and parser. Rather than having the parser execute each line of code immediately, it'll return the AST to the caller. As is usual in reentrant programs, the calling routine allocates a structure with space for the per-instance data and passes it along in each call to the scanner and parser.

Unfortunately, as of the time this book went to press (mid-2009), the code for flex pure scanners and yacc pure scanners is a mess. Bison's calling sequence for a pure `yylex()` is different from flex's, and the way they handle per-instance data is different. It's possible to paper over the problems in the existing code and persuade pure scanners and parsers to work together, which is what we will do in this chapter, but before doing so, check the latest flex and bison documentation. Most of the incompatibilities could be fixed by relatively simple changes to the code skeletons used to create scanners and parsers, and with any luck someone will have done it so you don't have to do it.

Pure Scanners in Flex

A single scanning job may involve many calls to `yylex()` because it returns tokens to the calling program. Since the scanner's state has to be saved between calls, you have to manage the per-scanner data yourself. Flex provides routines that create and destroy a scanner's context, as well as routines to access scanner values that used to be in static variables like `yyin` and `yytext` to allow routines outside `yylex()` to get and set them.

```
yyscan_t scaninfo;          a pointer to the per-instance scanner data

int yylex_init(&scaninfo);          create a scanner
int yylex_init_extra(userstuff, &scaninfo);  or create a scanner with a pointer to user data

yyset_in(stdin, scaninfo);  set the input file and other parameters

while( ... ) {
    tok = yylex(scaninfo);  call until done
}

yylex_destroy(scaninfo);    free the scanner data
```

The `yyscan_t` structure contains all of the per-scanner state such as the input and output files and pointers to remember where in the buffered input to resume scanning. It also includes a stack of pointers to `YY_BUFFER_STATE` structures to track the active input buffer. (As we saw in Chapter 2, the built-in buffer stack isn't too useful since you usually need to remember extra per-buffer information.)

The `userstuff` argument to `yylex_init_extra` allows you to provide your own per-instance data to the scanner, such as the address of the symbol table for it to use. It is a value of type `YY_EXTRA_TYPE`, by default defined to be `void` * but easily overridden with `%option extra-type`. The per-instance data is invariably stored in a structure, so the `userstuff` is a pointer to that structure. As we'll see in a moment, in one line you can retrieve it within the scanner and put it in a pointer variable with a reasonable name and type.

Within the scanner, flex defines macros for `yytext`, `yyleng`, and a few other fields that refer to the instance data. The values of `yylineno` and `yycolumn`, which is a variable not present in nonreentrant scanners, are stored in the current buffer structure, making it easier to track line and column information in multiple input files, while the rest are in the `yyscan_t` structure. Flex maintains `yylineno` as it does in nonreentrant scanners, but the only thing it does automatically to `yycolumn` is set it to zero when it sees a `\n` character, so you still have to track the column yourself using the techniques in Chapter 8.

Example 9-1 shows the word count program from Chapter 2, modified to use a pure scanner.

Example 9-1. Pure version of word count program

```
/* pure version of word count program */
%option noyywrap nodefault reentrant
%{
struct pwc {      our per-scanner data
    int chars;
    int words;
    int lines;
};
%}
%option extra-type="struct pwc *"

%%
%{                                 this code goes at the top of yylex
  struct pwc *pp = yyextra;    yyextra is a flex-defined macro
%}

[a-zA-Z]+          { pp->words++; pp->chars += strlen(yytext); }
\n                 { pp->chars++; pp->lines++; }
.                  { pp->chars++; }

%%
```

The three variables to count characters, words, and lines are now placed in a structure, with a copy allocated for each instance of the scanner and with %option extra-type making the userstuff in flex's scanner a pointer to that structure.

The first thing in the rules section is a line of code that flex will place at the top of yylex, after its own variable definitions but before any executable code. This line lets us declare a pointer to our own instance data and initialize it to yyextra, which is a macro provided by flex that refers to the extra data field in the scanner's current per-instance data. In the rules themselves, what were references to static variables are now references to our instance data.

```
main(argc, argv)
int argc;
char **argv;
{
  struct pwc mypwc = { 0, 0, 0 }; /* my instance data */
  yyscan_t scanner;              /* flex instance data */

  if(yylex_init_extra(&mypwc, &scanner)) {
    perror("init alloc failed");
    return 1;
  }

  if(argc > 1) {
    FILE *f;

    if(!(f = fopen(argv[1], "r"))) {
      perror(argv[1]);
      return (1);
    }
```

```
        yyset_in(f, scanner);
    } else
        yyset_in(stdin, scanner);

    yylex(scanner);
    printf("%8d%8d%8d\n", mypwc.lines, mypwc.words, mypwc.chars);

    if(argc > 1)
        fclose(yyget_in(scanner));

    yylex_destroy( scanner );
}
```

The main routine declares and initializes mypwc, our own instance data, and declares scanner, which will be the flex instance data. The call to yylex_init_extra takes a pointer to scanner, so it can fill it in with a pointer to the newly allocated instance, and the call returns 0 for success or 1 for failure (the malloc for the instance data failed).

If there's a file argument, we open the file and use yyset_in to store it in the yyin-ish field in the scanner data. Then we call yylex, passing it the flex instance data; print out the results that the scanner stored in our own instance data; and then free and deallocate the scanner.

This was more work than a regular nonpure scanner, but the changes were for the most part mechanical: move static data into a structure, change references to the static data to references to the structure, and add the code to create and destroy the scanner instance.

Pure Parsers in Bison

Pure parsers are a little easier to create than pure scanners, because an entire bison parse happens in a single call to yyparse. Hence, the parser can create its per-instance data at the start of the parse, do the parsing work, and then free it without needing explicit programmer help. The parser does typically need some application instance data, passed as an argument to yyparse. The static variables used to communicate with the scanner—yylval and, if the parser uses locations, yyloc—become instance variables that have to be passed to yylex, probably along with the application instance data.

Bison will create a pure parser if it sees the %define api.pure (formerly %pure_parser) declaration. This declaration makes the parser reentrant. To get a pure parser started, you pass in a pointer to the application per-instance data. The contents of the %parse-param declaration are placed between the parentheses in the definition of yyparse(), so you can declare as many arguments as you want, although one pointer to the per-instance data is usually all you need:

```
%define api.pure
%parse-param { struct pureparse *pp }
```

Pure parsers also change the calling sequence to yylex(), passing as arguments pointers to the current copies of yylval and, if locations are in use, yylloc.

```
/* generated calls within the parser */
token = yylex(YYSTYPE *yylvalp);                        without locations
token = yylex(YYSTYPE *yylvalp, YYLTYPE *yylocp);       with them
```

If you want to pass application data, you can declare it with `%lex-param{ }` or by `#define` YYLEX_PARAM. An ill-advised overoptimization strips the argument to `%lex-param` to the last token in the braces, so define YYLEX_PARAM instead. (The documentation shows that the implementer assumed you'd put a declaration there, as in `parse-param`, but since the argument for a flex scanner has to be the scanner's yyscan_t, I always fetch it from in a field in the application per-instance data.)

```
%code {
#define YYLEX_PARAM pp->scaninfo
%}
%%
    /* generated calls within the parser */
    token = yylex(YYSTYPE *yylvalp, pp->scaninfo);   without locations
    token = yylex(YYSTYPE *yylvalp, YYLTYPE *yylocp, pp->scaninfo);   with them
```

When the generated parser encounters a syntax error, it calls yyerror(), passing a pointer to the current location, if the parser uses locations, and the parser parameter in addition to the usual error message string: [1]

```
yyerror(struct pureparse *pp, "Syntax error");                without locations
yyerror(YYLTYPE &yyllocp, struct pureparse *pp, "Syntax error");   with them
```

If you're using a handwritten scanner, these are all the hooks you need for a pure parser. When you call internal routines from the scanner and parser, you'll want to pass along the instance data, as we'll see later in this chapter in the reentrant calculator. But since we're using a flex scanner, first we have to deal with flex and bison's incompatible calling sequence.

Using Pure Scanners and Parsers Together

If you compare the calling sequence for yylex in pure scanners and pure parsers, you'll note that they're incompatible. Flex wants the first argument to be the scanner instance data, but bison makes the first argument a pointer to yylval. While it is possible to use some undocumented C preprocessor symbols to fudge this, the maintainer of flex took pity on programmers and added the bison-bridge option to make its pure calling sequence compatible with bison's. If you use `%option bison-bridge`, the declaration of yylex becomes the following:

```
int yylex(YYSTYPE* lvalp, yyscan_t scaninfo);
```

If you use `%option bison-bridge bison-locations`, the declaration is as follows:

```
int yylex (YYSTYPE* lvalp, YYLTYPE* llocp, yyscan_t scaninfo);
```

---

1. If you pass multiple arguments to the parser, each one has to be in a separate `%parse-param`. If you put two arguments in the same `%parse-param`, bison won't report an error but the second parameter will disappear.

Flex defines the macros yylval and (optionally) yylloc, which are copies of the arguments, but they are both pointers to the bison value union and location structure, so yylval.field and yylloc.first_line have to become yylval->field and yylloc->first_line. This is also a bug, but it's documented in the flex and bison manuals, so it is unlikely to change.

Multiple Instances of Multiple Scanners and Parsers

The discussion of pure parsing in this chapter covers the way you can have several copies of a scanner or parser, all that use the same set of rules. It's also possible to have several instances of different scanners or parsers in a single program. The sections "Multiple Lexers in One Program" on page 127 and "Variant and Multiple Grammars" on page 163 describe how to put several different scanners parsers into a single program, renaming their symbols with a prefix other than "yy". You can use the same features to rename pure scanners and parsers and then call them as needed. This level of complexity will be a challenge to debug, but the features are there if you need them.

A Reentrant Calculator

To make the calculator from Chapter 3 reentrant, most of the changes are mechanical, putting static data into per-instance structures. Rather than executing the parsed ASTs within the parser, this version parses one expression or function definition at a time, and it returns the ASTs to the caller, where they can be run immediately or saved for later. The scanner, on the other hand, is managed as a single session, used for all the calls to **yyparse**, so that there's no problem of losing buffered input each time the parser restarts. This means that the program creates the scanner context when it starts, and then it passes the same context to the parser each time. Example 9-2 shows the modified header file for the calculator.

Example 9-2. Reentrant calc header file purecalc.h

```
/*
 * Declarations for a calculator, pure version
 */

/* per-parse data */
struct pcdata {
  yyscan_t scaninfo;          /* scanner context */
  struct symbol *symtab;      /* symbols for this parse */
  struct ast *ast;            /* most recently parsed AST */
};
```

The new structure pcdata contains the application context for the parser. It points to the symbol table, allowing different parses to have different namespaces; the scanner context that the parser passes to yylex; and a place for the parser to return the AST that it parsed. (Remember that the value of **yyparse** is 1 or 0 to report whether the parse succeeded, so it can't directly return the AST.)

The changes in the rest of the header add an initial context argument to all of the functions, both the ones specific to the calculator and **yyerror**.

```
/* symbol table */
struct symbol {          /* a variable name */
  char *name;
  double value;
  struct ast *func;      /* AST for the function */
  struct symlist *syms;  /* list of dummy args */
};

/* simple symtab of fixed size */
#define NHASH 9997
struct symbol symtab[NHASH];

struct symbol *lookup(struct pcdata *, char*);

/* list of symbols, for an argument list */
struct symlist {
  struct symbol *sym;
  struct symlist *next;
};

struct symlist *newsymlist(struct pcdata *, struct symbol *sym, struct symlist *next);
void symlistfree(struct pcdata *, struct symlist *sl);

/* node types
 *   + - * / |
 *   0-7 comparison ops, bit coded 04 equal, 02 less, 01 greater
 *   M unary minus
 *   L statement list
 *   I IF statement
 *   W WHILE statement
 *   N symbol ref
 *   = assignment
 *   S list of symbols
 *   F built in function call
 *   C user function call
 */

enum bifs {                       /* built-in functions */
  B_sqrt = 1,
  B_exp,
  B_log,
  B_print
};

/* nodes in the abstract syntax tree */
/* all have common initial nodetype */

   ... all nodes unchanged from the original version ...

/* build an AST */
struct ast *newast(struct pcdata *, int nodetype, struct ast *l, struct ast *r);
struct ast *newcmp(struct pcdata *, int cmptype, struct ast *l, struct ast *r);
```

```
struct ast *newfunc(struct pcdata *, int functype, struct ast *l);
struct ast *newcall(struct pcdata *, struct symbol *s, struct ast *l);
struct ast *newref(struct pcdata *, struct symbol *s);
struct ast *newasgn(struct pcdata *, struct symbol *s, struct ast *v);
struct ast *newnum(struct pcdata *, double d);
struct ast *newflow(struct pcdata *, int nodetype, struct ast *cond, struct ast *tl,
        struct ast *tr);

/* define a function */
void dodef(struct pcdata *, struct symbol *name, struct symlist *syms, struct ast *stmts);

/* evaluate an AST */
double eval(struct pcdata *, struct ast *);

/* delete and free an AST */
void treefree(struct pcdata *, struct ast *);

/* interface to the scanner */
void yyerror(struct pcdata *pp, char *s, ...);
```

The scanner has the `reentrant` and `bison-bridge` options to make a reentrant bison-compatible scanner. For the first time we also tell flex to create a header file analogous to the one that bison creates. The file contains declarations of the various routines used to get and set variables in a scanner context, as well as the definition of `yyscan_t` that the parser will need.

Don't Include the Scanner Header in Your Scanner!

If you create a scanner header file such as `purecalc.lex.h` in this example, be sure *not* to include the header directly or indirectly into the scanner itself. For some reason, the header has #undefs for several internal scanner macros, which will cause attempts to compile the scanner to fail with cryptic error messages about undefined variables. (Guess how I found this out.)

Either protect the `#include` statements with `#ifndef`/`#define` lines if you include the scanner header file in a common header file or do what this example does and include it directly only in the files that need it.

Example 9-3. Reentrant calculator scanner purecalc.l

```
/* recognize tokens for the calculator */
/* pure scanner and parser version */
/* $Header: /usr/home/johnl/flnb/RCS/ch09.tr,v 1.4 2009/05/19 18:28:27 johnl Exp $ */
%option noyywrap nodefault yylineno reentrant bison-bridge

%option header-file="purecalc.lex.h"
%option extra-type="struct pcdata*"

%{
#include "purecalc.tab.h"
#include "purecalc.h"
%}
```

```
/* float exponent */
EXP     ([Ee][-+]?[0-9]+)

%%
%{
  struct pcdata *pp = yyextra;
%}
 /* single character ops */
"+" |
"-" |
"*" |
"/" |
"=" |
"|" |
"," |
";" |
"(" |
")"     { return yytext[0]; }

 /* comparison ops */
">"     { yylval->fn = 1; return CMP; }
"<"     { yylval->fn = 2; return CMP; }
"<>"    { yylval->fn = 3; return CMP; }
"=="    { yylval->fn = 4; return CMP; }
">="    { yylval->fn = 5; return CMP; }
"<="    { yylval->fn = 6; return CMP; }

 /* keywords */

"if"    { return IF; }
"then"  { return THEN; }
"else"  { return ELSE; }
"while" { return WHILE; }
"do"    { return DO; }
"let"   { return LET;}

 /* built-in functions */
"sqrt"  { yylval->fn = B_sqrt; return FUNC; }
"exp"   { yylval->fn = B_exp; return FUNC; }
"log"   { yylval->fn = B_log; return FUNC; }
"print" { yylval->fn = B_print; return FUNC; }

 /* names */
[a-zA-Z][a-zA-Z0-9]*  { yylval->s = lookup(pp, yytext); return NAME; }

[0-9]+"."[0-9]*{EXP}? |
"."?[0-9]+{EXP}? { yylval->d = atof(yytext); return NUMBER; }

"//".*
[ \t]   /* ignore whitespace */
\\n    printf("c> "); /* ignore line continuation */
"\n"    { return EOL; }

.       { yyerror(pp, "Mystery character %c\n", *yytext); }
```

```
<<EOF>>  { exit(0); }
%%
```

Example 9-3 shows the scanner with modifications to make it reentrant. A line of code at the top of the rules puts the pointer to the application instance data accessed via macro **yyextra** into variable **pp**, which is of the right type in case we need to access fields in it. The references to yylval are adjusted to use it as a pointer, and the call to yyerror passes the instance data.

At the end of the lexer is an <<EOF>> rule that just exits. This is not a particularly elegant way to end the program, but for our purposes it will do. Possible alternative approaches to ending the program are discussed later.

Example 9-4 shows the parser, modified to be reentrant. It has two kinds of changes. Some of them are the mechanical changes to handle explicit state; the rest change the parser to handle one statement at a time.

Example 9-4. Reentrant calculator parser purecalc.y

```
/* calculator with AST */
%define api.pure
%parse-param { struct pcdata *pp }

%{
#   include <stdio.h>
#   include <stdlib.h>
%}

%union {
   struct ast *a;
   double d;
   struct symbol *s;           /* which symbol */
   struct symlist *sl;
   int fn;                     /* which function */
}

%{
#   include "purecalc.lex.h"
#   include "purecalc.h"
#define YYLEX_PARAM pp->scaninfo
%}

/* declare tokens */
%token <d> NUMBER
%token <s> NAME
%token <fn> FUNC
%token EOL

%token IF THEN ELSE WHILE DO LET

%nonassoc <fn> CMP
%right '='
%left '+' '-'
```

```
%left '*' '/'
%nonassoc '|' UMINUS

%type <a> exp stmt list explist
%type <sl> symlist

%start calc
%%
```

The parser file defines `api.pure` to generate a reentrant parser and uses `parse-param` to declare that the parser now takes an argument, which is the pointer to the application state. A few lines further down, a code block includes `purecalc.lex.h`, which is the header generated by flex, and defines `YYLEX_PARAM` to pass the scanner state, which is stored in the instance state, to the scanner.

```
calc: /* nothing */ EOL { pp->ast = NULL; YYACCEPT; }
   | stmt EOL { pp->ast = $1; YYACCEPT; }
   | LET NAME '(' symlist ')' '=' list EOL {
                   dodef(pp, $2, $4, $7);
                   printf("%d: Defined %s\n", yyget_lineno(pp->scaninfo),
                          $2->name);
                   pp->ast = NULL; YYACCEPT; }
   ;
```

The top-level rule is now `calc`, which handles an empty line, a statement that is parsed into an AST, or a function definition that is stored in the local symbol table. Normally a bison parser reads a token stream up to the end-of file-token. This parser uses `YYACCEPT` to end the parse. When the parser ends, it leaves the scanner's state unchanged, so the next time the parser starts up, using the same scanner state, it resumes reading where the previous parse left off. An alternate approach would be to have the lexer return an end-of-file token when the user types a newline, which would also work; in a situation like this, there's no strong reason to prefer one approach or the other.

The rest of the parser is the same as the nonreentrant version, except that every call to an external routine now passes the pointer to the instance state. As we will see, many of the routines don't do anything with the state variable, but it's easier to pass it to all of them than to try to remember which ones need it and which ones don't.

```
stmt: IF exp THEN list          { $$ = newflow(pp, 'I', $2, $4, NULL); }
   | IF exp THEN list ELSE list  { $$ = newflow(pp, 'I', $2, $4, $6); }
   | WHILE exp DO list          { $$ = newflow(pp, 'W', $2, $4, NULL); }
   | exp
   ;

list: /* nothing */ { $$ = NULL; }
   | stmt ';' list { if ($3 == NULL)
                        $$ = $1;
                     else
                        $$ = newast(pp, 'L', $1, $3);
                   }
   ;

exp: exp CMP exp          { $$ = newcmp(pp, $2, $1, $3); }
```

```
            |  exp '+' exp        { $$ = newast(pp, '+', $1,$3); }
            |  exp '-' exp        { $$ = newast(pp, '-', $1,$3);}
            |  exp '*' exp        { $$ = newast(pp, '*', $1,$3); }
            |  exp '/' exp        { $$ = newast(pp, '/', $1,$3); }
            |  '|' exp            { $$ = newast(pp, '|', $2, NULL); }
            |  '(' exp ')'        { $$ = $2; }
            |  '-' exp %prec UMINUS { $$ = newast(pp, 'M', $2, NULL); }
            |  NUMBER             { $$ = newnum(pp, $1); }
            |  FUNC '(' explist ')' { $$ = newfunc(pp, $1, $3); }
            |  NAME               { $$ = newref(pp, $1); }
            |  NAME '=' exp       { $$ = newasgn(pp, $1, $3); }
            |  NAME '(' explist ')' { $$ = newcall(pp, $1, $3); }
         ;

      explist: exp
         | exp ',' explist { $$ = newast(pp, 'L', $1, $3); }
         ;
      symlist: NAME        { $$ = newsymlist(pp, $1, NULL); }
         | NAME ',' symlist { $$ = newsymlist(pp, $1, $3); }
         ;
      %%
```

Example 9-5 shows the helper functions, adjusted for a reentrant scanner and parser.
There is now a symbol table per instance state, so the routines that do symbol table
lookups need to get the symbol table pointer from the state structure.

Example 9-5. Helper functions purecalcfuncs.c

```
/*
 * helper functions for purecalc
 */
#  include <stdio.h>
#  include <stdlib.h>
#  include <stdarg.h>
#  include <string.h>
#  include <math.h>

#  include "purecalc.tab.h"
#  include "purecalc.lex.h"
#  include "purecalc.h"

/* symbol table */
/* hash a symbol */
static unsigned
symhash(char *sym)
{
  unsigned int hash = 0;
  unsigned c;

  while(c = *sym++) hash = hash*9 ^ c;

  return hash;
}

struct symbol *
```

```
lookup(struct pcdata *pp, char* sym)
{
  struct symbol *sp = &(pp->symtab)[symhash(sym)%NHASH];
  int scount = NHASH;              /* how many have we looked at */

  while(--scount >= 0) {
    if(sp->name && !strcmp(sp->name, sym)) { return sp; }

    if(!sp->name) {                /* new entry */
      sp->name = strdup(sym);
      sp->value = 0;
      sp->func = NULL;
      sp->syms = NULL;
      return sp;
    }

    if(++sp >= pp->symtab+NHASH) sp = pp->symtab; /* try the next entry */
  }
  yyerror(pp, "symbol table overflow\n");
  abort(); /* tried them all, table is full */

}

struct ast *
newast(struct pcdata *pp, int nodetype, struct ast *l, struct ast *r)
{
  struct ast *a = malloc(sizeof(struct ast));

  if(!a) {
    yyerror(pp, "out of space");
    exit(0);
  }
  a->nodetype = nodetype;
  a->l = l;
  a->r = r;
  return a;
}

struct ast *
newnum(struct pcdata *pp, double d)
{
  struct numval *a = malloc(sizeof(struct numval));

  if(!a) {
    yyerror(pp, "out of space");
    exit(0);
  }
  a->nodetype = 'K';
  a->number = d;
  return (struct ast *)a;
}

struct ast *
newcmp(struct pcdata *pp, int cmptype, struct ast *l, struct ast *r)
{
```

```
  struct ast *a = malloc(sizeof(struct ast));

  if(!a) {
    yyerror(pp, "out of space");
    exit(0);
  }
  a->nodetype = '0' + cmptype;
  a->l = l;
  a->r = r;
  return a;
}

struct ast *
newfunc(struct pcdata *pp, int functype, struct ast *l)
{
  struct fncall *a = malloc(sizeof(struct fncall));

  if(!a) {
    yyerror(pp, "out of space");
    exit(0);
  }
  a->nodetype = 'F';
  a->l = l;
  a->functype = functype;
  return (struct ast *)a;
}

struct ast *
newcall(struct pcdata *pp, struct symbol *s, struct ast *l)
{
  struct ufncall *a = malloc(sizeof(struct ufncall));

  if(!a) {
    yyerror(pp, "out of space");
    exit(0);
  }
  a->nodetype = 'C';
  a->l = l;
  a->s = s;
  return (struct ast *)a;
}

struct ast *
newref(struct pcdata *pp, struct symbol *s)
{
  struct symref *a = malloc(sizeof(struct symref));

  if(!a) {
    yyerror(pp, "out of space");
    exit(0);
  }
  a->nodetype = 'N';
  a->s = s;
  return (struct ast *)a;
}
```

```
struct ast *
newasgn(struct pcdata *pp, struct symbol *s, struct ast *v)
{
  struct symasgn *a = malloc(sizeof(struct symasgn));

  if(!a) {
    yyerror(pp, "out of space");
    exit(0);
  }
  a->nodetype = '=';
  a->s = s;
  a->v = v;
  return (struct ast *)a;
}

struct ast *
newflow(struct pcdata *pp, int nodetype, struct ast *cond, struct ast *tl, struct ast *el)
{
  struct flow *a = malloc(sizeof(struct flow));

  if(!a) {
    yyerror(pp, "out of space");
    exit(0);
  }
  a->nodetype = nodetype;
  a->cond = cond;
  a->tl = tl;
  a->el = el;
  return (struct ast *)a;
}

struct symlist *
newsymlist(struct pcdata *pp, struct symbol *sym, struct symlist *next)
{
  struct symlist *sl = malloc(sizeof(struct symlist));

  if(!sl) {
    yyerror(pp, "out of space");
    exit(0);
  }
  sl->sym = sym;
  sl->next = next;
  return sl;
}

void
symlistfree(struct pcdata *pp, struct symlist *sl)
{
  struct symlist *nsl;

  while(sl) {
    nsl = sl->next;
    free(sl);
    sl = nsl;
```

```
    }
  }

/* define a function */
void
dodef(struct pcdata *pp, struct symbol *name, struct symlist *syms, struct ast *func)
{
  if(name->syms) symlistfree(pp, name->syms);
  if(name->func) treefree(pp, name->func);
  name->syms = syms;
  name->func = func;
}

static double callbuiltin(struct pcdata *pp, struct fncall *);
static double calluser(struct pcdata *pp, struct ufncall *);

double
eval(struct pcdata *pp, struct ast *a)
{
  double v;

  if(!a) {
    yyerror(pp, "internal error, null eval");
    return 0.0;
  }

  switch(a->nodetype) {
    /* constant */
  case 'K': v = ((struct numval *)a)->number; break;

    /* name reference */
  case 'N': v = ((struct symref *)a)->s->value; break;

    /* assignment */
  case '=': v = ((struct symasgn *)a)->s->value =
      eval(pp, ((struct symasgn *)a)->v); break;

    /* expressions */
  case '+': v = eval(pp, a->l) + eval(pp, a->r); break;
  case '-': v = eval(pp, a->l) - eval(pp, a->r); break;
  case '*': v = eval(pp, a->l) * eval(pp, a->r); break;
  case '/': v = eval(pp, a->l) / eval(pp, a->r); break;
  case '|': v = fabs(eval(pp, a->l)); break;
  case 'M': v = -eval(pp, a->l); break;

    /* comparisons */
  case '1': v = (eval(pp, a->l) > eval(pp, a->r))? 1 : 0; break;
  case '2': v = (eval(pp, a->l) < eval(pp, a->r))? 1 : 0; break;
  case '3': v = (eval(pp, a->l) != eval(pp, a->r))? 1 : 0; break;
  case '4': v = (eval(pp, a->l) == eval(pp, a->r))? 1 : 0; break;
  case '5': v = (eval(pp, a->l) >= eval(pp, a->r))? 1 : 0; break;
  case '6': v = (eval(pp, a->l) <= eval(pp, a->r))? 1 : 0; break;

  /* control flow */
  /* null if/else/do expressions allowed in the grammar, so check for them */
```

```
  case 'I':
    if( eval(pp,  ((struct flow *)a)->cond) != 0) {
      if( ((struct flow *)a)->tl) {
        v = eval(pp,  ((struct flow *)a)->tl);
      } else
        v = 0.0;                  /* a default value */
    } else {
      if( ((struct flow *)a)->el) {
        v = eval(pp, ((struct flow *)a)->el);
      } else
        v = 0.0;                  /* a default value */
    }
    break;

  case 'W':
    v = 0.0;              /* a default value */

    if( ((struct flow *)a)->tl) {
      while( eval(pp, ((struct flow *)a)->cond) != 0)
        v = eval(pp, ((struct flow *)a)->tl);
    }
    break;                          /* last value is value */

  case 'L': eval(pp, a->l); v = eval(pp, a->r); break;

  case 'F': v = callbuiltin(pp, (struct fncall *)a); break;

  case 'C': v = calluser(pp, (struct ufncall *)a); break;

  default: printf("internal error: bad node %c\n", a->nodetype);
  }
  return v;
}

static double
callbuiltin(struct pcdata *pp, struct fncall *f)
{
  enum bifs functype = f->functype;
  double v = eval(pp, f->l);

 switch(functype) {
 case B_sqrt:
   return sqrt(v);
 case B_exp:
   return exp(v);
 case B_log:
   return log(v);
 case B_print:
   printf("= %4.4g\n", v);
   return v;
 default:
   yyerror(pp, "Unknown built-in function %d", functype);
   return 0.0;
 }
}
```

```
static double
calluser(struct pcdata *pp, struct ufncall *f)
{
  struct symbol *fn = f->s;       /* function name */
  struct symlist *sl;             /* dummy arguments */
  struct ast *args = f->l;        /* actual arguments */
  double *oldval, *newval;        /* saved arg values */
  double v;
  int nargs;
  int i;

  if(!fn->func) {
    yyerror(pp, "call to undefined function", fn->name);
    return 0;
  }

  /* count the arguments */
  sl = fn->syms;
  for(nargs = 0; sl; sl = sl->next)
    nargs++;

  /* prepare to save them */
  oldval = (double *)malloc(nargs * sizeof(double));
  newval = (double *)malloc(nargs * sizeof(double));
  if(!oldval || !newval) {
    yyerror(pp, "Out of space in %s", fn->name); return 0.0;
  }

  /* evaluate the arguments */
  for(i = 0; i < nargs; i++) {
    if(!args) {
      yyerror(pp, "too few args in call to %s", fn->name);
      free(oldval); free(newval);
      return 0;
    }

    if(args->nodetype == 'L') { /* if this is a list node */
      newval[i] = eval(pp, args->l);
      args = args->r;
    } else {                    /* if it's the end of the list */
      newval[i] = eval(pp, args);
      args = NULL;
    }
  }

  /* save old values of dummies, assign new ones */
  sl = fn->syms;
  for(i = 0; i < nargs; i++) {
    struct symbol *s = sl->sym;

    oldval[i] = s->value;
    s->value = newval[i];
    sl = sl->next;
  }
```

```
    free(newval);

    /* evaluate the function */
    v = eval(pp, fn->func);

    /* put the dummies back */
    sl = fn->syms;
    for(i = 0; i < nargs; i++) {
      struct symbol *s = sl->sym;

      s->value = oldval[i];
      sl = sl->next;
    }

    free(oldval);
    return v;
}

void
treefree(struct pcdata *pp, struct ast *a)
{
  switch(a->nodetype) {

    /* two subtrees */
  case '+':
  case '-':
  case '*':
  case '/':
  case '1':  case '2':  case '3':  case '4':  case '5':  case '6':
  case 'L':
    treefree(pp, a->r);

    /* one subtree */
  case '|':
  case 'M': case 'C': case 'F':
    treefree(pp, a->l);

    /* no subtree */
  case 'K': case 'N':
    break;

  case '=':
    free( ((struct symasgn *)a)->v);
    break;

  case 'I': case 'W':
    free( ((struct flow *)a)->cond);
    if( ((struct flow *)a)->tl) free( ((struct flow *)a)->tl);
    if( ((struct flow *)a)->el) free( ((struct flow *)a)->el);
    break;

  default: printf("internal error: free bad node %c\n", a->nodetype);
  }
```

```
  free(a); /* always free the node itself */
}
```

The yyerror function now gets the current line number that was in the static yylineno from the scanner state using yyget_lineno.

```
void
yyerror(struct pcdata *pp, char *s, ...)
{
  va_list ap;
  va_start(ap, s);

  fprintf(stderr, "%d: error: ", yyget_lineno(pp->scaninfo));
  vfprintf(stderr, s, ap);
  fprintf(stderr, "\n");
}
```

The main function needs to create instance data and link it together, putting a pointer to the application instance data into the scanner instance via yylex_init_extra and storing the pointer to the scanner instance into p.scaninfo. Then it allocates a fresh symbol table, and it's ready to start parsing.

In this simple example, each time it calls the parser, if the parser returns an AST, it immediately evaluates the AST and frees it.

```
int
main()
{
  struct pcdata p = { NULL, 0, NULL };

  /* set up scanner */
  if(yylex_init_extra(&p, &p.scaninfo)) {
    perror("init alloc failed");
    return 1;
  }

  /* allocate and zero out the symbol table */
  if(!(p.symtab = calloc(NHASH, sizeof(struct symbol)))) {
    perror("sym alloc failed");
    return 1;
  }

  for(;;) {
    printf("> ");
    yyparse(&p);
    if(p.ast) {
      printf("= %4.4g\n", eval(&p, p.ast));
      treefree(&p, p.ast);
      p.ast = 0;
    }
  }
}
```

Makefile for Pure Applications

This Makefile is slightly more complex than the ones in previous chapters, because the purecalc scanner and parser each use a header file created from the other.

```
CFLAGS = -g

all:     purewc purecalc

purewc: purewc.lex.o
        cc -g -o $@ purewc.lex.c

purewc.lex.c: purewc.l
        flex -opurewc.lex.c purewc.l

purecalc:      purecalc.lex.o purecalc.tab.o purecalcfuncs.o
        cc -g -o $@ purecalc.tab.o purecalc.lex.o purecalcfuncs.o -lm

purecalc.lex.o: purecalc.lex.c purecalc.tab.h purecalc.h

purecalc.tab.o: purecalc.tab.c purecalc.lex.h purecalc.h

purecalc.lex.c purecalc.lex.h: purecalc.l
        flex -opurecalc.lex.c purecalc.l

purecalc.tab.c purecalc.tab.h: purecalc.y
        bison -vd purecalc.y
```

Push and Pull Parsers

Bison has an experimental *push parse* option that turns the flow of control inside out. A regular *pull* parser starts up and repeatedly calls yylex to "pull" each token into the parser. In a *push* parser, you create a yypstate parser state, and then you call the parser for each token, passing it the token and the state to "push" the token into the parser. The parser does what it can with the token, shifting, reducing, and calling any action routines, and returns after each token. Push parsers are usually also reentrant and are intended to be called from event routines in GUIs and the like. Since they're experimental, the details are likely to change; therefore consult the bison manual for the current calling sequence.

There's no flex push scanner at this point. Each call to a push scanner would pass it a chunk of input text, which it would process and turn into tokens. Since the flow of control in a push scanner would be inside out relative to a pull scanner, each action rather than returning would call the push parser, passing it the current token and value. When the scanner ran out of input, it would remember where it was, either saving the current position in the scanning automaton or just backing up to the end of the last token recognized, saving the remaining text for next time, and returning to the caller.

There's no reason that one couldn't modify flex to do this. It's open source, so if you're interested, you can do it!

GLR Parsing

> ## With Great Power Comes Great Responsibility
>
> A big reason that parser generators such as yacc and bison became popular is that they create parsers that are much more reliable than handwritten parsers. If you feed a grammar to bison and it has no conflicts, you can be completely sure that the language that the generated parser accepts is exactly the one described by the grammar. It won't have any of the holes that handwritten parsers tend to have, particularly when diagnosing erroneous input. If you use precedence declarations sparingly to resolve conflicts in known situations, expression grammars, and if/then/else, you can still be sure that your parser is handling the language as you think it is.
>
> On the other hand, if you use GLR parsing, you can hand any grammar to bison, and it will create a parser that parses something, resolving the conflicts at parse time. But the more conflicts it has, the less likely it is that the language it's parsing is the language you want, and the less likely it is that your parser will resolve the conflicts the way you want. Before switching to GLR, be sure you understand why your grammar has the conflicts you're expecting GLR to handle and that you understand how you are resolving them. Otherwise, you risk the embarrassing situation of finding out much later that your parser gives up unexpectedly when it runs into a conflict you didn't anticipate or that because of an incorrect conflict resolution, the language it's parsing isn't quite the one you wanted.
>
> GLR parsers can in theory be extremely slow, since running N parses in parallel is roughly N times as slow as a single parse, and a particularly ambiguous grammar could split on each token. Useful GLR grammars typically have only a few ambiguities that are resolved within a few tokens, so the performance is adequate.

A normal bison LALR parser doesn't have to deal with shift/reduce or reduce/reduce conflicts, since any conflicts were resolved one way or the other when the parser was built. (See Chapter 8.) But when a GLR parser encounters a conflict, it conceptually splits and continues both possible parses, with each parser consuming the input tokens in parallel. When there are several conflicts, it can create a tree of partial parses, splitting each time there is a conflict.

If the grammar is actually unambiguous and it just needs more lookahead than the single token that LALR(1) offers, most of the parses will come to a point when they can't match the next input token and will fail. Bison silently discards a failing parse and continues so long as there's at least one other still active. If all possible parses fail, bison reports an error in the usual way. For grammars like this, a GLR parser works very much like a regular LALR parser, and you need only add a few lines to tell it to use the GLR parser and tell it how many conflicts to expect.

On the other hand, if the grammar really is ambiguous, the parser will reach states where there are two or more possible reductions of rules with the same LHS symbol, and it has to decide what to do. If you know that it should always use the same rule, you can put `%dprec N` tags in each of the rules to set the precedence among them. If all of the rules in an ambiguous reduction have `%dprec`, the parser reduces the rule with the highest `N`. Your other option is to use `%merge`, which tells it to call a routine you write that examines the results of all the rules and "merges" the results into the value to use for the LHS symbol.

While a GLR parser is handling multiple possible parses, it remembers what reductions it would make for each parse but doesn't call the action routines. When it resolves the ambiguity, either by having all but one of the parses fail or by `%dprec` tags, it then calls the action routines and catches up. Normally this makes no difference, but if your parser feeds back information to the scanner, setting start states or flags that the scanner tests, you may have hard-to-diagnose bugs since the parser won't be setting the states or flags when it logically would do so.

GLR Version of the SQL Parser

The SQL parser in Chapter 4 has a few lexical hacks to deal with the limits of LALR parsers. We'll take the hacks out and use a GLR parser instead. One hack made `ONDUPLICATE` a single token because of a lookahead limitation. The other made `NOT EXISTS` a single token that was a variant of `EXISTS` because of ambiguity in the expression grammar. This version of the scanner simply takes out those hacks and makes `EXISTS`, `ON`, and `DUPLICATE` ordinary keyword tokens.

```
EXISTS    { return EXISTS; }
ON        { return ON; }
DUPLICATE { return DUPLICATE; }
```

In the parser, the grammar becomes more straightforward with `ON DUPLICATE` as separate tokens and a separate rule for `NOT EXISTS`.

```
opt_ondupupdate: /* nil */
    | ON DUPLICATE KEY UPDATE insert_asgn_list { emit("DUPUPDATE %d", $5); }
    ;
    ...
expr: ...
    | NOT expr                         { emit("NOT"); }
    | EXISTS '(' select_stmt ')'       { emit("EXISTS 1"); }
    | NOT EXISTS '(' select_stmt ')'   { emit("EXISTS 0"); }
    ;
```

The next step is to run the grammar through bison, using the `-v` switch to create a bison listing, and to see what it says. In this case, it says there were 2 shift/reduce conflicts and 59 reduce/reduce:

```
State 249 conflicts: 1 shift/reduce
State 317 conflicts: 1 shift/reduce
State 345 conflicts: 59 reduce/reduce
```

Before throwing the switch to GLR, it's important to be sure that the conflicts are the ones we were expecting, so we look at those three states in the listing file:

```
state 249

    55 join_table: table_reference STRAIGHT_JOIN table_factor .
    56             | table_reference STRAIGHT_JOIN table_factor . ON expr

   ON  shift, and go to state 316

   ON          [reduce using rule 55 (join_table)]
   $default  reduce using rule 55 (join_table)

state 317

    54 join_table: table_reference opt_inner_cross JOIN table_factor . opt_join_condition

   ON      shift, and go to state 377
   USING   shift, and go to state 378

   ON          [reduce using rule 70 (opt_join_condition)]
   $default  reduce using rule 70 (opt_join_condition)

   opt_join_condition   go to state 379
   join_condition       go to state 380

state 345

   263 expr: EXISTS '(' select_stmt ')' .
   264     | NOT EXISTS '(' select_stmt ')' .

   NAME                 reduce using rule 263 (expr)
   NAME                 [reduce using rule 264 (expr)]

       ... 57 more reduce/reduce conflicts ...

   ')'                  reduce using rule 263 (expr)
   ')'                  [reduce using rule 264 (expr)]
   $default             reduce using rule 263 (expr)
```

States 249 and 317 are indeed limited lookahead for ON, and state 345 is the ambiguity of treating NOT EXISTS as one operator or two. (The large number of conflicts is because the token that follows NOT EXISTS can be any token that's valid in or after an expression.) Having confirmed that the conflicts are the expected ones, we add three lines to the definition section, one to make it a GLR parser and the other two to tell bison how many conflicts to expect. If you change the grammar and the number of conflicts changes, bison will fail, which is a good thing; then you can go back and be sure the new set of conflicts is still the expected one.

```
%glr-parser
%expect 2
%expect-rr 59
```

With these additions, the parser will now build, and it mostly works. Here it correctly parses two statements that use ON and ON DUPLICATE, but we haven't quite finished with the expression ambiguity:

```
insert into foo select a from b straight_join c on d;
rpn: NAME a
rpn: TABLE b
rpn: TABLE c
rpn: NAME d
rpn: JOIN 128
rpn: SELECT 0 1 1
rpn: INSERTSELECT 0 foo
rpn: STMT

insert into foo select a from b straight_join c on duplicate key update x=y;
rpn: NAME a
rpn: TABLE b
rpn: TABLE c
rpn: JOIN 128
rpn: SELECT 0 1 1
rpn: NAME y
rpn: ASSIGN x
rpn: DUPUPDATE 1
rpn: INSERTSELECT 0 foo
rpn: STMT

select not exists(select a from b);
rpn: NAME a
rpn: TABLE b
rpn: SELECT 0 1 1
Ambiguity detected.
Option 1,
  expr -> <Rule 247, tokens 2 .. 9>
    NOT <tokens 2 .. 2>
    expr -> <Rule 263, tokens 3 .. 9>
      EXISTS <tokens 3 .. 3>
      '(' <tokens 4 .. 4>
      select_stmt <tokens 5 .. 8>
      ')' <tokens 9 .. 9>

Option 2,
  expr -> <Rule 264, tokens 2 .. 9>
    NOT <tokens 2 .. 2>
    EXISTS <tokens 3 .. 3>
    '(' <tokens 4 .. 4>
    select_stmt <tokens 5 .. 8>
    ')' <tokens 9 .. 9>

1: error: syntax is ambiguous
SQL parse failed
```

Bison produces excellent diagnostics in GLR parsers. Here we can see the two possible parses: the first treating NOT EXISTS as separate operators, and the second treating it as one operator. This problem is easily fixed with `%dprec` since the one-operator version is always the one we want:

```
expr: ...
    | NOT expr { emit("NOT"); } %dprec 1
    ...
    | NOT EXISTS '(' select_stmt ')'  { emit("EXISTS 0"); } %dprec 2
```

Now the parser works correctly. The other way to resolve ambiguous parses is to provide your own function that takes the results of both rules and returns the result to be used as the value of the reduced rule. The arguments to the function and its value are of type `YYSTYPE`, which is the name that flex gives to the union created from `%union` declarations. If there are multiple reduce/reduce conflicts, you need a separate function for each one you want to resolve yourself. Each rule involved has a `%merge` tag, and all of the tags have to be the same for the rules involved in a conflict to be resolved:

```
%{
YYSTYPE exprmerge(YYSTYPE x1, YYSTYPE x2);
%}
expr: ...
    | NOT expr { emit("NOT"); } %merge <exprmerge>
    ...
    | NOT EXISTS '(' select_stmt ')'  { emit("EXISTS 0"); } %merge <exprmerge>
```

It's hard to come up with an application of `%merge` that isn't either contrived or extremely complicated. Since the merge function is called after all of the possible rules have been reduced, the values for rules have to be ASTs or something similar that contain all of the necessary information about all of the possible parses. The function would look at the ASTs and probably pick one to return and throw the other away, remembering to free its allocated storage first. The classic ambiguous syntax handled by GLR parsers is C++ declarations, which can be syntactically identical to an assignment with a typecast, but since the resolution rule is that anything that can be a declaration is a declaration, `%dprec` handles it just fine with no merging needed.

In many cases, GLR parsers are overkill, and you're better off tweaking your scanner and parser to run in a regular LALR parser, but if you have a predefined input language that just isn't LALR, GLR can be a lifesaver.

C++ Parsers

Bison can create parsers in C++. Although flex appears to be able to create C++, scanners, the C++ code doesn't work.[2] Fortunately, C scanners created by flex compile under C++ and it is not hard to use a flex C scanner with a bison C++ parser, which is what we'll do in the next example.

---

2. This is confirmed by the guy who wrote it. It will probably be fixed eventually, but it turned out to be surprisingly hard to design a good C++ interface for flex scanners.

All bison C++ parsers are reentrant, so bison creates a class for the parser. As with reentrant C parsers, the programmer can create as many instances as needed and usually passes in per-instance application data kept in a separate class.

Every time you create a C++ parser, bison creates four class headers; location.hh and position.hh to define the location structure, stack.hh for the internal parser stack, and the header for the parser itself. The first three always have the same contents; the last has specific values from the parser, as its C equivalent does. The parser header includes the other files, so they're separate files mostly; therefore they can be included by the lexer and other modules that need to handle locations. (One could ask why they didn't just make those three files standard library include files.) Creating the parser header is mandatory, since the generated C++ source includes it, although you still have to tell bison to do so.

A C++ Calculator

C++ parsers are somewhat more complex than C parsers, so to keep the code manageable, the example is based on the very simple calculator from Chapter 1. To make it slightly more interesting, the calculator can work in any radix from 2 to 10, with the radix being stored in the per-parser application context.

The application class cppcalc_ctx is defined in the header file cppcalc-ctx.hh, shown in Example 9-6.

Example 9-6. Application context class for the C++ calculator cppcalc-ctx.hh

```
class cppcalc_ctx {
public:
  cppcalc_ctx(int r) { assert(r > 1 && r <= 10); radix = r; }

  inline int getradix(void) { return radix; }

private:
  int radix;

};
```

C++ Parser Naming

Unless otherwise instructed, bison creates the parser in the yy namespace, specifically in a class called parser. The parser itself is a class method called parse, which you call after creating an instance of the class. The namespace can be changed by the declaration %define namespace, and the class can be changed by %define parser_class_name. In this example we change the class name to cppcalc. The class contains the private data for a parser. It also has some debugging methods enabled by defining the preprocessor symbol YYDEBUG, notably set_debug_level(N), which turns on parser tracing if N is nonzero.

A C++ Parser

The C++ parser, shown in Example 9-7, uses some new declarations.

Example 9-7. C++ calculator parser cppcalc.yy

```
/* C++ version of calculator */

%language "C++"
%defines
%locations

%define parser_class_name "cppcalc"

%{
#include <iostream>
using namespace std;
#include "cppcalc-ctx.hh"
%}

%parse-param { cppcalc_ctx &ctx }
%lex-param   { cppcalc_ctx &ctx }

%union {
      int ival;
};

/* declare tokens */
%token <ival> NUMBER
%token ADD SUB MUL DIV ABS
%token OP CP
%token EOL

%type <ival> exp factor term

%{
extern int yylex(yy::cppcalc::semantic_type *yylval,
        yy::cppcalc::location_type* yylloc,
        cppcalc_ctx &ctx);

void myout(int val, int radix);
%}

%initial-action {
 // Filename for locations here
 @$.begin.filename = @$.end.filename = new std::string("stdin");
}
%%
%%
```

The parser uses %language to declare that it's written in C++ rather than in C, %defines to create the header file, %locations to put code to handle locations into the parser, and %define to call the class cppcalc rather than the default parser. Then some C++ code includes the iostream library and the context header described earlier.

The %parser-param and %lex-param declarations are the ones we met in the section "Pure Parsers in Bison" on page 212, and we define an extra argument to the parser (the parser's class constructor) and to yylex. In this example we're not using a reentrant lexer, but if we were, the parameter to the lexer would have to be a flex scanner context yyscan_t as it was in the previous example. It would use the same trick of storing it in a field in the parser parameter, which is now an instance of the context class.

We declare a %union, which works the same way it does in C. In this simple case it has one member, the integer value of an expression. Following that are the token and nonterminal declarations.

C++ and %union

Although C allows a union to include structures, C++ doesn't permit a union to include class instances, so you can't use a class directly in a %union. Pointers to class instances are fine and are quite common in C++ parsers. Since the class instances pointed to will be dynamically allocated with new, remember that in each action where RHS symbols have class pointer values, each pointer value has to be saved somewhere it can be referenced later or has to be deleted. If you use parser error recovery, use %destructor declarations to tell bison how to free values that are discarded during error recovery. Otherwise, the program will have storage leaks.

These are the same rules that apply to malloced C structures, as in the AST we built in Chapter 3.

For some reason, bison doesn't create the declaration of yylex that C++ requires, so we do it manually here. Its arguments are the same as in the pure C example: pointers to the token value, token location, and the lex-param context pointer. In a C++ parser, token values and locations have the types semantic_type and location_type, both members of the parser class. We also define myout, an output routine defined later that prints values using a particular radix.

In a C parser that uses locations, if you want to report the filename, you have to add your own code to do so, as in section "More Sophisticated Locations with Filenames" on page 202, but the C++ version of locations fixes that oversight, adding a filename string field to the begin and end positions in each location. The %initial-action sets the filename for the initial location in $@, which is the location that's passed to the scanner. That is all we need since the scanner in this example reads only one file and never updates the location filename.

```
// bison rules for the C++ parser
calclist: /* nothing */
 | calclist exp EOL { cout << "= "; myout(ctx.getradix(), $2); cout << "\n> "; }
 | calclist EOL { cout << "> "; } /* blank line or a comment */
 ;

exp: factor
 | exp ADD factor { $$ = $1 + $3; }
```

```
    | exp SUB factor { $$ = $1 - $3; }
    | exp ABS factor { $$ = $1 | $3; }
    ;

factor: term
    | factor MUL term { $$ = $1 * $3; }
    | factor DIV term { if($3 == 0) {
                            error(@3, "zero divide");
                            YYABORT;
                        }
                        $$ = $1 / $3; }
    ;

term: NUMBER
    | ABS term { $$ = $2 >= 0? $2 : - $2; }
    | OP exp CP { $$ = $2; }
    ;
%%
```

The rules in the parser are the same as they were in Chapter 1, with the action code changed from C to C++. Note that the rule that prints a top-level `calclist` expression now calls `myout`, passing it the radix fetched from the `ctx` structure. The rule for division now has a zero divide test, calling parser class member function `error`, which replaces `yyerror`. (Because of a bug in the C++ parser skeleton, it always calls `error` with a location argument even if you don't use `%location`. The easiest workaround is always to use locations in a C++ parser.)

```
// C++ code section of parser
main()
{
  cppcalc_ctx ctx(8);      // work in octal today

  cout << "> ";

  yy::cppcalc parser(ctx); // make a cppcalc parser

  int v = parser.parse();  // and run it

  return v;
}

// print an integer in given radix
void
myout(int radix, int val)
{
  if(val < 0) {
    cout << "-";
    val = -val;
  }
  if(val > radix) {
    myout(radix, val/radix);
    val %= radix;
  }
  cout << val;
```

```
}

int
myatoi(int radix, char *s)
{
  int v = 0;

  while(*s) {
    v = v*radix + *s++ - '0';
  }
  return v;
}

namespace yy {
  void
  cppcalc::error(location const &loc, const std::string& s) {
    std::cerr << "error at " << loc << ": " << s << std::endl;
  }
}
```

Unlike a C pure parser, a C++ pure parser requires that you first create an instance of the parser then call it. Hence, the main program creates a `ctx` structure with an appropriate radix, creates an instance of `yy::cppcalc` called `parser` using that context, and then calls the `parse` method to do the actual parsing.

Two helper routines, `myout` and `myatoi`, do radix to binary conversion, and finally we define `yy::error`, the error routine analogous to `yyerror`. For some reason, bison declares `error` as a private member function in the parser class, which means you can't call it from elsewhere; in particular, you can't call it from the scanner. The bison manual suggests that `yy::error` call the real error routine, which is defined in a context visible to the scanner and is probably the best workaround. Notice, incidentally, that the error routine outputs the location of the error using the normal C++ `<<` operator. This works because the `location` class defines a variety of operators including output formatting.

Interfacing a Scanner with a C++ Parser

The flex scanner, shown in Example 9-8, is written in C++-compatible C.

Example 9-8. C++ calculator scanner cppcalc.l

```
/* recognize tokens for the C++ calculator and print them out */

%option noyywrap
%{
# include <cstdlib>

# include "cppcalc-ctx.hh"
# include "cppcalc.tab.hh"

#define YY_DECL int yylex(yy::cppcalc::semantic_type *yylval, \
    yy::cppcalc::location_type *yylloc, cppcalc_ctx &ctx)
```

```
// make location include the current token
# define YY_USER_ACTION  yylloc->columns (yyleng);

typedef yy::cppcalc::token token;
extern int myatoi(int radix, char *s); // defined in the parser
%}
%%
```

The declaration part of the scanner includes the standard C library and the header files for the context and parser classes. It defines YY_DECL to declare the calling sequence for yylex to match what the parser expects, and it defines YY_USER_ACTION, the macro invoked before the action for each token, to set the location based on the length of the token. This is the same trick we did in Chapter 8, but the code is much shorter since C++ locations have a method that does what we want.

The parser token numbers are defined in the token member of the parser class, so a typedef for the plain name token will make the token values easier to type.

```
// rules for C++-compatible scanner
%{
    // start where previous token ended
    yylloc->step ();
%}

"+"     { return token::ADD; }
"-"     { return token::SUB; }
"*"     { return token::MUL; }
"/"     { return token::DIV; }
"|"     { return token::ABS; }
"("     { return token::OP; }
")"     { return token::CP; }
[0-9]+  { yylval->ival = myatoi(ctx.getradix(), yytext); return token::NUMBER; }

\n      { yylloc->lines(1); return token::EOL; }

  /* skip over comments and whitespace */
"//".*  |
[ \t]   {  yylloc->step (); }

.       { printf("Mystery character %c\n", *yytext); }
%%
```

The code at the beginning of the rules section is copied near the beginning of yylex. The step method sets the beginning of the location equal to the end, so the location now points to the end of the previous token. (An alternative would be what we did in Chapter 8, tracking the line and column in local variables and copying them into the location for each token, but this takes advantage of predefined methods on C++ locations to make the code shorter.)

The action code prefixes the token names with token:: since the token names are now parser class members. The action for a newline uses the lines method to update the location line number, the action for comments and whitespace invokes step since they don't return from the scanner, and the previous step is invoked only when yylex has returned and is called again.

The last catchall rule prints an error message. In the original C version of the scanner it called yyerror, but since this scanner isn't part of the C++ parser class, it can't call the parser error routine. Rather than write glue routines to allow the various parts of the program to call the same error reporting routine, for simplicity we just call printf.

Should You Write Your Parser in C++ ?

As should be apparent by now, the C++ support in bison is nowhere near as mature as the C support, which is not surprising since it's about 30 years newer. The fact that %union can't include class instances can require some extra work, and the less than seamless integration between C++ bison and C flex requires careful programming, particularly if they need to share significant data structures accessed from C in the scanner and C++ in the parser or if they need to have the scanner read its input using C stdio while the rest of the program uses C++ library I/O. A good object design would wrap a class around the application context (ctx in this example), the parser, and probably the scanner to present a unified interface to the rest of the program.

Nonetheless, C++ bison parsers do work, and the design of the parser class is a reasonable one. If you're integrating your parser into a larger C++ project or if you want to use C++ libraries that don't have C equivalents, a C++ parser can work well.

Java and Beyond

Bison currently (2009) has experimental support for parsers written in Java. By the time you read this, it may support other languages as well. The Java support is modeled on that for C++, with adjustments for the Java environment, which has no preprocessor or unions, but does have garbage collection. Since the details are likely to have changed, consult the bison manual for the current Java interface.

Exercises

1. Modify the parser in the pure calculator to parse one statement at a time and return without using YYACCEPT. You'll probably want to change the scanner so it returns a zero token at end-of-line rather than using EOL.

2. Does the GLR version of the SQL parser accept the same language as the original version? Come up with an example that would be accepted and one that wouldn't. (Hint: Try putting comments between tokens that usually just have a space between them.)

SQL Parser Grammar and Cross-Reference

Since the grammar for the SQL parser in Chapter 4 is so large, here's a list of the rules in the order they appear in the source file, as well as a cross-reference of each token and nonterminal symbol with the rules where they appear. This cross-reference is for the slightly extended version in Chapter 8 that includes error recovery rules.

The listing in Example A-1 and the cross-references in Example A-2 are extracted from the listing file `lpmysql.output` created when bison compiled the grammar. The listing also includes a list of unused tokens, of which this grammar has quite a few since it defines SQL keywords not used in the subset we parse, and it includes the complete set of parser states and shift and reduce actions. The entire listing is more than 10,000 lines long, much too long to include in this book, but is invaluable for reference when debugging a grammar.

Example A-1. SQL grammar listing

```
 0 $accept: stmt_list $end

 1 stmt_list: stmt ';'
 2          | stmt_list stmt ';'
 3          | error ';'
 4          | stmt_list error ';'

 5 stmt: select_stmt

 6 select_stmt: SELECT select_opts select_expr_list
 7            | SELECT select_opts select_expr_list FROM table_references opt_where
                opt_groupby opt_having opt_orderby opt_limit opt_into_list

 8 opt_where: /* empty */
 9          | WHERE expr

10 opt_groupby: /* empty */
11            | GROUP BY groupby_list opt_with_rollup
```

```
12 groupby_list: expr opt_asc_desc
13              | groupby_list ',' expr opt_asc_desc

14 opt_asc_desc: /* empty */
15              | ASC
16              | DESC

17 opt_with_rollup: /* empty */
18                 | WITH ROLLUP

19 opt_having: /* empty */
20            | HAVING expr

21 opt_orderby: /* empty */
22             | ORDER BY groupby_list

23 opt_limit: /* empty */
24           | LIMIT expr
25           | LIMIT expr ',' expr

26 opt_into_list: /* empty */
27               | INTO column_list

28 column_list: NAME
29             | STRING
30             | column_list ',' NAME
31             | column_list ',' STRING

32 select_opts: /* empty */
33             | select_opts ALL
34             | select_opts DISTINCT
35             | select_opts DISTINCTROW
36             | select_opts HIGH_PRIORITY
37             | select_opts STRAIGHT_JOIN
38             | select_opts SQL_SMALL_RESULT
39             | select_opts SQL_BIG_RESULT
40             | select_opts SQL_CALC_FOUND_ROWS

41 select_expr_list: select_expr
42                  | select_expr_list ',' select_expr
43                  | '*'

44 select_expr: expr opt_as_alias

45 table_references: table_reference
46                  | table_references ',' table_reference

47 table_reference: table_factor
48                 | join_table

49 table_factor: NAME opt_as_alias index_hint
50             | NAME '.' NAME opt_as_alias index_hint
51             | table_subquery opt_as NAME
52             | '(' table_references ')'
```

```
53 opt_as: AS
54       | /* empty */

55 opt_as_alias: AS NAME
56              | NAME
57              | /* empty */

58 join_table: table_reference opt_inner_cross JOIN table_factor opt_join_condition
59            | table_reference STRAIGHT_JOIN table_factor
60            | table_reference STRAIGHT_JOIN table_factor ON expr
61            | table_reference left_or_right opt_outer JOIN table_factor
                   join_condition
62            | table_reference NATURAL opt_left_or_right_outer JOIN table_factor

63 opt_inner_cross: /* empty */
64                | INNER
65                | CROSS

66 opt_outer: /* empty */
67          | OUTER

68 left_or_right: LEFT
69              | RIGHT

70 opt_left_or_right_outer: LEFT opt_outer
71                        | RIGHT opt_outer
72                        | /* empty */

73 opt_join_condition: join_condition
74                   | /* empty */

75 join_condition: ON expr
76               | USING '(' column_list ')'

77 index_hint: USE KEY opt_for_join '(' index_list ')'
78           | IGNORE KEY opt_for_join '(' index_list ')'
79           | FORCE KEY opt_for_join '(' index_list ')'
80           | /* empty */

81 opt_for_join: FOR JOIN
82             | /* empty */

83 index_list: NAME
84           | index_list ',' NAME

85 table_subquery: '(' select_stmt ')'

86 stmt: delete_stmt

87 delete_stmt: DELETE delete_opts FROM NAME opt_where opt_orderby opt_limit

88 delete_opts: delete_opts LOW_PRIORITY
89            | delete_opts QUICK
90            | delete_opts IGNORE
91            | /* empty */
```

```
92 delete_stmt: DELETE delete_opts delete_list FROM table_references opt_where

93 delete_list: NAME opt_dot_star
94             | delete_list ',' NAME opt_dot_star

95 opt_dot_star: /* empty */
96             | '.' '*'

97 delete_stmt: DELETE delete_opts FROM delete_list USING table_references
   opt_where

98 stmt: insert_stmt

99 insert_stmt: INSERT insert_opts opt_into NAME opt_col_names VALUES
   insert_vals_list opt_ondupupdate

100 opt_ondupupdate: /* empty */
101                | ONDUPLICATE KEY UPDATE insert_asgn_list

102 insert_opts: /* empty */
103            | insert_opts LOW_PRIORITY
104            | insert_opts DELAYED
105            | insert_opts HIGH_PRIORITY
106            | insert_opts IGNORE

107 opt_into: INTO
108         | /* empty */

109 opt_col_names: /* empty */
110             | '(' column_list ')'

111 insert_vals_list: '(' insert_vals ')'
112                 | insert_vals_list ',' '(' insert_vals ')'

113 insert_vals: expr
114            | DEFAULT
115            | insert_vals ',' expr
116            | insert_vals ',' DEFAULT

117 insert_stmt: INSERT insert_opts opt_into NAME SET insert_asgn_list
             opt_ondupupdate
118          | INSERT insert_opts opt_into NAME opt_col_names select_stmt
             opt_ondupupdate

119 insert_asgn_list: NAME COMPARISON expr
120                 | NAME COMPARISON DEFAULT
121                 | insert_asgn_list ',' NAME COMPARISON expr
122                 | insert_asgn_list ',' NAME COMPARISON DEFAULT

123 stmt: replace_stmt

124 replace_stmt: REPLACE insert_opts opt_into NAME opt_col_names VALUES
   insert_vals_list opt_ondupupdate
125             | REPLACE insert_opts opt_into NAME SET insert_asgn_list
```

```
                  opt_ondupupdate
126              |  REPLACE insert_opts opt_into NAME opt_col_names select_stmt
                  opt_ondupupdate

127 stmt: update_stmt

128 update_stmt: UPDATE update_opts table_references SET update_asgn_list opt_where
    opt_orderby opt_limit

129 update_opts: /* empty */
130              |  insert_opts LOW_PRIORITY
131              |  insert_opts IGNORE

132 update_asgn_list: NAME COMPARISON expr
133                   |  NAME '.' NAME COMPARISON expr
134                   |  update_asgn_list ',' NAME COMPARISON expr
135                   |  update_asgn_list ',' NAME '.' NAME COMPARISON expr

136 stmt: create_database_stmt

137 create_database_stmt: CREATE DATABASE opt_if_not_exists NAME
138                       |  CREATE SCHEMA opt_if_not_exists NAME

139 opt_if_not_exists: /* empty */
140                   |  IF EXISTS

141 stmt: create_table_stmt

142 create_table_stmt: CREATE opt_temporary TABLE opt_if_not_exists
                       NAME '(' create_col_list ')'
143                   |  CREATE opt_temporary TABLE opt_if_not_exists NAME '.'
                       NAME '(' create_col_list ')'
144                   |  CREATE opt_temporary TABLE opt_if_not_exists
                       NAME '(' create_col_list ')' create_select_statement
145                   |  CREATE opt_temporary TABLE opt_if_not_exists
                       NAME create_select_statement
146                   |  CREATE opt_temporary TABLE opt_if_not_exists NAME '.'
                       NAME '(' create_col_list ')' create_select_statement
147                   |  CREATE opt_temporary TABLE opt_if_not_exists NAME '.'
                       NAME create_select_statement

148 create_col_list: create_definition
149                 |  create_col_list ',' create_definition

150 $@1: /* empty */

151 create_definition: $@1 NAME data_type column_atts
152                   |  PRIMARY KEY '(' column_list ')'
153                   |  KEY '(' column_list ')'
154                   |  INDEX '(' column_list ')'
155                   |  FULLTEXT INDEX '(' column_list ')'
156                   |  FULLTEXT KEY '(' column_list ')'

157 column_atts: /* empty */
158             |  column_atts NOT NULLX
```

```
159              | column_atts NULLX
160              | column_atts DEFAULT STRING
161              | column_atts DEFAULT INTNUM
162              | column_atts DEFAULT APPROXNUM
163              | column_atts DEFAULT BOOL
164              | column_atts AUTO_INCREMENT
165              | column_atts UNIQUE '(' column_list ')'
166              | column_atts UNIQUE KEY
167              | column_atts PRIMARY KEY
168              | column_atts KEY
169              | column_atts COMMENT STRING

170 opt_length: /* empty */
171           | '(' INTNUM ')'
172           | '(' INTNUM ',' INTNUM ')'

173 opt_binary: /* empty */
174           | BINARY

175 opt_uz: /* empty */
176       | opt_uz UNSIGNED
177       | opt_uz ZEROFILL

178 opt_csc: /* empty */
179        | opt_csc CHAR SET STRING
180        | opt_csc COLLATE STRING

181 data_type: BIT opt_length
182          | TINYINT opt_length opt_uz
183          | SMALLINT opt_length opt_uz
184          | MEDIUMINT opt_length opt_uz
185          | INT opt_length opt_uz
186          | INTEGER opt_length opt_uz
187          | BIGINT opt_length opt_uz
188          | REAL opt_length opt_uz
189          | DOUBLE opt_length opt_uz
190          | FLOAT opt_length opt_uz
191          | DECIMAL opt_length opt_uz
192          | DATE
193          | TIME
194          | TIMESTAMP
195          | DATETIME
196          | YEAR
197          | CHAR opt_length opt_csc
198          | VARCHAR '(' INTNUM ')' opt_csc
199          | BINARY opt_length
200          | VARBINARY '(' INTNUM ')'
201          | TINYBLOB
202          | BLOB
203          | MEDIUMBLOB
204          | LONGBLOB
205          | TINYTEXT opt_binary opt_csc
206          | TEXT opt_binary opt_csc
207          | MEDIUMTEXT opt_binary opt_csc
208          | LONGTEXT opt_binary opt_csc
```

```
209            | ENUM '(' enum_list ')' opt_csc
210            | SET '(' enum_list ')' opt_csc

211 enum_list: STRING
212            | enum_list ',' STRING

213 create_select_statement: opt_ignore_replace opt_as select_stmt

214 opt_ignore_replace: /* empty */
215                    | IGNORE
216                    | REPLACE

217 opt_temporary: /* empty */
218                | TEMPORARY

219 stmt: set_stmt

220 set_stmt: SET set_list

221 set_list: set_expr
222            | set_list ',' set_expr

223 set_expr: USERVAR COMPARISON expr
224          | USERVAR ASSIGN expr

225 expr: NAME
226      | USERVAR
227      | NAME '.' NAME
228      | STRING
229      | INTNUM
230      | APPROXNUM
231      | BOOL
232      | expr '+' expr
233      | expr '-' expr
234      | expr '*' expr
235      | expr '/' expr
236      | expr '%' expr
237      | expr MOD expr
238      | '-' expr
239      | expr ANDOP expr
240      | expr OR expr
241      | expr XOR expr
242      | expr COMPARISON expr
243      | expr COMPARISON '(' select_stmt ')'
244      | expr COMPARISON ANY '(' select_stmt ')'
245      | expr COMPARISON SOME '(' select_stmt ')'
246      | expr COMPARISON ALL '(' select_stmt ')'
247      | expr '|' expr
248      | expr '&' expr
249      | expr '^' expr
250      | expr SHIFT expr
251      | NOT expr
252      | '!' expr
253      | USERVAR ASSIGN expr
254      | expr IS NULLX
```

```
255      | expr IS NOT NULLX
256      | expr IS BOOL
257      | expr IS NOT BOOL
258      | expr BETWEEN expr AND expr

259 val_list: expr
260         | expr ',' val_list

261 opt_val_list: /* empty */
262             | val_list

263 expr: expr IN '(' val_list ')'
264      | expr NOT IN '(' val_list ')'
265      | expr IN '(' select_stmt ')'
266      | expr NOT IN '(' select_stmt ')'
267      | EXISTS '(' select_stmt ')'
268      | NAME '(' opt_val_list ')'
269      | FCOUNT '(' '*' ')'
270      | FCOUNT '(' expr ')'
271      | FSUBSTRING '(' val_list ')'
272      | FSUBSTRING '(' expr FROM expr ')'
273      | FSUBSTRING '(' expr FROM expr FOR expr ')'
274      | FTRIM '(' val_list ')'
275      | FTRIM '(' trim_ltb expr FROM val_list ')'

276 trim_ltb: LEADING
277         | TRAILING
278         | BOTH

279 expr: FDATE_ADD '(' expr ',' interval_exp ')'
280      | FDATE_SUB '(' expr ',' interval_exp ')'

281 interval_exp: INTERVAL expr DAY_HOUR
282             | INTERVAL expr DAY_MICROSECOND
283             | INTERVAL expr DAY_MINUTE
284             | INTERVAL expr DAY_SECOND
285             | INTERVAL expr YEAR_MONTH
286             | INTERVAL expr YEAR
287             | INTERVAL expr HOUR_MICROSECOND
288             | INTERVAL expr HOUR_MINUTE
289             | INTERVAL expr HOUR_SECOND

290 expr: CASE expr case_list END
291      | CASE expr case_list ELSE expr END
292      | CASE case_list END
293      | CASE case_list ELSE expr END

294 case_list: WHEN expr THEN expr
295          | case_list WHEN expr THEN expr

296 expr: expr LIKE expr
297      | expr NOT LIKE expr
298      | expr REGEXP expr
299      | expr NOT REGEXP expr
300      | CURRENT_TIMESTAMP
```

```
301      | CURRENT_DATE
302      | CURRENT_TIME
303      | BINARY expr
```

Example A-2. SQL grammar terminal symbol cross-reference

```
Terminals, with rules where they appear

$end (0) 0
'!' (33) 252
'%' (37) 236
'&' (38) 248
'(' (40) 52 76 77 78 79 85 110 111 112 142 143 144 146 152 153 154
    155 156 165 171 172 198 200 209 210 243 244 245 246 263 264 265
    266 267 268 269 270 271 272 273 274 275 279 280
')' (41) 52 76 77 78 79 85 110 111 112 142 143 144 146 152 153 154
    155 156 165 171 172 198 200 209 210 243 244 245 246 263 264 265
    266 267 268 269 270 271 272 273 274 275 279 280
'*' (42) 43 96 234 269
'+' (43) 232
',' (44) 13 25 30 31 42 46 84 94 112 115 116 121 122 134 135 149 172
    212 222 260 279 280
'-' (45) 233 238
'.' (46) 50 96 133 135 143 146 147 227
'/' (47) 235
';' (59) 1 2 3 4
'^' (94) 249
'|' (124) 247
error (256) 3 4
NAME (258) 28 30 49 50 51 55 56 83 84 87 93 94 99 117 118 119 120 121
    122 124 125 126 132 133 134 135 137 138 142 143 144 145 146 147
    151 225 227 268
STRING (259) 29 31 160 169 179 180 211 212 228
INTNUM (260) 161 171 172 198 200 229
BOOL (261) 163 231 256 257
APPROXNUM (262) 162 230
USERVAR (263) 223 224 226 253
ASSIGN (264) 224 253
OR (265) 240
XOR (266) 241
ANDOP (267) 239
REGEXP (268) 298 299
LIKE (269) 296 297
IS (270) 254 255 256 257
IN (271) 263 264 265 266
NOT (272) 158 251 255 257 264 266 297 299
BETWEEN (273) 258
COMPARISON (274) 119 120 121 122 132 133 134 135 223 242 243 244 245
    246
SHIFT (275) 250
MOD (276) 237
UMINUS (277)
ADD (278)
ALL (279) 33 246
ALTER (280)
ANALYZE (281)
```

```
AND (282) 258
ANY (283) 244
AS (284) 53 55
ASC (285) 15
AUTO_INCREMENT (286) 164
BEFORE (287)
BIGINT (288) 187
BINARY (289) 174 199 303
BIT (290) 181
BLOB (291) 202
BOTH (292) 278
BY (293) 11 22
CALL (294)
CASCADE (295)
CASE (296) 290 291 292 293
CHANGE (297)
CHAR (298) 179 197
CHECK (299)
COLLATE (300) 180
COLUMN (301)
COMMENT (302) 169
CONDITION (303)
CONSTRAINT (304)
CONTINUE (305)
CONVERT (306)
CREATE (307) 137 138 142 143 144 145 146 147
CROSS (308) 65
CURRENT_DATE (309) 301
CURRENT_TIME (310) 302
CURRENT_TIMESTAMP (311) 300
CURRENT_USER (312)
CURSOR (313)
DATABASE (314) 137
DATABASES (315)
DATE (316) 192
DATETIME (317) 195
DAY_HOUR (318) 281
DAY_MICROSECOND (319) 282
DAY_MINUTE (320) 283
DAY_SECOND (321) 284
DECIMAL (322) 191
DECLARE (323)
DEFAULT (324) 114 116 120 122 160 161 162 163
DELAYED (325) 104
DELETE (326) 87 92 97
DESC (327) 16
DESCRIBE (328)
DETERMINISTIC (329)
DISTINCT (330) 34
DISTINCTROW (331) 35
DIV (332)
DOUBLE (333) 189
DROP (334)
DUAL (335)
EACH (336)
```

ELSE (337) 291 293
ELSEIF (338)
ENCLOSED (339)
END (340) 290 291 292 293
ENUM (341) 209
ESCAPED (342)
EXISTS (343) 140 267
EXIT (344)
EXPLAIN (345)
FETCH (346)
FLOAT (347) 190
FOR (348) 81 273
FORCE (349) 79
FOREIGN (350)
FROM (351) 7 87 92 97 272 273 275
FULLTEXT (352) 155 156
GRANT (353)
GROUP (354) 11
HAVING (355) 20
HIGH_PRIORITY (356) 36 105
HOUR_MICROSECOND (357) 287
HOUR_MINUTE (358) 288
HOUR_SECOND (359) 289
IF (360) 140
IGNORE (361) 78 90 106 131 215
INDEX (362) 154 155
INFILE (363)
INNER (364) 64
INOUT (365)
INSENSITIVE (366)
INSERT (367) 99 117 118
INT (368) 185
INTEGER (369) 186
INTERVAL (370) 281 282 283 284 285 286 287 288 289
INTO (371) 27 107
ITERATE (372)
JOIN (373) 58 61 62 81
KEY (374) 77 78 79 101 152 153 156 166 167 168
KEYS (375)
KILL (376)
LEADING (377) 276
LEAVE (378)
LEFT (379) 68 70
LIMIT (380) 24 25
LINES (381)
LOAD (382)
LOCALTIME (383)
LOCALTIMESTAMP (384)
LOCK (385)
LONG (386)
LONGBLOB (387) 204
LONGTEXT (388) 208
LOOP (389)
LOW_PRIORITY (390) 88 103 130
MATCH (391)

MEDIUMBLOB (392) 203
MEDIUMINT (393) 184
MEDIUMTEXT (394) 207
MINUTE_MICROSECOND (395)
MINUTE_SECOND (396)
MODIFIES (397)
NATURAL (398) 62
NO_WRITE_TO_BINLOG (399)
NULLX (400) 158 159 254 255
NUMBER (401)
ON (402) 60 75
ONDUPLICATE (403) 101
OPTIMIZE (404)
OPTION (405)
OPTIONALLY (406)
ORDER (407) 22
OUT (408)
OUTER (409) 67
OUTFILE (410)
PRECISION (411)
PRIMARY (412) 152 167
PROCEDURE (413)
PURGE (414)
QUICK (415) 89
READ (416)
READS (417)
REAL (418) 188
REFERENCES (419)
RELEASE (420)
RENAME (421)
REPEAT (422)
REPLACE (423) 124 125 126 216
REQUIRE (424)
RESTRICT (425)
RETURN (426)
REVOKE (427)
RIGHT (428) 69 71
ROLLUP (429) 18
SCHEMA (430) 138
SCHEMAS (431)
SECOND_MICROSECOND (432)
SELECT (433) 6 7
SENSITIVE (434)
SEPARATOR (435)
SET (436) 117 125 128 179 210 220
SHOW (437)
SMALLINT (438) 183
SOME (439) 245
SONAME (440)
SPATIAL (441)
SPECIFIC (442)
SQL (443)
SQLEXCEPTION (444)
SQLSTATE (445)
SQLWARNING (446)

```
SQL_BIG_RESULT (447) 39
SQL_CALC_FOUND_ROWS (448) 40
SQL_SMALL_RESULT (449) 38
SSL (450)
STARTING (451)
STRAIGHT_JOIN (452) 37 59 60
TABLE (453) 142 143 144 145 146 147
TEMPORARY (454) 218
TEXT (455) 206
TERMINATED (456)
THEN (457) 294 295
TIME (458) 193
TIMESTAMP (459) 194
TINYBLOB (460) 201
TINYINT (461) 182
TINYTEXT (462) 205
TO (463)
TRAILING (464) 277
TRIGGER (465)
UNDO (466)
UNION (467)
UNIQUE (468) 165 166
UNLOCK (469)
UNSIGNED (470) 176
UPDATE (471) 101 128
USAGE (472)
USE (473) 77
USING (474) 76 97
UTC_DATE (475)
UTC_TIME (476)
UTC_TIMESTAMP (477)
VALUES (478) 99 124
VARBINARY (479) 200
VARCHAR (480) 198
VARYING (481)
WHEN (482) 294 295
WHERE (483) 9
WHILE (484)
WITH (485) 18
WRITE (486)
YEAR (487) 196 286
YEAR_MONTH (488) 285
ZEROFILL (489) 177
FSUBSTRING (490) 271 272 273
FTRIM (491) 274 275
FDATE_ADD (492) 279
FDATE_SUB (493) 280
FCOUNT (494) 269 270


Nonterminals, with rules where they appear

$accept (254)
    on left: 0
stmt_list (255)
```

        on left: 1 2 3 4, on right: 0 2 4
stmt (256)
        on left: 5 86 98 123 127 136 141 219, on right: 1 2
select_stmt (257)
        on left: 6 7, on right: 5 85 118 126 213 243 244 245 246 265 266
        267
opt_where (258)
        on left: 8 9, on right: 7 87 92 97 128
opt_groupby (259)
        on left: 10 11, on right: 7
groupby_list (260)
        on left: 12 13, on right: 11 13 22
opt_asc_desc (261)
        on left: 14 15 16, on right: 12 13
opt_with_rollup (262)
        on left: 17 18, on right: 11
opt_having (263)
        on left: 19 20, on right: 7
opt_orderby (264)
        on left: 21 22, on right: 7 87 128
opt_limit (265)
        on left: 23 24 25, on right: 7 87 128
opt_into_list (266)
        on left: 26 27, on right: 7
column_list (267)
        on left: 28 29 30 31, on right: 27 30 31 76 110 152 153 154 155
        156 165
select_opts (268)
        on left: 32 33 34 35 36 37 38 39 40, on right: 6 7 33 34 35 36
        37 38 39 40
select_expr_list (269)
        on left: 41 42 43, on right: 6 7 42
select_expr (270)
        on left: 44, on right: 41 42
table_references (271)
        on left: 45 46, on right: 7 46 52 92 97 128
table_reference (272)
        on left: 47 48, on right: 45 46 58 59 60 61 62
table_factor (273)
        on left: 49 50 51 52, on right: 47 58 59 60 61 62
opt_as (274)
        on left: 53 54, on right: 51 213
opt_as_alias (275)
        on left: 55 56 57, on right: 44 49 50
join_table (276)
        on left: 58 59 60 61 62, on right: 48
opt_inner_cross (277)
        on left: 63 64 65, on right: 58
opt_outer (278)
        on left: 66 67, on right: 61 70 71
left_or_right (279)
        on left: 68 69, on right: 61
opt_left_or_right_outer (280)
        on left: 70 71 72, on right: 62
opt_join_condition (281)

```
      on left: 73 74, on right: 58
join_condition (282)
      on left: 75 76, on right: 61 73
index_hint (283)
      on left: 77 78 79 80, on right: 49 50
opt_for_join (284)
      on left: 81 82, on right: 77 78 79
index_list (285)
      on left: 83 84, on right: 77 78 79 84
table_subquery (286)
      on left: 85, on right: 51
delete_stmt (287)
      on left: 87 92 97, on right: 86
delete_opts (288)
      on left: 88 89 90 91, on right: 87 88 89 90 92 97
delete_list (289)
      on left: 93 94, on right: 92 94 97
opt_dot_star (290)
      on left: 95 96, on right: 93 94
insert_stmt (291)
      on left: 99 117 118, on right: 98
opt_ondupupdate (292)
      on left: 100 101, on right: 99 117 118 124 125 126
insert_opts (293)
      on left: 102 103 104 105 106, on right: 99 103 104 105 106 117
      118 124 125 126 130 131
opt_into (294)
      on left: 107 108, on right: 99 117 118 124 125 126
opt_col_names (295)
      on left: 109 110, on right: 99 118 124 126
insert_vals_list (296)
      on left: 111 112, on right: 99 112 124
insert_vals (297)
      on left: 113 114 115 116, on right: 111 112 115 116
insert_asgn_list (298)
      on left: 119 120 121 122, on right: 101 117 121 122 125
replace_stmt (299)
      on left: 124 125 126, on right: 123
update_stmt (300)
      on left: 128, on right: 127
update_opts (301)
      on left: 129 130 131, on right: 128
update_asgn_list (302)
      on left: 132 133 134 135, on right: 128 134 135
create_database_stmt (303)
      on left: 137 138, on right: 136
opt_if_not_exists (304)
      on left: 139 140, on right: 137 138 142 143 144 145 146 147
create_table_stmt (305)
      on left: 142 143 144 145 146 147, on right: 141
create_col_list (306)
      on left: 148 149, on right: 142 143 144 146 149
create_definition (307)
      on left: 151 152 153 154 155 156, on right: 148 149
$@1 (308)
```

```
        on left: 150, on right: 151
column_atts (309)
      on left: 157 158 159 160 161 162 163 164 165 166 167 168 169, on right:
      151 158 159 160 161 162 163 164 165 166 167 168 169
opt_length (310)
      on left: 170 171 172, on right: 181 182 183 184 185 186 187 188
      189 190 191 197 199
opt_binary (311)
      on left: 173 174, on right: 205 206 207 208
opt_uz (312)
      on left: 175 176 177, on right: 176 177 182 183 184 185 186 187
      188 189 190 191
opt_csc (313)
      on left: 178 179 180, on right: 179 180 197 198 205 206 207 208
      209 210
data_type (314)
      on left: 181 182 183 184 185 186 187 188 189 190 191 192 193 194
      195 196 197 198 199 200 201 202 203 204 205 206 207 208 209 210,
      on right: 151
enum_list (315)
      on left: 211 212, on right: 209 210 212
create_select_statement (316)
      on left: 213, on right: 144 145 146 147
opt_ignore_replace (317)
      on left: 214 215 216, on right: 213
opt_temporary (318)
      on left: 217 218, on right: 142 143 144 145 146 147
set_stmt (319)
      on left: 220, on right: 219
set_list (320)
      on left: 221 222, on right: 220 222
set_expr (321)
      on left: 223 224, on right: 221 222
expr (322)
      on left: 225 226 227 228 229 230 231 232 233 234 235 236 237 238
      239 240 241 242 243 244 245 246 247 248 249 250 251 252 253 254
      255 256 257 258 263 264 265 266 267 268 269 270 271 272 273 274
      275 279 280 290 291 292 293 296 297 298 299 300 301 302 303, on right:
      9 12 13 20 24 25 44 60 75 113 115 119 121 132 133 134 135 223 224
      232 233 234 235 236 237 238 239 240 241 242 243 244 245 246 247
      248 249 250 251 252 253 254 255 256 257 258 259 260 263 264 265
      266 270 272 273 275 279 280 281 282 283 284 285 286 287 288 289
      290 291 293 294 295 296 297 298 299 303
val_list (323)
      on left: 259 260, on right: 260 262 263 264 271 274 275
opt_val_list (324)
      on left: 261 262, on right: 268
trim_ltb (325)
      on left: 276 277 278, on right: 275
interval_exp (326)
      on left: 281 282 283 284 285 286 287 288 289, on right: 279 280
case_list (327)
      on left: 294 295, on right: 290 291 292 293 295
```

Glossary

action

The C or C++ code associated with a flex pattern or a bison rule. When the pattern or rule matches an input sequence, the action code is executed.

alphabet

A set of distinct symbols. For example, the ASCII character set is a collection of 128 different symbols. In a flex specification, the alphabet is the native character set of the computer. In a bison grammar, the alphabet is the set of tokens and nonterminals used in the grammar.

ambiguity

An *ambiguous* grammar is one with more than one rule or set of rules that match the same input. In a bison grammar, ambiguous rules cause shift/reduce or reduce/reduce conflicts. The parsing mechanism that bison normally uses cannot handle ambiguous grammars. The programmer can use %prec declarations and bison's own internal rules to resolve conflicts when creating a parser, or the programmer can use a GLR parser, which can handle ambiguous grammars directly.

ASCII

American **S**tandard **C**ode for **I**nformation Interchange; a collection of 128 symbols representing the common symbols found in the American alphabet: lowercase and uppercase letters, digits, and punctuation, plus additional characters for formatting and control of data communication links. Most

systems that run flex and bison use ASCII or extended 8-bit codes in the ISO-8859 series that include ASCII as a subset.

bison

A program that translates a dialect of BNF into LALR(1) or GLR parsers.

BNF

Backus-**N**aur **F**orm; a method of representing context-free grammars. It is commonly used to specify formal grammars of programming languages. The input syntax of bison is a simplifed version of BNF.

compiler

A program that translates a set of instructions (a *program*) in one language into some other representation; typically, the output of a compiler is in the native binary language that can be run directly on a computer. Compare to *interpreter*.

conflict

An error within the bison grammar in which two (or more) parsing actions are possible when parsing the same input token. There are two types of conflicts: *shift/reduce* and *reduce/reduce*. (See also *ambiguity*.)

context-free grammar

A grammar in which each rule has a single symbol on the LHS; hence, one in which the RHS can match input regardless of what might precede or follow the material it matches. Also called a *phrase structure grammar*. Context-sensitive grammars, containing rules with several symbols on the

LHS, are not practical for parsing computer languages.

empty

The special case of a string with zero symbols, sometimes written as a Greek epsilon. Bison rules can match the empty string, but flex patterns cannot.

finite automaton

An abstract machine that consists of a finite number of instructions (or *transitions*). Finite automata are useful in modeling many commonly occurring computer processes and have useful mathematical properties. Flex and bison create scanners and parsers based on finite automata.

flex

A program for producing lexical analyzers, also known as *scanners*, that match patterns defined by regular expressions to a character stream.

GLR

Generalized **L**eft to **R**ight; a powerful parsing technique that bison can optionally use. Unlike LALR(1), it can parse grammars that are ambiguous or need indefinite lookahead by maintaining all possible parses in parallel of the input read so far.

grammar

A set of *rules* that together define a language.

input

A stream of data read by a program. For instance, the input to a flex scanner is a sequence of bytes, while the input to a bison parser is a sequence of *tokens*.

interpreter

A program that reads instructions in a language (a *program*) and decodes and acts on them one at a time. Compare to *compiler*.

LALR(1)

Look **A**head **L**eft to **R**ight; the parsing technique that bison normally uses. The (1) denotes that the lookahead is limited to a single token.

language

Formally, a well-defined set of strings over some alphabet; informally, some set of instructions for describing tasks that can be executed by a computer.

left-hand side (LHS)

The left-hand side or LHS of a bison *rule* is the symbol that precedes the colon. During a parse, when the input matches the sequence of symbols on the RHS of the rule, that sequence is *reduced* to the LHS symbol.

lex

A program that produced lexical analyzers that match patterns defined by regular expressions to a character stream. Now superseded by flex, which is more reliable and more powerful.

lexical analyzer

A program that converts a character stream into a token stream. Flex takes a description of individual tokens as regular expressions, divides the character stream into tokens, and determines the types and values of the tokens. For example, it might turn the character stream a = 17; into a token stream consisting of the name a, the operator =, the number 17, and the single character token ;. Also called a *lexer* or *scanner*.

lookahead

Input read by a parser or scanner but not yet matched to a pattern or rule. Bison parsers have a single token of lookahead, while flex scanners can have indefinitely long lookahead.

nonterminal

Symbols in a bison grammar that do not appear in the input but instead are defined by *rules*. Contrast to *tokenizing*.

parser stack

In a bison parser, the symbols for partially matched rules are stored on an internal stack. Symbols are added to the stack when the parser *shifts* and are removed when it *reduces*.

parsing

The process of taking a stream of *tokens* and logically grouping them into *statements* within some language.

pattern

In a flex scanner, a *regular expression* that the scanner matches against the input.

precedence

The order in which some particular operation is performed; for example, when interpreting mathematical statements, multiplication and division are assigned higher precedence than addition and subtraction. Thus, the statement 3+4*5 is 23 as opposed to 35.

production

See *rule*.

program

A set of instructions that perform a certain defined task.

reduce

In a bison parser, when the input matches the list of symbols on the RHS of a rule, the parser *reduces* the rule by removing the RHS symbols from the *parser stack* and replacing them with the LHS symbol.

reduce/reduce conflict

In a bison grammar, the situation where two or more rules match the same string of tokens. Bison resolves the conflict by reducing the rule that occurs earlier in the grammar.

regular expression

A language for specifying *patterns* that match a sequence of characters. Regular expressions consist of normal characters, which match the same character in the input; character classes, which match any single character in the class; and other characters, which specify the way that parts of the expression are to be matched against the input.

right-hand side (RHS)

The right-hand side or RHS of a bison *rule* is the list of symbols that follow the colon.

During a parse, when the input matches the sequence of symbols on the RHS of the rule, that sequence is *reduced* to the LHS symbol.

rule

In bison, *rules* are the abstract description of the grammar. Bison rules are also called *productions*. A rule is a single *nonterminal* called the LHS, a colon, and a possibly empty set of symbols called the RHS. Whenever the input matches the RHS of a rule, the parser *reduces* the rule.

semantic meaning

See *value*.

shift

A bison parser *shifts* an input symbol, placing it onto the parser stack in expectation that the symbol will match one of the rules in the grammar.

shift/reduce conflict

In a bison grammar, the situation where a symbol completes the RHS of one rule, which the parser needs to *reduce*, and is an intermediate symbol in the RHS of other rules, for which the parser needs to *shift* the symbol. Shift/reduce conflicts occur either because the grammar is ambiguous or because the parser would need to look more than one token ahead to decide whether to reduce the rule that the symbol completes. Bison resolves the conflict by doing the shift.

specification

A flex *specification* is a set of patterns to be matched against an input stream. Flex turns a specification into a scanner.

start

The single symbol to which a bison parser reduces a valid input stream. Rules with the start symbol on the LHS are called *start rules*.

start state

In a flex specification, patterns can be tagged with start states. At any point one start state is active, and patterns tagged with that start state can match the input. In an exclusive start state, only tagged patterns can match, while in an inclusive state, untagged patterns can also match the input.

symbol

In bison terminology, *symbols* are either *tokens* or *nonterminals*. In the rules for the grammar, any name found on the right-hand side of a rule is always a symbol.

In bison terminology, *tokens* or *terminals* are the symbols provided to the parser by the scanner. Compare to a *nonterminal*, which is defined within the parser.

symbol table

A data structure containing information about names occurring in the input so that all references to the same name can be related to the same object.

tokenizing

The process of converting a stream of characters into a stream of tokens is termed *tokenizing*. A scanner tokenizes its input.

value

Each *token* in a bison grammar has both a *syntactic* and a *semantic* value; its semantic value is the actual data contents of the token. For instance, the syntactic type of a certain operation may be INTEGER, but its semantic value might be 3.

yacc

Yet **A**nother **C**ompiler **C**ompiler; the predecessor to bison, a program that generates a parser from a list of rules in BNF-like format.

Index

Symbols

" (quotation mark), 20, 159
$ (dollar sign), 20, 122, 134, 158, 160
% (percent sign), 119, 120, 158
%code, 147
%code blocks, 147
%destructor, 148
%expect, 145
%initial-action, 149
%name-prefix, 165
%parse-param, 152
%start, 159
%type, 162
%union
    bison, 65, 163
    C++, 237
%union construct, 53
' (single quotes), 91, 159
( ) (parenthesis), 20, 133
(Generalized Left to Right (see GLR)
* (asterisk), 20, 133
+ (plus sign), 20, 133
-p flag, 165
. (period), 19, 132, 159
/ (slash), 21, 122, 134
: (colon), 47, 159
:= (assignment operator), 98
; (semicolon), 159
< > (angle brackets), 134, 159, 160
? (question mark), 133
@ (at sign), 158
[ ] (brackets), 19, 133
\ (backslash), 20, 133
^ (caret), 20, 121, 134

_ (underscore), 159
{ } (braces), 20, 120, 122, 133, 159
| (vertical bar), 20, 47, 120, 134, 159

A

abstract syntax tree (see AST)
actions
    bison grammar, 142, 158
    defined, 2, 259
    embedded, 146
alphabet
    defined, 259
ambiguity
    bison, 144
    and bison grammars, 154
    defined, 259
    example of, 34
    grammars, 14
    reduce/reduce conflicts, 178
ambiguous patterns
    regular expressions, 22
angle brackets < >, 134, 159, 160
ASCII (American Standard Code for
        Information Interchange)
    defined, 259
assignment operator (:=), 98
associativity
    declarations, 154
    operators, 59
AST (abstract syntax tree)
    about, 51
    calculator example, 52–57, 61–78
asterisk (*), 20, 133
at sign (@), 158
attributes

We'd like to hear your suggestions for improving our indexes. Send email to *index@oreilly.com*.

G

glossary, 259–262
GLR (Generalized Left to Right)
    defined, 260
    parsing, 145, 230
grammar
    ambiguity, 14, 178
    bison syntax, 65–67, 141
    changing, 15
    defined, 260
    and parsing, 9–13
    parsing SQL, 243–258
    porting bison grammars, 153
    reserved words, 69
    variant and multiple bison grammars, 163

H

hashing with linear probing, 35
header files
    including in scanners, 216
"Hello World" flex program, 2

I

I/O
    flex input sources, 123
    flex scanner structure, 25
    in flex scanners, 23
    start states and nested input files, 28–31
IF/THEN/ELSE conflict resolution technique, 185, 188
IN operator
    SQL, 99
indexes
    CREATE DATABASE statement, 112
    SQL tables, 105
infinite recursion, 146
inherited attributes
    bison, 148
input
    defined, 260
input buffers
    flex, 123
input() function, 125
input() macro, 27
INSERT statement
    SQL parsing, 107–109
interpreter
    defined, 260

J

Java parsers
    bison support for, 241
joins
    SQL tables, 105

K

keywords
    C keywords, 41
    SQL, 86–90, 93

L

LALR (Look Ahead Left to Right)
    defined, 260
language
    defined, 260
left context
    flex, 121
left recursion, 66, 156
left-hand side (see LHS)
lex
    defined, 260
    history, xiii
lexers
    calculator example, 69
    locations feature in bison, 201
    multiple, 127
    multiple bison parsers, 165
    parsing SQL, 85–94
    portability, 129
lexical analysis
    parsing, 1
lexical analyzer
    defined, 260
lexical feedback
    bison, 150
LHS (left-hand side)
    defined, 260
    reduce/reduce conflicts, 192
libraries
    bison library, 167
    flex library, 24, 125
    portability of bison library, 153
limited lookahead
    shift/reduce conflicts, 191
line numbers
    flex, 126
lists of values

synthesized attributes, 148

T

tables
    CREATE TABLE statement, 111–114
    relational databases, 82
    SELECT table references, 102–106
    symbol tables, 32–38
terminal symbols, 141
    bison, 161
tokenizing
    defined, 262
tokens
    about, 7
    bison, 161
    content-dependent tokens, 22
    error tokens, 207
    interchanging precedence, 146
    literal character tokens, 54–57
    literal tokens in bison, 151
    SQL, 85
    symbols as, 141
tuple calculus
    SQL, 82

U

unary expressions
    SQL, 97
underscore (_), 159
unput() macro, 27, 137
unterminated quoted strings
    detecting, 198
UPDATE statement
    SQL parsing, 110
user defined functions
    bison parser example, 76
user variables
    SQL parsing, 114

V

value types
    declaring, 162
values
    in bison parsers, 53
    defined, 262
    tokens, 7
variable-length lists of expressions
    SQL, 98

variables
    names in SQL expressions, 97
    user variables in SQL parsing, 114
vertical bar (|), 20, 47, 120, 134, 159

W

whitespace
    scanning, 94
word count example, 2, 24

Y

y.output files
    bison, 166
yacc (Yet Another Compiler Compiler)
    defined, 262
    history, xiii
YYABORT, 168
YYACCEPT, 168
YYBACKUP macro, 168
yyclearin, 169
yydebug, 169
YYDEBUG, 169
yyerrok, 169
YYERROR macro, 170
yyerror(), 167, 170, 200
yyin, 26
yyinput() and yyunput() macros, 137
yyleng, 137
yyless() function, 122
yyless() macro, 137
yylex() function, 120, 130, 135, 138, 210
yylineno, 31, 126
yymore(), 139
yyout, 27
yyparse(), 152, 165, 168, 171
YYRECOVERING() macro, 171
yyrestart(), 24, 139
YYSTYPE, 160
yywrap(), 24, 139
YY_BUFFER_STATE, 26
YY_BUF_SIZE, 129
YY_DECL macro, 138
YY_INPUT macro, 27, 125
yy_scan_buffer function, 139
yy_scan_string function, 139
YY_USER_ACTION macro, 139, 201

About the Author

John R. Levine is the author of several dozen books, including *lex and yacc* and *qmail* published by O'Reilly, and *The Internet for Dummies*. He writes, consults, and lectures on computer software, network and email security, and policy topics.

Colophon

Our look is the result of reader comments, our own experimentation, and feedback from distribution channels. Distinctive covers complement our distinctive approach to technical topics, breathing personality and life into potentially dry subjects.

The animals on the cover of *flex & bison* are Nicobar pigeons (*Caloenas nicobarica*). This large (approximately 40 cm) bird with gray, yellow, and iridescent green plumage resides on islands from the Bay of Bengal and Malaysia through New Guinea. DNA analysis suggests that it is the closest living relative of the Dodo (*Raphus cucullatus*).

The cover image is adapted from part of a plate in *The Royal Natural History*, written by English naturalist Richard Lydekker in 1895. The cover font is Adobe ITC Garamond. The text font is Linotype Birka; the heading font is Adobe Myriad Condensed; and the code font is LucasFont's TheSansMonoCondensed.

Get even more for your money.

Join the O'Reilly Community, and register the O'Reilly books you own. It's free, and you'll get:

- $4.99 ebook upgrade offer
- 40% upgrade offer on O'Reilly print books
- Membership discounts on books and events
- Free lifetime updates to ebooks and videos
- Multiple ebook formats, DRM FREE
- Participation in the O'Reilly community
- Newsletters
- Account management
- 100% Satisfaction Guarantee

Signing up is easy:

1. **Go to: oreilly.com/go/register**
2. **Create an O'Reilly login.**
3. **Provide your address.**
4. **Register your books.**

Note: English-language books only

To order books online:
oreilly.com/store

For questions about products or an order:
orders@oreilly.com

To sign up to get topic-specific email announcements and/or news about upcoming books, conferences, special offers, and new technologies:
elists@oreilly.com

For technical questions about book content:
booktech@oreilly.com

To submit new book proposals to our editors:
proposals@oreilly.com

O'Reilly books are available in multiple DRM-free ebook formats. For more information:
oreilly.com/ebooks

Spreading the knowledge of innovators   oreilly.com

Milton Keynes UK
Ingram Content Group UK Ltd.
UKHW051056240424
441648UK00001B/2